COSMOLOGY
IN THEOLOGICAL
PERSPECTIVE

COSMOLOGY IN THEOLOGICAL PERSPECTIVE

Understanding Our Place in the Universe

Olli-Pekka Vainio

Baker Academic

a division of Baker Publishing Group
Grand Rapids, Michigan

© 2018 by Olli-Pekka Vainio

Published by Baker Academic
a division of Baker Publishing Group
PO Box 6287, Grand Rapids, MI 49516-6287
www.bakeracademic.com

Printed in the United States of America

Library of Congress Cataloging-in-Publication Data
Names: Vainio, Olli-Pekka, author.
Title: Cosmology in theological perspective : understanding our place in the universe / Olli-Pekka
   Vainio.
Description: Grand Rapids : Baker Publishing Group, 2018. | Includes bibliographical references
   and index.
Identifiers: LCCN 2017052478 | ISBN 9780801099434 (pbk. : alk. paper)
Subjects: LCSH: Biblical cosmology. | Cosmology. | Religion and science.
Classification: LCC BS651 .V26 2018 | DDC 261.5/5—dc23
LC record available at https://lccn.loc.gov/2017052478

18 19 20 21 22 23 24   7 6 5 4 3 2 1

If you have a religion it must be cosmic.

C. S. Lewis, "Unreal Estates"

In God's hand were all the ends of the world:
. . . when his hand was opened by the key of love, the
creatures came forth.

Thomas Aquinas, *In sententiarum*, prologue

And therefore as a stranger give it welcome.
There are more things in heaven and earth, Horatio,
Than are dreamt of in your philosophy.

William Shakespeare, *Hamlet*

But whether thus these things, or whether not;
whether the sun, predominant in heaven,
Rise on the earth, or earth rise on the sun . . .
Solicit not thy thoughts with matters hid.
Leave them to God above, him serve and fear.

John Milton, *Paradise Lost*

Contents

Preface

A great deal of writing of this book took place under the auspices of the Center of Theological Inquiry (CTI), Princeton, New Jersey, which hosted a program on the societal implications of astrobiology. Having followed debates on cosmology and religion from a distance, I was privileged to spend a year thinking through some of the theological and philosophical issues that are related to the possibility of life outside our own planet. Theologians and philosophers have been dealing with these themes for a very long time. More recently, C. S. Lewis addressed many of these questions in the mid-twentieth century, both in his science fiction and academic writings. His more analytical writings on the subject remain relevant to us today as guides how to think about the role of humans in the cosmos, while his fiction still has the power to stir our imagination. For these reasons, I decided to use Lewis as an example and as a conversation partner while writing this book. This is, however, not a book on Lewis but an experiment in thinking with him about cosmological issues of our own time.

The program at CTI was funded by NASA and the John Templeton Foundation. I am thankful for all of them and our merry band of scholars, with whom it was a great pleasure to discuss, debate, and marvel at the wonders of our cosmos. I am especially grateful for the following people who read parts of the manuscript and offered valuable advice and support: Max Baker-Hytch, Jesse Couenhoven, Andrew Davison, David Fergusson, Eric Gregory, Rope Kojonen, Zoë Lehmann Imfeld, Timothy Jenkins, Andreas Losch, Robin Lovin, John McCarthy, Gerald McKenny, Douglas Ottati, Timo Nisula, Vesa Palonen, Erik Persson, Adam Pryor, Frank Rosenzweig, Susan Schneider, William Storrar, Fred Simmons, Aku Visala, and the anonymous referee. R. David Nelson and Eric Salo from Baker were immensely helpful during both the writing and the editing processes. Albion Butters helped me with English. All remaining mistakes are my own.

Chapters 8, 9, 10, and 11 use portions of my previously published articles, respectively: "Dark Light: Mystical Theology of Edith Stein," *Journal of Analytic Theology* 4 (2016); "The Curious Case of Analogia Entis: How Metaphysics Affects Ecumenics," *Studia Theologica* 69 (2016); "Imago Dei and Human Rationality," *Zygon* 49 (2014); and "Reason and Imagination in the Thought of C. S. Lewis," in *Origins of Religion*, ed. Hanne Appelqvist (Helsinki: SLAG, 2018). They are all used with permission.

A Note on the Chapter Titles

Each chapter title is an allusion to or a quote from a different science fiction movie or television show, in this order: *Close Encounters of the Third Kind* (1977), *Star Wars: Phantom Menace* (1999), *Star Trek IV: The Voyage Home* (1986), *Star Trek: First Contact* (1996), *2010: Odyssey Two* (1984), *Contact* (1997), *Event Horizon* (1997), *Alien* (1979), *Gattaca* (1997), *The Terminator* (1984), and *Star Trek: The Original Series* (1966).

Abbreviations

ANF	*Ante-Nicene Fathers*
ca.	*circa*, approximately
CR	Corpus Reformatorum
d.	died
fl.	*floruit*, flourished
Gr.	Greek
Lat.	Latin
LW	*Luther's Works*
NPNF[1]	*Nicene and Post-Nicene Fathers*, Series 1
NPNF[2]	*Nicene and Post-Nicene Fathers*, Series 2
sec.	section
ST	Thomas Aquinas, *Summa Theologiae*
WA	Weimarer Ausgabe (Weimar edition of *Luther's Works*)

Introduction

Close Encounters

In a widely read and commented-on *Huffington Post* blog, an author claimed that evidence of alien life would mark the end of religion.

> Let us be clear that the Bible is unambiguous about creation: the earth is the center of the universe, only humans were made in the image of god, and all life was created in six days. All life in all the heavens. In six days. So when we discover that life exists or existed elsewhere in our solar system or on a planet orbiting another star in the Milky Way, or in a planetary system in another galaxy, we will see a huge effort to square that circle with amazing twists of logic and contorted justifications. But do not buy the inevitable historical edits: Life on another planet is completely incompatible with religious tradition. Any other conclusion is nothing but *ex post facto* rationalization to preserve the myth.[1]

Although the author's remarks portrayed a poor understanding of religion, theology, and the history of philosophy, the popularity of the blog post demonstrated the importance of inquiry about the interface between contemporary cosmology, astrobiology, and religious-existential questions. He is right

---

1. Jeff Schweitzer, "Earth 2.0: Bad News for God," *Huff Post Science Blog*, July 23, 2015, http://www.huffingtonpost.com/jeff-schweitzer/earth-20-bad-news-for-god_b_7861528.html. See also Davies, *Are We Alone?*, xi–xii, 54: "Even the discovery of a single extra-terrestrial microbe, if it could be shown to have evolved independently of life on Earth, would drastically alter our world view and change our society as profoundly as the Copernican and Darwinian revolutions. It could truly be described as the greatest scientific discovery of all time. . . . It is hard to see how the world's great religions could continue in anything like their present form should an alien message be received."

1

in pointing out that these questions deserve serious investigation.[2] However, it might surprise him that this investigation has been ongoing for some time now and the results so far have been less than dramatic.[3]

Instead of rushing off to discuss the question of life outside the known human sphere (which is just one question among many), we need to start from the beginning in order to properly grasp the scale and depth of this line of inquiry. We humans have always had a special connection with the stars and other entities beyond our immediate reach. The earliest cave paintings reveal glimpses of cultures that felt part of something larger than their earthly existence. Cosmology was among the topics addressed by the first philosophers, and perhaps the most important of the early philosophical cosmologies, Plato's *Timaeus*, still has the power to stir our imagination. Yet nowadays many people consider questions about the cosmos to be scientific, not philosophical.

This is not how it was in the beginning. Before the development of the empirical scientific method, cosmology was something that you could (almost) do without leaving your proverbial armchair. Our modern scientific narrative claims that when science slowly started to gain momentum by offering better explanations, philosophy was left behind, and soon it will become forgotten altogether. There is no denying that science has brought us wonderful things and opened vistas that we barely could have imagined before. But how in fact has our philosophical worldview changed and to what extent is the change attributable to the progress of science?

In the history of philosophy, there have been various ways of trying to distinguish different types of inquiry. One example is to differentiate between two approaches:

Philosophy: value, meaning

Science: empirical facts

2. Also, NASA's *Astrobiology Strategy* paper (October 2015) states, "The results of astrobiology research will have broad societal impact, affecting the way we think about life in the context of ethics, law, philosophy, theology, and a host of other issues. Our place in the universe, as a species and as a planet, speaks to our fundamental understanding of ourselves" (155), https://nai.nasa.gov/media/medialibrary/2016/04/NASA_Astrobiology_Strategy_2015_FINAL_041216.pdf. NASA has pursued these multidisciplinary questions in, e.g., Dick, *Impact of Discovering Life beyond Earth*.

3. The question of alien life has been a popular topic since the early Enlightenment, and Christian theologians have actively participated in the debate; see, e.g., Crowe, *Extraterrestrial Life Debate*. For a contemporary discussion, see Weintraub, *Religions and Extraterrestrial Life*; O'Meara, *Vast Universe*; Wilkinson, *Science*; and Arnould, "Extraterrestrial Intelligent Life."

The distinction sounds intuitively plausible, but the actual interaction between philosophy and science is a more complicated matter and the borderline between values and facts is vague. This is not only a problem of definition. Many worldviews tend to be emancipatory, which means that they are likely to take over other realms of knowledge. Scientism will try to reduce philosophical questions to scientific ones, and religious or ideological fundamentalism will try to base science on religious or ideological principles. These extremes should be avoided, not because they are extremes (extreme views can sometimes be right), but because they are deficient methods of knowledge acquisition.[4]

In ordinary use, the word *cosmology* refers to the account of everything that exists.[5] The boundary between the disciplines has always been slippery, and even today when scientists are doing cosmology, they are often, implicitly or explicitly, doing metaphysics.[6] I argue that philosophy cannot be divorced from cosmology and that you cannot do cosmology without philosophy. Therefore, cosmology, no matter how it is done, will always have (at least) one foot in a religious stream.

One of the topics in this book is to investigate how our knowledge of the world has enabled different interpretations of it. Even when people agree about some fact, they may still give different meanings to it. This gives rise to different cosmologies. The cosmology of a modern person is obviously very different from the one held by a person who lived in Mesopotamia three thousand years ago. Of course, we think that our cosmology is immensely better than that earlier one, and it is not uncommon to sneer at previous generations in this regard. Yet after another three thousand years pass, we might find ourselves sitting next to the author of the *Epic of Gilgamesh*, being laughed at by more enlightened minds.

To my mind, this condescending attitude toward cosmologies is utterly wrongheaded and misses something of great importance. Cosmology is—and it always has been—an attempt to make sense of the human place in the universe. Ancient cosmologies may sound odd to us, but they were the best holistic accounts of the world that people with minds not worse than ours could construct with the evidence they had at the time. C. S. Lewis offers a balanced approach to looking at how cosmologies were—and are—constructed.

---

4. Already Aristotle accused Pythagoreans of basing science on their (false) theories, which were not sufficiently attentive to the empirical evidence (Aristotle, *On the Heavens* 2.13). For a discussion on the contemporary demarcation problem, see Stenmark, *Scientism*.

5. See also the similar analysis of the concept of *world* in Lewis, *Studies in Words*, 214.

6. This is especially evident in several recent popular science books. See, e.g., Krauss, *Universe from Nothing*; Vilenkin, *Many Worlds in One*.

I am only suggesting considerations that may induce us to regard all [cosmo-logical] Models in the right way, respecting each and idolizing none. We are all, very properly, familiar with the idea that in every age the human mind is deeply influenced by the accepted Model of the universe. But there is a two-way traffic; the Model is also influenced by the prevailing temper of mind. We must recognize that what has been called "a taste in universes" is not only pardon-able but inevitable. We can no longer dismiss the change of Models as a simple progress from error to truth. No Model is a catalogue of ultimate realities, and none is a mere fantasy. Each is a serious attempt to get in all the phenomena known at a given period, and each succeeds in getting in a great many. But also, no less surely, each reflects the prevalent psychology of an age almost as much as it reflects the state of that age's knowledge.[7]

In this book, I will not try to offer an account of how scientific and reli-gious views should be related.[8] Suffice it to say that philosophy can have an effect on the ways in which we pursue scientific questions, and science can make some philosophical theories and religious views appear to be probable or improbable. The aim of this book is to examine the interface between philosophical and scientific convictions about our universe as we know it, paying specific attention to questions in the fields of philosophical and theo-logical cosmology.

This book does not try to be a comprehensive account of theological cos-mology. Instead, I will be mostly focusing on the questions that are related to the human place in the universe as we know it. Various topics are important for theological cosmology, like the questions concerning the big bang, the metaphysics of time, and the quantum theory, but in my opinion these ques-tions have already been well scrutinized elsewhere.[9] Thus, I have decided to leave these themes aside and concentrate more on topics that are, in a way, old, but that have received renewed attention, especially because of the recent discoveries of exoplanets.

On Method

My method is broadly "Lewisian." Among popular audiences, C. S. Lewis is well known for his fantasy novels and popular apologetics, but the fact that his academic works concentrated on medieval thought is often overlooked.

7. Lewis, *Discarded Image*, 222.
8. On specifically this methodological question, see, e.g., Stenmark, *Science and Religion*; McGrath, *Science of God*.
9. See, e.g., Drees, *Beyond the Big Bang*.

In fact, many of his texts are still counted among the best available studies on the medieval worldview. One feature of the medieval cosmos is that it was Christocentric through and through; humans were never the real center of the universe. It was Lewis's understanding of the cosmos as created through the divine Logos (the true Cosmic center) that enabled him to imagine other possible worlds filled with life more or less like our own. The medieval world was, to use Lewis's word, "anthropoperipheral," and we were "creatures of the Margin."[10] Obviously, this opens immense possibilities for the imagination.

In his essays, Lewis offered reasoned commentaries on our place in the cosmos that drew from the ancient Christian tradition, encountering head-on the contemporary challenges, which he showed to be often based on misunderstandings or superficial knowledge of history. He resisted the scientistic worldview as "all fact and no meaning"—that is to say, a worldview that tries to be too secure and is thereby paradoxically vacated of those things that really matter to us. By mixing elements from the contemporary and ancient cosmologies, he wished to underline the meaning that was lost, as "pure facts" had taken over the collective imagination. In a way, his science fiction was a project that tried to re-enchant the world after the disenchantment brought by scientism and crude materialism.[11]

I do not intend to offer here a close reading of Lewis's cosmology per se, but I will be using him as an example of how to think about cosmological matters in a scientific age while trying to understand the meaning of Christian cosmological convictions. Turning what I take to be Lewis's philosophical style (which I do not think was unique to just him) into a proper method, I wish to highlight three *formal* epistemic desiderata:

---

10. Lewis, *Discarded Image*, 58.

11. Lewis, "Transposition," 114–15:

> You will have noticed that most dogs cannot understand *pointing*. You point to a bit of food on the floor; the dog, instead of looking at the floor, sniffs at your finger. A finger is a finger to him, and that is all. His world is all fact and no meaning. And in a period when factual realism is dominant we shall find people deliberately inducing upon themselves this doglike mind. A man who has experienced love from within will deliberately go about to inspect it analytically from outside and regard the results of this analysis as truer than his experience. The extreme limit of this self-blinding is seen in those who, like the rest of us, have consciousness, yet go about to study the human organism as if they did not know it was conscious. As long as this deliberate refusal to understand things from above, even where such understanding is possible, continues, it is idle to talk of any final victory over materialism. The critique of every experience from below, the voluntary ignoring of meaning and concentration on fact, will always have the same plausibility. There will always be evidence, and every month fresh evidence, to show that religion is only psychological, justice only self-protection, politics only economics, love only lust, and thought itself only cerebral biochemistry.

See also Nagel, *Secular Philosophy*, 7.

1. Understanding of history
2. Coherence of knowledge
3. Intellectual virtue

The first one pertains to our dependence on history. Every attempt at constructing a cosmology takes place in a historical context, with people typically trying to answer specific questions that are germane to that time. In order to grasp what the development of cosmologies means, we need to understand the past. This is especially important for the Christian church, which is a living tradition.[12] The faith of the church today is a part of a living organism; we cannot be separated from the tradition, lest we cease to exist, yet we cannot simply reiterate the past either.

There are apparent dangers in nostalgia.[13] We are often prone to remember things incorrectly, so that things and times appear better than they were. Moreover, nostalgia misleads us if we fail to recognize that the things that we try to bring back from the past to our own time are not viable anymore, having lost their philosophical credentials. A good kind of nostalgia requires that we locate an idea, portray it correctly, and have a clear understanding of why it is a good thing. Moreover, we need an account for why this thing was lost, which is connected to its viability today. Is the thing of the past genuinely good for us, and does it help us solve some of our present problems?

History as such does not offer us a clear, unified picture, but an understanding of history gives us a sense of borders and the rules of the playing field. Even if the historical traditions of the church are not uniform, they portray a type of unity. Lewis calls this "mere Christianity," and G. K. Chesterton, "orthodoxy." I take the coherence of knowledge in this context to mean a balance between three *material* elements that are constitutive of Christian identity. These include the following:

1. Canonical witness
2. Ecumenical tradition
3. Ecumenical consensus

For a church to be a Christian church, it needs acknowledgment of these three elements that form its identity. The church is founded on the witness of

12. When I speak about "the church," I refer to the ecumenical tradition of Christianity, not to any particular denomination. Sometimes I use "church" to refer to, e.g., the Catholic Church, but that should be obvious in each context.

13. For an argument against seeing Lewis as engaging in unwarranted nostalgia in his science fiction, see Schwartz, C. S. Lewis.

the apostles, which is recorded in the biblical canon. The Bible is the "norming norm," which controls and guides the theological deliberation of the church. However, this norm does not exist in a vacuum. Knowledge of the tradition is crucial for understanding the reception history of biblical doctrines, how they have been interpreted at different times and why, and why we have received *this* form of the doctrine. As the church thinks about and rethinks its identity in our own time, it needs to be reminded what the church outside any single denominational tradition is doing. It is normal for us humans to be limited by our location and our in-group, so that we are unable to see all possible solutions. Therefore, churches need each other in their reflection.

On the one hand, the model that I am suggesting is a form of theological inquiry, which is an ongoing project in all Christian communities. On the other hand, it is not necessarily employed properly and consciously everywhere, always, and by everyone. Even if I cannot pursue the question of the ecumenical nature of theological thinking any further here, I believe that this is a rough outline that in principle should be able to be affirmed by all Christian churches.[14]

History and coherence offer us the material elements, which are then balanced by intellectual virtues. These include values like honesty, open-mindedness, critical thinking, courage, and wisdom. Without virtues, we end up in either relativism or dogmatism, both of which fail to pass as the proper epistemic attitude supported by both the Christian tradition and the best available means of knowledge acquisition.[15] Knowledge acquisition is always a balancing act. We find ways to relate new things we have found with the old things that we currently hold on to. The history of the church offers several examples, both good and bad, on how this can be done.

Structure of the Book

I have split this book into ten short chapters, each of which discusses one topic that is important for the human role in the universe. Chapter 1 discusses how humans of the ancient world built their cosmologies. This includes a survey of cosmologies that existed before and during the writing of the Old Testament, and the more advanced prescientific cosmologies of Plato and Aristotle, which had an influence on the early church.

14. For more on this question from a historical and contemporary perspective, see Guarino, *Vincent of Lérins*.

15. Roberts and Wood, *Intellectual Virtues*; Baehr, *Intellectual Virtues and Education*; Kort, *C. S. Lewis*, 63.

Chapter 2 examines how the early church understood the core message of the biblical cosmogonies and what kinds of philosophical and hermeneutical tools the first Christians employed in interpreting them. Special attention is paid to two major works on early Christian cosmology, by Basil the Great and Saint Augustine.

Chapter 3 takes up three cases where science and theology seem to have been at odds. The debates surrounding the work of Galileo, Newton, and Darwin are still with us, and they can teach us many things about how to think—and how not to think—about the relation of theological convictions and cosmological facts. These first chapters function as introductions that try to make transparent how the tradition has deliberated these themes before. When this foundation has been laid, I turn to more contemporary issues.

Chapter 4 moves through historical debates on the plurality of worlds to our own time, where multiverse theories are widely debated. How does the idea of the multiverse fit together with Christian theism? Here I formulate a version of the principle of plenitude, according to which a benevolent Creator is likely to create good things in abundance. This principle is also used later in the book when the possibility of the existence of other rational beings is discussed.

Theistic religions view the human being as created in the image of God. Interestingly, there has never been a single definition for this term, *imago Dei*, since it has been used to perform various theological tasks at different times. In chapter 5, after providing a loose framework of how the concept might be used today, I ask whether animals, aliens, and artificial intelligences might be taken to be bearers of the image of God.

Chapter 5 investigates how the possibility of alien life might fit together with Christian theism, or if Christianity implies that we are alone in the universe. I argue that Christian theism is compatible with both views, but each of them actualizes different challenges that require a response. I offer a set of brief answers to these challenges.

Chapter 7 continues this same deliberation, but this time from the point of view of the immensity of the cosmos. Should God have created a human-sized cosmos? Why all the empty space? The scale of the cosmos raises questions about human value and significance. How can we think about our lives as meaningful in the grand cosmic perspective?

Chapters 8 and 9 discuss properly theological doctrines. How should we understand the relation of God and creation? Where can God be found? As God is not a being among other beings, how should we understand

God's nature? Could God reveal himself or become incarnate more than once?[16]

Chapter 10 returns to C. S. Lewis and uses his distinction between reason and imagination to offer a framework for how to continue thinking about cosmology from a theological perspective. Given everything we know at this point in history, how should we pursue our quest for a greater understanding of God and the cosmos?

16. I refer to God with male pronouns because Christ identified God as the Father, which is an authoritative metaphor (but not the only one). This does not mean that I think that God is gendered in the same sense as humans are. God is beyond gender distinctions, and I understand this to be an ecumenically shared view of Christian faith. My own language (Finnish) is not gendered, which makes *theo*-logy a lot easier in this respect. For discussion, see Rea, "Gender"; Soskice, *Kindness of God*.

1

Every Saga Has a Beginning

Philosophical Cosmologies in the Ancient World

In order to grasp the relationship between contemporary science and the Christian worldview, it is helpful to look back and see how cosmologies were constructed in the past. In this chapter, I will briefly examine cosmologies in the ancient Near East and their similarities and dissimilarities with the Old Testament. Plato and Aristotle offer the first major philosophical accounts of cosmology, and they had significant influence on early Christianity. For the first Christians, these were the "scientific" models of the world that they tried to reconcile with their faith. On several points, they were in fundamental agreement. Nonetheless, Christians came to deny the existence of a past-eternal universe, and their view of God—namely, that God is one and personal—differed from that in the Greek tradition.

Cosmos in Ancient Mesopotamia, Egypt, and the Old Testament

The Greek word *cosmos* in its mundane usage referred to skillfully and beautifully composed objects, like jewels, statues, or machines. For example, in Homer's *Odyssey* (8.492), the Trojan horse is called a *cosmos*. The opposite of *cosmos* is chaos and disorder. Charles Taylor aptly captures the idea of prescientific cosmologies: "I use 'cosmos' for our forebearers' idea of the totality of existence because it contains the idea of an ordered whole. It is not that our own universe isn't in its own way ordered, but in the cosmos the order of things was a humanly meaningful one. That is, the principle of order in the cosmos was closely related to, often identical with, that which gives shape to our lives."[1]

While the first cosmologies were anthropocentric, later developments have to some extent left this perspective behind; they are not directly concerned about the place and meaning of humans in the grand scheme of things. As we approach our own time, cosmology starts to focus more on things like the structure and evolution of the universe and the origin of matter. Nevertheless, questions concerning the nature of consciousness and the origin and the meaning of life are always lurking around the corner, and many cosmologists find it hard not to say something about these issues, which lie outside proper scientific method. It is, in fact, hard to tell when a cosmology is purely scientific and when it borders on the philosophical or religious. Cosmological questions are, and always have been, deeply connected with existential questions.[2]

Prescientific cosmologies included some claims about the nature and movements of the heavenly bodies, but they were not exclusively interested in stars alone; they sought to tell a story about everything that exists. This is common for all origin myths; they tell where we came from and what our relation to the whole is, while the most advanced ones typically point us in the direction of how we should go about living our lives.[3]

Prescientific cosmologies typically proceeded from perception of the immediate features of reality and aimed to provide a holistic account of everything that exists. Therefore, it is natural that such accounts were anthropocentric. A fundamental feature of these cosmologies is what a person sees and experiences, which was then inserted into a mythic framework. The same stance is portrayed in old medieval maps where the words *hic sunt dracones* (here be dragons) may appear on the edges. The maps portray what is known, what has been seen, and what matters. Here is the world of knowledge; there is the world of surprise. However, we should not take old maps too seriously. The old genre of *mappa mundi* was not meant to serve the same function as our

---

1. Taylor, *Secular Age*, 60.

2. For brief accounts, see, e.g., Carr, "Cosmology and Religion"; Halvorson and Kragh, "Cosmology and Theology." On cosmological narratives in different religious traditions, see Kärkkäinen, *Creation and Humanity*.

3. We obviously know very little about the religions of the cultures that predated the axial revolution (from the eighth to the third century BC). Based on the cave paintings, it has been suggested that early on the human cosmology was split between this-worldly and other-worldly realms, and the latter could be visited by shamans with the help of spirits. The world or cosmos was the sum of these two realms. However, these claims are speculative. See Lewis-Williams and Pearce, *Inside the Neolithic Mind*; Bellah, *Religion in Human Evolution*, 117–74; and van Huyssteen, *Alone in the World?*, 233–70.

Figure 1.1. Hereford Mappa Mundi, a medieval map of the world dating from ca. 1300. The map, along with a commentary, can be browsed at https://www.themappamundi.co.uk.

modern maps. For example, the famous Hereford Map depicts the world with Jerusalem at its center, and it also gives the location of Eden (see fig. 1.1). It is obvious that the author of the map did not even care about geographical details, for places seem to appear in random locations. It focuses on the meanings and relations of things, not where they are. Thus, these maps illustrate a different way of placing oneself in the universe, which might at first sound strange for us. For the illustrator, the meaning of things was more important than accurate depictions of them as physical objects.

To get a better grasp of the first actual cosmologies, we need to go back to ancient Mesopotamia and Egypt. Ancient Near Eastern cosmologies often used the human body as a model for the cosmos (a pattern that has continued in a mutated form until this very day). The human body offers a way of structuring the world in a hierarchical manner, where certain parts are higher while others are lower. The act of creation is also typically depicted with the help of sexual images, such as in intercourse between gods and earthly elements.[4]

The old languages of these regions did not have a specific word for cosmos, but the world was typically divided between heaven and earth. Gods, often linked to the celestial bodies, were believed to reside in heaven, with earth consisting of the world of humans and the subterranean netherworld, the dwelling place of the dead. In the hierarchy of the Babylonian *Enuma Elish*, the regions closest to humans are also dwelling places of more anthropomorphic deities, whereas the peripheries are inhabited by strange gods and demonic creatures. In the story, our world is created when the hero of the story, Marduk, slays Tiamat, a chaos monster often depicted as a dragon, and builds the world from different parts of her body. As a whole, the story can be read as a theodicy that explains the birth of our world from chaos through the guiding hands of very powerful, but not ultimately perfect, deities: the world is created out of matter that is subject to change as such and also subject to the whims of gods.[5]

The early cosmologies typically consisted of elements and images that were familiar at the time of their writing. The Sumerian *Epic of Gilgamesh* depicts the earth as a mountain surrounded by primeval waters; other texts portray the human world as a reed raft floating on water. The early cosmologies are a mixture of elementary knowledge of the movements of the stars and existential accounts of the place of humans in the grand scheme of things. Even if the texts are openly mythical and poetic, they express a familiar need to offer a systematic account of the totality of things, with an emphasis on existential questions. The depictions of wars between gods and other beings are not mere stories; they are explanations of why we humans behave as we do. In this, they are fine examples of human curiosity and cognitive capacity.[6]

---

4. Pongratz-Leisten et al., "Creation and Cosmogony." For example, the Sumerian *Enki and the World Order* tells how the world was created from the semen of an ocean god. For a collection of Sumerian and Akkadian texts with a commentary, see Horowitz, *Mesopotamian Cosmic Geography*; Black, *Literature of Ancient Sumer*, 210–44.

5. Lambert, "Mesopotamian Creation Stories." For a comparison with Genesis 1, see Sparks, "Enūma Elish." On how ancient cosmogonic myths function as theodicies, see Laato and de Moor, *Theodicy*, 27–150.

6. As Robert W. Jenson states,
    All cultures do in fact tell just such primal aetiological stories as appear in Genesis 1–11, and around much the same set of motifs. How are we to understand this? What is common

The Egyptian cosmologies, which are slightly more developed and philo-sophically explicit than the Mesopotamian ones, portray the same tendencies, but they also offer a normative account of human good.[7] The stars, as well as forces of nature like the primordial ocean, are gods. A central philosophical concept in Egyptian cosmology is *ma'at*, which refers to the balance of the cosmos. When there is balance, there is also justice, harmony, and prosper-ity. The opposite of *ma'at* is chaos, which presents itself in war, famine, and a lack of various virtues. In the beginning, humans lived peacefully under the reign of the sun god Re, the ruler of both gods and men. When humans rebelled, gods were sent to destroy the human race. Re pitied humans and decided not to execute his sentence, but the alliance between gods and men was still broken. The gods left Earth for the sky, and humans were destined to remain behind. The earthly king, Pharaoh, ruled as a steward of divine order, and he was supposed to represent *ma'at* in his rule as well as he could, lest the world succumb to chaos.

In its post-fall state, the Egyptian cosmos consists of the following elements. The world of humans is a disk that floats on an immense ocean. The god of the air, Shu, holds up the god of the sky, Hathor, who forms a cupola over the Earth. Her belly glitters with stars by night, and by day Re sails his boat across the horizon. During the night, Re enters the underworld where the dead reside. The Egyptians thought that the Earth-disk is the physical center of the universe, around which everything else revolves. However, this was not a place of great value, as the divine realm was held to be the true, nonphysical center. Humans had value only relative to order and the hierarchy of the cosmos.

The Nordic mythologies portray the cosmos in a similar fashion. Above us is a cupola formed out of the skull of the giant Ymir, who was slain by Odin and his brothers. Ymir's body was used to form Midgard, the world

---

to all the race, and emerges in the need to tell aetiological stories of primal times, is, we may suggest, a set of *worries*. Thus the fragility of the physical circumstances in which human life is possible is felt by all cultures; and stories are everywhere told about the bare aversion of universal catastrophe. Or again, encounter with peoples whose speech cannot be understood is always a threatening puzzle. In Israel, as elsewhere, stories like those of Genesis 1–11 are told to bring such anxieties to word and so make them bearable, that is, to certify reality as it is now experienced. Among the universally felt fragilities of existence, one is metaphysical. Not only is our human world ambiguous and threatening in certain dominating but contingent features, so also is the precondition of our human history, the world in its mere givenness prior to all our action in it: there is a sort of absolute worry. We have already cited Heidegger citing Leibniz: "Why is there anything at all? Why not just nothing?" (Jenson, *Systematic Theology*, 2:9–10. See also M. Robinson, *Absence of Mind*, 25–26)

7. Quirke, "Creation Stories"; el-Aswad, "Archaic Egyptian Cosmology"; Redford, *Ancient Gods Speak*, 189–91.

of humans, at the edges of which also live giants, elves, and dwarves. Below Midgard is Nilfheim, the world of the dead, and above is Asgard, the home of the gods. Midgard resides on a plane surrounded by the sea and the giant serpent Jörmungandr. Whether the Vikings thought that the world is literally flat is hard to answer. Humans do not play a great role in the Nordic myths; they are mostly objects of the gods' whims and other events happening in the world. After the end of the world, Ragnarök (translated in English as the "twilight of the gods"), only two humans survive, and they, with a few lesser surviving gods, establish an era of peace and tranquility. However, this ending is suspected to be an influence of Christianity, as the poems were collected relatively late in the thirteenth century.[8]

The idea of Earth being flat can be traced back to these ancient myths. Being the way the world was ordinarily viewed, the ancient Near Eastern cosmology is repeated almost unchanged in the Old Testament. The world is depicted as a flat disk supported by pillars. Below our feet is *sheol*, the place of the dead, and above us is the dome of heaven. The lower heaven is the realm of birds but also planets and stars. The upper heaven is the abode of divine beings. Nevertheless, the fact that the idea of a flat Earth never got much traction in the later Mediterranean (especially Greek) philosophies, as well as the early church, shows the power of natural philosophy over simple experience and a good story.[9]

Ancient cosmogonies were openly mythical, taking place in primordial time and offering detailed descriptions of the divine councils and lives of the gods. Comparing these to the Old Testament, it is obvious that their tone is different, even if there are several similarities. For the Judeo-Christian tradition, the obvious source for cosmological speculation is, of course, the two creation stories in the beginning of Genesis (1:1–2:3 and 2:4–25), but the psalms (esp. Pss. 8, 19, 29, 65, 104, 139), Proverbs 3:8, Job, and Isaiah 40–55 also contain material that is relevant for the understanding of creation.[10] It is well known that the creation accounts of the Old Testament employ the same material as other contemporary and older accounts. However, the authors of Genesis used it to tell a different story.[11] For example, nowhere in the Old Testament

8. See, e.g., the poem "Voluspa" in Crawford, *Poetic Edda*.

9. For an overview of the Old Testament cosmology, see Greenwood, *Scripture and Cosmology*, 71–102. The church fathers and the medieval church took the idea of a spherical Earth as a fact proved by common sense, and there were very few exceptions to this rule. The claim that the church had believed in a flat Earth is a rather recently invented myth. See J. Russell, *Inventing the Flat Earth*; Grant, *Planets, Stars and Orbs*, 626.

10. Clifford, *Creation Accounts*, 137–97; Enns, *Evolution of Adam*, 35–61; Walton, "Genesis."

11. Gunton, *Triune Creator*, 17–18; Fergusson, *Cosmos and the Creator*, 7; Walton, *Genesis 1*, 193–98; Jaki, *Genesis 1*, 8–31.

are planets or the forces of nature deified. However, some passages, such as Isaiah 51:9–10, use the language of primordial fight:

> Awake, as in days gone by,
> as in generations of old.
> Was it not you who cut Rahab to pieces,
> who pierced that monster through?
> Was it not you who dried up the sea,
> the waters of the great deep,
> who made a road in the depths of the sea
> so that the redeemed might cross over?

Furthermore, Genesis 1 employs language and themes reminiscent of Mesopotamian creation narratives, including primordial matter, which God uses to create the world and effect the separation of various elements and the sky as a "vault":

> In the beginning God created the heavens and the earth. Now the earth was formless and empty, darkness was over the surface of the deep, and the Spirit of God was hovering over the waters.
> And God said, "Let there be light," and there was light. God saw that the light was good, and he separated the light from the darkness. God called the light "day," and the darkness he called "night." And there was evening, and there was morning—the first day.
> And God said, "Let there be a vault between the waters to separate water from water." So God made the vault and separated the water under the vault from the water above it. And it was so. God called the vault "sky." And there was evening, and there was morning—the second day. (Gen. 1:1–3)

It is not possible to offer a detailed interpretation of Genesis here. Considering our theme, it suffices to note that the creation accounts of the Old Testament are thoroughly theological, and actual cosmological details are not at the center of the story, enabling the liberal use of contemporary images and language. The focus is on God as the sole benevolent Creator, who creates an orderly, good world where humans can live. The world does not come into being through theomachy, a battle between gods; even though the primordial powers are real powers, they yield to God without resistance. Thus, despite use of the language of that era, the way in which the narrator employed it is clearly different, such that familiar concepts were given a new theological meaning.[12]

---

12. On the patristic accounts of creation, where the emphasis is on theological anthropology and Christology, see Bouteneff, *Beginnings*, 55–87. On the early interpretations of the Old

John Walton points out something obvious in the Bible—namely, that God never reveals things that would be scientifically ahead of that period. Revelation takes place in the culture in which people were living at the time. Moreover, revelation also serves the needs of that culture, which often makes it hard for other cultures to understand it properly, or at least grasp all the details in it. For example, Walton makes a helpful distinction between material and functional ontologies. While material ontology is concerned about the absolute origin of things, functional ontology is about what makes a thing what it is. It is framed by offering an account of how things are related to one another and how they form a functional whole.[13] These two types of ontologies do not exclude each other, but they are different ways of looking at things. Walton's point is that material ontology would have been foreign at the time of the writing of Genesis, while functional ontology would have been the most natural way of approaching the question of things coming into existence. Therefore, the text of Genesis addresses an issue that is larger than the question about mere material origins.

Let us note here an important point: while it is true that the Bible does not contain any new scientific discoveries, this does not mean that it does not contain ideas that are philosophically new and revolutionary. For example, Genesis provides a comprehensive worldview where everything is "good." Being good refers to the purpose of things; everything is in its right place. Goodness is something that is built into the fabric of the cosmos; it is not accidental or contingent.[14] Moreover, the six days of creation followed by the Sabbath refer to the liturgical function of the cosmos. The whole creation is God's temple. This can be seen as an affirmation of absolute monotheism, as the other gods are effectively made homeless; they have no temple.[15]

Genesis does not explicitly state that everything was created out of nothing (ex nihilo), but the later tradition found that to be a doctrine that could be supported by Genesis. The earliest reference to ex nihilo is found in 2 Maccabees (second century BC): "So I urge you, my child, to look at the sky and the earth. Consider everything you see there, and realize that God made it all from nothing, just as he made the human race" (2 Macc.

Testament creation accounts, see also Walton, *Genesis 1*; Walton, *Lost World*; Fretheim, *God and World*; and Anderson, *Creation*.

13. Walton, *Lost World*, 18–19, 23–37.

14. This issue is related to the origin stories where the world comes about as a consequence of a primordial fight between the principalities. In the Christian story, violence and war are not at the center, compared to the ultimate primacy of God over everything else. As Paul Ricoeur states, "Creation is not a victory over an Enemy older than the creator." Quoted in Gunton, *Triune Creator*, 26.

15. Smith, *Priestly Vision of Genesis 1*.

7:28 GNT).[16] In the Shepherd of Hermas, it is stated, "First of all, believe that God is One, who created all things and set them in order, and made out of what did not exist everything that is, and who contains all things but is himself alone uncontained."[17] However, the early Jewish interpretations differed on the exact meaning of "nothing," and there was no consensus regarding what nothingness in fact referred to.[18]

During the first Christian centuries, the Platonic narratives of creation, which presupposed eternal matter, provided a reason to formulate the actual doctrine. However, the official status came quite late, in the Fourth Lateran Council (1215), where it was stated: "God . . . creator of all visible and invisible things, of the spiritual and of the corporal; who by His own omnipotent power at once from the beginning of time created each creature from nothing, spiritual and corporal, namely, angelic and mundane, and finally the human, constituted as it were, alike of the spirit and the body."[19] Nevertheless, the teaching had had strong support among the early church, which had to resist gnostic interpretations of the creation.[20] The early Christian interpreters of Genesis noted a resemblance between mythical concepts and the biblical text, but they were quick to point out how their meaning and use were different.[21] The canonical origins of *creatio ex nihilo* are ultimately in the New Testament, such as in Hebrews 11:3 ("By faith we understand that the universe was formed at God's command, so that what is seen was not made out of what was visible") and Revelation 4:11 ("You are worthy, our Lord and God, to receive glory and honor and power, for you created all things, and by your will they were created and have their being").[22]

Similar primacy and the providential presence of God are also prevalent in the Old Testament, where creation has a teleology and order.[23] Everything in

16. In the Septuagint: ὅτι οὐκ ἐξ ὄντων ἐποίησεν αὐτὰ ὁ θεός (*hoti ouk ex ontōn epoiēsen auta ho theos*).

17. Shepherd of Hermas, Mandate 1.1, in Holmes, *Apostolic Fathers*, 505.

18. For discussion, see May, *Creatio Ex Nihilo*; W. Brown, *Ethos of Cosmos*, 40; Oord, *Theologies of Creation*; Reno, *Genesis*, 29–46; and Burrell, *Creation*. For a philosophical defense of creation ex nihilo, see Copan and Craig, *Creation out of Nothing*. Copan and Craig argue that even if the concept of ex nihilo does not as such appear in Genesis, the account of Genesis even in its original meaning fits well together with the later doctrine.

19. Denzinger, *Compendium of Creeds*, §428.

20. For Philo, Justin, Theophilus, and Irenaeus on ex nihilo, see Steenberg, *Irenaeus on Creation*, 38–44. The reason for the late formulation was the rise of Platonism in the early Middle Ages. See Fiorenza and Gavin, *Systematic Theology*, 219–20.

21. See, e.g., Basil, *Hexaemeron* 2.2; 2.4, where he argues that the "deep" does not refer to primordial powers. See also Irenaeus, *Against Heresies* 4.20.1–2; Origen, *De principiis* 1.3.3; 2.1.4.

22. Gunton, *Triune Creator*, 20–24; Copan and Craig, *Creation out of Nothing*, 71–91.

23. W. Brown, *Ethos of Cosmos*, 36–132. On the same order in New Testament accounts of creation, see Coloe, *Creation Is Groaning*, 71–115.

the created order is oriented toward God, as Psalms 24:1 claims: "The earth is the LORD's, and everything in it, the world, and all who live in it." A central concept that includes not only humans but all life is *nephesh*, a sacred life force, which suffers if the relationship with the Creator is broken and which seeks to return to God (Ps. 33:19). Humans are generally called images of God, which in the ancient world was a title reserved for the representatives of the divine realm—that is, kings and queens.

In general, the ancient Israelites adopted the contemporary worldview because there was not much in their covenant with Yahweh that seriously challenged it, except their philosophical claims concerning the nature of God as one and the relation between God and the created order. Interestingly, the Israelite cosmology was more minimalistic and less explicit than its Egyptian and Mesopotamian counterparts.[24] This enabled an easy and natural connection between Israelite religious cosmology and Platonism.[25]

Plato's Lively Cosmos

Plato's *Timaeus* (360 BC) is the first major philosophical treatise of cosmology in the history of Western philosophy. It predates the scientific method, but it offers quite acute observations about reality and portrays an inquiring mindset that constantly seeks greater understanding. In the Platonic cosmology, the chaotic primal matter, the Ideas or Forms, and the demiurge have existed for all eternity.[26] Movement toward a better grasp of the real is based on the distinction between two levels of reality: unchangeable Forms and changeable matter. Our world, which is subject to change and decay, has been made into the image of the unchangeable.

> Now if so be that this Cosmos is beautiful and its Constructor good, it is plain that he fixed his gaze on the Eternal; but if otherwise (which is an impious supposition), his gaze was on that which has come into existence. But it is clear to

24. The Old Testament contains several cosmic depictions that suggest there was no single cosmology to which Israelites were supposed to adhere. Cf. Ps. 24:1–2; 136:6 (the earth is established "on the waters"), and Ps. 104 (the firmament that holds the waters). See Pongratz-Leisten et al., "Creation and Cosmogony." The plurality of images made it easier to adopt a more metaphorical approach to the narratives.

25. The Jewish philosopher Philo of Alexandria (25 BC–AD 50) wrote an influential commentary on Genesis in which he argued for a form of creation ex nihilo that was influenced by Platonism: matter was not eternal even if the ideas that were used to form the matter were. Effectively there was thus a primary creation of ideas in eternity that preceded the creation of matter in time. Philo of Alexandria, *Creation of the Cosmos* 1, 4 (pp. 7, 16).

26. Plato, *Timaeus* 31ab, 37c, 52, 92c.

everyone that his gaze was on the Eternal; for the Cosmos is the fairest of all that has come into existence, and He the best of all the Causes. So having in this wise come into existence, it has been constructed after the pattern of that which is apprehensible by reason and thought and is self-identical. Again, if these premises be granted, it is wholly necessary that this Cosmos should be a Copy of something.[27]

The world as we know it was created by the *demiourgos*, which is a name for the manifestation of the perfectly good and beautiful divine mind; often this has been simply translated as "God," but it is clear that Plato did not have in mind the concept of a theistic Creator; the demiurge is instead an impersonal symbol of organizing force, which is not an object of worship. The demiurge, being perfect in every way and lacking nothing, guarantees that the world is created in the image of divine reality, which effectively makes this world both the only and the best possible world.[28]

Being the best means that the world follows certain mathematical ideals. The idea of the world as spherical, and thereby perfect, was first suggested by Parmenides on philosophical grounds. It was only later, when it became possible to make actual measurements and experiments, that Plato's friend Eudoxus of Cnidus proved this initially philosophical claim to be empirically true. Thus, Plato very likely believed that our world is spherical, like the other heavenly bodies.[29]

Neither the demiurge nor the Ideas or Forms (most of all Goodness, Beauty, Truth) are part of our physical cosmos; instead, they reside in the realm beyond it.[30] Since the temporal world resembles the eternal world so much, it is possible for us to contemplate the world such that it functions like an icon, offering us access to the eternal. Even if the depiction of cosmology is anthropocentric, this is only the case because cosmological contemplation is the only way for our souls to find their way back to their original state. In fact, we are not the centerpiece in the cosmos, and the cosmos was not created for our sake. However, the demiurge has created our minds and bodies and the cosmos so that they have an indissoluble connection. Our task in this earthly life is to use our demiurge-given senses to bring our chaotic selves back into harmony with the universe. "But the cause and purpose of that best good, as we must maintain, is this,—that God devised and bestowed upon us vision to

27. Plato, *Timaeus* 29ab (trans. Bury, 53).
28. Cornford, *Plato's Cosmology*, 37–38. Later, the demiurge came to mean a lesser creator god or the highest of the this-worldly gods. This was not Plato's usage of the term.
29. Grant, *Science and Religion*, 75. Plato, *Timaeus* 33b.
30. Plato, *Timaeus* 42e.

the end that we might behold the revolutions of Reason in the Heaven and use them for the revolvings of the reasoning that is within us, these being akin to those, the perturbable to the imperturbable; and that, through learning and sharing in calculations which are correct by their nature, by imitation of the absolutely unvarying revolutions of the God we might stabilize the variable revolutions within ourselves."[31]

The world is an organism like the human body and therefore intelligible.[32] The human body is a *microcosmos* that reflects in its physical appearance the nature of the cosmos. The human head is the seat of reason, the highest of the cognitive faculties, and therefore spherical, like the planets, which move in perfect and perpetual circular motion. Lower animals, such as horses and birds, who lack this capacity, have nonspherical heads. The lowest of animals—fish and everything that lives in the water—are at the farthest end of the scale.

By means of their intellect, humans can—and should—transcend their bodily existence. The body is a prison of the soul, and the soul belongs to the higher realm.[33] Return takes place by meditation on the features of the physical world, which are a reflection of the divine perfection and order. Incidentally, the Greek word *physis* also means "order" or "law" (*nomos*).[34] For Plato, as in Greek thought in general, natural philosophy was not a science in the sense that we use the term, but it combined elements from philosophy, political theory, mathematics, and religion. The purpose of natural philosophy was the education of the soul so that it could escape earthly existence and once again become united with Ideas.[35] The same approach to philosophy was widely adopted by the early Christians, who interpreted the ascent of the soul to God in ways that heavily drew on Platonic cosmology.[36]

Plato held that the cosmos is a living thing that has a soul and reason, and planets are also animate, godlike beings.[37] The cosmos is thus full of life. This later became known as "the principle of plenitude."[38] Plato writes, "For since God desired to make it resemble most closely that intelligible Creature which is fairest of all and in all ways most perfect, He constructed it as a Living

31. Plato, *Timaeus* 47bc (trans. Bury, 109). See also 88c.

32. Plato, *Timaeus* 39e.

33. Plato, *Timaeus* 81d–e.

34. Plato, *Gorgias* 492a.

35. Grant, *History of Natural Philosophy*, 21–26.

36. On the use of Platonist themes by Origen, Gregory of Nyssa, and Athanasius, see Louth, *Christian Mystical Tradition*, 51–94.

37. Plato, *Timaeus* 30c, 39a. A good treatment of what this personification of planetary bodies meant and how it has been employed in modern fiction by C. S. Lewis can be found in M. Ward, *Planet Narnia*.

38. Lovejoy, *Great Chain of Being*, 50–55.

Creature, one and visible, containing within itself all the living creatures which are by nature akin to itself."[39]

The principle of plenitude was taken up in the twentieth century by Arthur Lovejoy and put forward as a quintessential Platonic idea. Lovejoy argued that the principle is a natural outcome of Plato's metaphysics, and he charted its appearances throughout Western intellectual history. Lovejoy thus summarized Plato's logic behind the idea: "The idea of Good is a necessary reality; it cannot be other than what its essence implies; and it therefore must, by virtue of its own nature, necessarily engender finite existents. And the number of kinds of these is predetermined logically; the Absolute would not be what it is if it gave rise to anything less than a complete world in which the 'model,' i.e., the totality of ideal Forms, is translated into concrete realities. It follows that every sensible thing that is, is because it—or at all events, its sort—cannot but be, and be precisely what it is."[40]

Although Lovejoy's interpretation of the principle of plenitude can be contested when it comes to the details, it is nonetheless true that this way of thinking about the world had considerable influence on later Platonic tradition and also on Basil, Augustine, and Aquinas.[41] The principle became the subject of increased criticism, especially after the late Middle Ages.[42] We do not need to delve into the intricacies of this particular theory; it suffices to note that it resonated well with Judeo-Christian theism, which had close affinity with Platonism during the first centuries of Christianity. In its theological form, the principle means that it is good that God creates things in abundance, or that we have no reason to think that God should only create those things that are absolutely needed—and nothing else. The Platonic cosmology was remarkably

39. Plato, *Timaeus* 30d (trans. Bury, 57).

40. Lovejoy, *Great Chain of Being*, 54.

41. Basil, *Hexaemeron* 5.7; Augustine, *City of God* 11.22–23. To be precise, Augustine does not think that given enough time everything that is potential will become actualized; see *City of God* 11.5. Nevertheless, he does think that the cosmos contains beings in plenitude, and many of those are odd, strange, and even dangerous, and this is something that reflects God's nature as the Creator who is ultimately Good. Aquinas writes (*ST* 1.47.1): "God planned to create many distinct things, in order to share with them and reproduce in them his goodness. Because no one creature could do this, he produced many diverse creatures, so that what was lacking in one expression of his goodness could be made up by another; for the goodness which God has whole and together, creatures share in many different ways. And the whole universe shares and expresses that goodness better than any individual creature."

42. However, the reasons for this were quite complicated. Among these was the question of which things the plenitude exactly refers to. Should we expect a plenitude of possible individual beings or events? If the former, this resembles atomism, which was rejected by Plato and Aristotle. If the latter, then we are not very far from hard determinism (which late medieval voluntarists claimed to restrict the freedom of God). Also, the principle has had various interpretations and suggestions of how and to what it can be applied. See Hintikka, "Great Chain of Being."

close to the Judeo-Christian idea of creation. They both acknowledged the goodness and purpose of creation. However, the eternity of matter caused problems during the first centuries of Christianity, as that seemed to suggest the existence of a coeternal entity alongside God.

Aristotle and the Ptolemaic Cosmos

Aristotle's (384–322 BC) main work dealing with cosmology is his early *On the Heavens (Peri ouranou)*. The work shares a lot in common with Plato when it comes to the basic elements of cosmology, even if there are clear differences.[43] The most obvious dissimilarity is the order in which the philosophers proceed in giving their accounts. Plato began with the eternal world, which is reflected in the harmony of the cosmos, in its laws and shapes. Aristotle instead started with immediate empirical phenomena and tried to provide an account that makes sense of what we see. His cosmological model had immense historical influence, for it came to dominate, with only minor changes, Western scientific inquiry for almost two thousand years.

Aristotle held that the cosmos has existed from all eternity, it has no beginning, and it will never end. The cosmos is the sum of everything that exists. Therefore, our cosmos is also the only one that exists, and its center is the spherical Earth, which is minuscule compared to other heavenly bodies.[44] The cosmos is divided between sublunary Nature (*physis*) and translunary Sky (*ouranos*). The world of Nature is the world of change, whereas the Sky is immutable and unchanging. In Nature, things come into being and go out of existence, they live and they die, and they grow and decay. In the Sky, nothing changes. The word *nova*, which counterintuitively from our perspective refers to a new (*novum*) star, illustrates this point. The appearance of the first supernova in 1572 was quite literally a world-shattering event. In the place where nothing was supposed to change, a change occurred.

Like Plato, Aristotle held that the sublunary world consists of four elements— Earth, Air, Fire, and Water—and all other substances are mixtures of these. The element of Sky is aether, also known as the "fifth element," which is eternal. Everything in the cosmos has a natural way of moving into its correct place by

43. Some early interpreters tried to harmonize *Timaeus* and *On the Heavens* so that they would define the cosmos in the same way. See Baltes, *Die Weltentstehung*.

44. Aristotle's estimate for Earth's circumference was 400,000 stadia. The exact length of a stadium varied from 150 to 300 meters, but in any case Aristotle's calculations made the earth significantly bigger than it actually is. Still, Aristotle thought that the other bodies are much bigger than Earth, which hints at the cosmological scales in the ancient world. Aristotle, *On the Heavens* 2.14.

its own powers: pieces of earth fall downward, fire rises upward. Movement is not due to external influence but rather to the inherent inclination of an object toward its natural state. Outward influence can prohibit movement by blocking the object, like when a rock is held by the hand, but when the hand is removed, the rock will fall. Unlike all other movements, circular movement, perceived in perfect form only in the planets, does not have a contradicting or opposing movement, and thus it is eternal, like the uncreated matter through which the stars travel.

The Aristotelian model of the cosmos was laid out in detail by Ptolemy in his work *Almagest*.[45] The Ptolemaic model was taken as the standard schema for the universe, and it was also adopted by the early church. This model was the best available scientific explanation of the universe, and it remained dominant until challenged by Copernicus, Kepler, and Galileo. Ptolemy's theory was a mixture of philosophy and empirical calculations. One example of this was the idea that the earth is not in fact in the exact mathematical center of the cosmos, since this so-called deferent center and the earth do not exist in the same location. Moreover, the planets do not move in their orbits like trains but orbit the epicycle center, which follows a perfectly circular route around the earth. These theories were introduced to accommodate the irregularities of the planetary movements, which resulted from elliptical orbits. In this, Ptolemy's model admittedly did a good job, but it did not remove the inherent tension between his complex mathematics and the presupposition of perfection that was fundamental in Aristotelian philosophy.[46]

In the Ptolemaic model of the cosmos, the earth is spherical and surrounded by the Seven Heavens (see fig. 1.2). These heavens are translucent globes, each of which is home to a shining planet. Looking up from the earth, these heavens are the moon, Mercury, Venus, the sun, Mars, Jupiter, and Saturn. The planets were also held to be gods, following the Platonic fashion of according to moving objects a soul that animates them. Thus, the whole cosmos was seen to be alive as a sum of different souls that could affect each other to create a harmonious whole. The theory of astrology—that is, the influence of stars on the life of humans—was based on this Greek holistic cosmology.[47]

45. Toomer, *Ptolemy's Almagest*, 150. Even though Aristotle's works became lost for centuries in the West and were rediscovered later in the early Middle Ages, Ptolemy's works remained in the public knowledge.

46. Scharf, *Copernicus Complex*, 15.

47. Even if Aristotle thought that heavenly bodies influence terrestrial bodies, he never taught that we could use this connection to make predictions. However, this was argued by Ptolemy in his work *Tetrabiblos*. Grant, *Science and Religion*, 101.

Figure 1.2. Ptolemaic cosmos, from Peter Apian's book *Cosmographia* (published 1524).

Beyond Saturn was the *stellatum*, where all the stars that did not move resided. Sometimes an extra layer was added for planetary constellations. If one goes through the *stellatum*, one finds the First Moved (*primum mobile*), which is the first ultimate thing that is still part of our cosmos. After this, human categories break down. Aristotle offers this fascinating account, which tries to strike a balance between what must be said and what cannot be said:

It is therefore evident that there is also no place or void or time outside the heaven. For in every place body can be present; and void is said to be that in which the presence of body, though not actual, is possible; and time is the number of movement. But in the absence of natural body there is no movement, and outside the heaven, as we have shown, body neither exists nor can come to exist. It is clear then that there is neither place, nor void, nor time, outside the heaven. Hence whatever is there, is of such a nature as not to occupy any place, nor does time age it; nor is there any change in any of the things which lie beyond the outermost motion; they continue through their entire duration unalterable and unmodified, living the best and most self-sufficient of lives.[48]

The later Christian centuries read this as an account of heaven or the nature of God. However, even if Aristotle believed in God, his idea differed from that of both Plato and the Christian understanding of the divine. For Aristotle,

48. Aristotle, *On the Heavens* 1.9.

God is totally disinterested of the cosmos; God is totally self-sufficient thought that thinks only about itself. It has neither any need nor awareness of us. We are insignificant.[49] Nevertheless, the Aristotelian God and its creation had enough common features with the Judeo-Christian doctrine of creation that Christian theologians could recognize some familiarity with it and use Aristotle's thought as a framework for theological deliberation.

Biblical cosmogonies evidently differ from other ancient Near Eastern origin myths. Granted, they share certain elements, but they were used differently to underline the difference of Yahweh from creation. Regarding factual cosmology, the Bible remains relatively silent. It does not contain the kind of deliberation that we find in the texts of Plato and Aristotle, which makes the biblical tradition flexible and able to coexist with different cosmologies. Effectively, various cosmological accounts were quite early on interpreted as allegories and metaphors. For example, the talk about pillars of the earth (Job 9:6; 1 Sam. 2:8) was ordinarily interpreted as references to the divine power and providence, even if the original audience might have taken the expressions literally. This hermeneutical openness has been a great advantage for the Christian tradition, which has been adamant on certain philosophical points on creation but has shown considerable freedom on where the line between allegory and concrete history should be drawn.

---

49. Gilson, *God and Philosophy*, 31–37. For a thorough treatment of how Greek philosophy was divided on the issue of whether the world needs a designer, see Sedley, *Creationism*.

2

The Voyage Home

Cosmos in Early Christian Thought

The early church was not particularly interested in philosophical or scientific cosmology. This is understandable, since the church was persecuted until the fourth century and it did not have a position in society that could have enabled creation of a systematic cosmology. Similarly, the church did not produce any noteworthy art that was preserved for later generations (or if it did, such was destroyed quite early on). What the church produced and what have been preserved are the canonical and other theological texts. But not even the key texts of the Apologists—like Justin Martyr's *First and Second Apology* and *Dialogue with Trypho*, and Tertullian's *Apology*—address cosmological issues in detail, as they are more focused on proving that Christians are not a public threat (to the Romans) and on working out Christianity's relationship with Judaism. After the Constantinian turn, Christians quite rapidly rose to the cultural elite. It is at this point that cosmological issues were first raised in earnest.

In this chapter, I offer an overview of early Christian cosmological thinking, with special attention given to Basil's and Augustine's theological cosmologies. I also offer brief accounts of how the early Christians understood the relationship of theology and secular philosophy and to what extent Christian cosmology was anthropocentric.

Genesis Interpreted

An obvious theme for the early church that required attention was the interpretation of the book of Genesis and its depiction of the creation of the world in six days. Natural counterparts in the contemporary culture were, of course, Plato's *Timaeus* and Aristotle's *On the Heavens*, as well as their commentaries. The gnostics and other groups that were close to the church also offered their own accounts and interpretations about the nature of the world, often using material from the canonical texts of the church.[1]

It is worth noting that the challenge that came from Greek philosophy cannot be defined in terms of "science" versus "religion," as is often done nowadays. The main reason for this is the fact that the philosophy of that time included religious elements, and consequently pure categories of science and religion were not available until the nineteenth century.[2] Influential Epicurean and Stoic schools were philosophies that aimed for the examined life. This was naturally something that the early church could relate to, and in the first apologies for the Christian faith, the Apologists portrayed Christian faith as "true philosophy."[3] The influence of those schools started to wane in the first century, and they were slowly replaced by different forms of Platonism and Aristotelianism, which were mixed with aspects of religious mysticism. Out of these traditions came gnostic and Manichean doctrines, which argued for a strong dualism between two basic principles: matter was transient and evil, whereas spirit was eternal and good. With the help of secret knowledge (Gr. *gnosis*), the follower of a religious lifestyle could be freed from the shackles of matter and rise back into the spiritual realm.

When Christians began to have more public visibility and could address more philosophical issues, the dominant school from about 250 onward was Neoplatonism, which formed the most important intellectual background for early Christian philosophy. The effect of Neoplatonism was most prevalent in the debates about Christology and the trinitarian relationship. Regarding the doctrine of creation, Plotinus's (204–270) doctrine of the One was important. On the one hand, the idea of One as ultimate principle was easy to connect to the Judeo-Christian tradition; on the other, the Plotinian One was impersonal, and the creation—or emanation—of the world out of the One was a necessary act, not a willed one.[4]

1. Kenny, *New History*, 77–94.
2. For helpful deconstructions of simple categories of science and religion in antiquity, see Harrison, *Territories*; Nongbri, *Before Religion*.
3. E.g., Justin Martyr, *Dialogue with Trypho* 8.
4. Cox, *By the Same Word*, 31–43.

Given that the church was challenged from both within and without, it is interesting that it never landed on one true interpretation of the details of Genesis and did not give creedal status to any comprehensive cosmological model. The early treatises were focused on objecting to gnostic and Manichean interpretations of Genesis, and this philosophical opposition unites them. The church was, on the one hand, tied to the language of the ancient Near East cosmology that the Bible used, but, on the other hand, it felt that these claims had to be squared, at least to some extent, with Plato and Aristotle.[5] The problematic passages were typically allegorized, and quite rapidly the doctrinal core of the early Christian doctrine of creation boiled down to the following basic claims:

1. Created matter (i.e., "the heavens and the earth") is not eternal.
2. Created matter is good.
3. The existence of the cosmos is not an accident, for it exists because of divine will.

These led to three further fundamental cosmological convictions:

4. God is one.
5. The evil in the world is not created by God.
6. Everything is created with a purpose.[6]

This may not sound like much, but it was in the denial of these points that the church felt that its core message was threatened. The early church did not put its foot down when it came to interpreting various cosmological images and tropes of the Bible.[7] A modern reader may be surprised to learn that the early Christian interpretations of Genesis were heavily allegorical. For example, Origen (185–254) writes in *First Principles* (*De principiis*),

5. Greenwood, *Scripture and Cosmology*, 132, 157–58.
6. Thus, among others, Basil, *Hexaemeron* 1.2; 2.2–3; Justin Martyr, *First Apology* 1.10; Theophilus, *To Autoclytus* 2.10; Irenaeus, *Against Heresies* 4.39.2. See also Steenberg, *Irenaeus on Creation*, 32–38; Bouteneff, *Beginnings*, 86–87. The themes remained almost unchanged for over a thousand years. For example, Philipp Melanchthon's *Loci Communes* 1521 and Martin Chemnitz's *Loci Theologici* (which was a widely read expansion of Melanchthon's work) consider these as central themes on the doctrine of creation. Chemnitz, *Loci Theologici*, 1:152–72. For contemporary expositions of the doctrine of creation along these same lines, see Jenson, *Systematic Theology*, 2:1–16; Fergusson, *Cosmos and the Creator*, 1–22; Gunton, *Triune Creator*, 14–40; Hart, *The Hidden and the Manifest*, 338–50; and Backhaus, "'Before Abraham,'" 84.
7. Neither did the medieval church, which tolerated various opinions on the details of Genesis. See Grant, *Planets, Stars and Orbs*, 85.

which was the first systematic account of theology (or at least close to one),
as follows:

> For who that has understanding will suppose that the first, and second, and
> third day, and the evening and the morning, existed without a sun, and moon,
> and stars? And that the first day was, as it were, also without a sky? And who is
> so foolish as to suppose that God, after the manner of a husbandman, planted
> a paradise in Eden, towards the east, and placed in it a tree of life, visible and
> palpable, so that one tasting of the fruit by the bodily teeth obtained life? And
> again, that one was a partaker of good and evil by masticating what was taken
> from the tree? And if God is said to walk in the paradise in the evening, and
> Adam to hide himself under a tree, I do not suppose that anyone doubts that
> these things figuratively indicate certain mysteries, the history having taken
> place in appearance, and not literally.[8]

However, the fathers had diverging views regarding what parts of Genesis
should be interpreted allegorically. Did God *really* give clothes made of skins
to Adam and Eve after the fall? Was Eden a place that could be located geo-
graphically? Questions like these were pondered, and theologians criticized each
other's readings, but these questions never caused significant intra-Christian
debate. Nevertheless, it is good to remember that while the allegorical sense
and literal sense were not mutually exclusive (and the proper use of allegory
required the reality of the historical events, even if the exact mode of historicity
was debated) for the fathers, the early church never settled on one ratified view
regarding which things in Scripture were literal and which were allegorical.[9]

On the Outskirts of Athens and Jerusalem

The early church was not hostile toward secular philosophy in general. However, Tertullian's comments are often used to make the church sound more
critical than it actually was. His remarks about the mutual exclusivity of Athens

---

8. Origen, *De principiis* 4.16 (*ANF* 4:365).
9. A good hermeneutical rule of thumb is expressed by Augustine: "No one, then, forbids
us to understand Paradise according to these, and perhaps other, more appropriate, allegorical interpretations, while also believing in the truth of that story as presented to us in a most
faithful narrative of events." Augustine, *City of God* 13.21 (trans. Dyson, 568–69). See also
Augustine, *Literal Meaning of Genesis* 8.1.1.1. Even Origen (*De principiis* 2.3.6), who was fond
of allegory, denies that allegorical reading of Genesis means denying the bodily reality of the
blessed state. Purely allegorical interpretations were used by gnostics and generally rejected
by the fathers. It was nonetheless important for the early church to avoid anthropomorphisms
like God's bodily movement and breathing. For a discussion, see Sheridan, *Language for God*,
127–42; Bouteneff, *Beginnings*, 69–70.

and Jerusalem are sometimes used as examples of Christian opposition to all rational thought.[10] His rhetoric is admittedly extreme, but in the end his constructive position is not all that dramatic. Tertullian is not opposed to philosophy qua philosophy, but rather the forms of Greek philosophy being done in a way that is not philosophically sound. In his *Apology*, he expresses the epistemic stance of Christian faith, which can be summarized as follows:[11]

1. Theology is interested in truth.
2. Theological matters should be approached with the help of proofs, arguments, and evidence.
3. Arguments should be formed so that they rely on premises that are held by all parties.

His account is especially interesting since he is regarded as holding the most extreme position among the fathers.[12] Clearly, according to him, there is no room for irrationality in theology. Instead, the fathers typically pointed out how philosophers disagreed with one another and contradicted themselves. In effect, the debate went as follows: If a philosopher claimed that a Christian doctrine was spurious, one of the rhetorical tricks to disarm the charge was to point out that the opponent's own tradition was hardly unified, containing multiple contradictory—and often ridiculous—positions. The disagreement of the philosophers was then contrasted with the alleged unity of revelation.[13]

While philosophy was sometimes disparaged, several church fathers considered it an indispensable tool that could not be disregarded by Christians. A prominent Greek father, Clement of Alexandria (150–215), states the following in the section of *Miscellanies* called "Philosophy, the Handmaiden of Theology":

> Accordingly, before the advent of the Lord, philosophy was necessary to the Greeks for righteousness. And now it becomes conducive to piety; being a kind

10. Tertullian, *Prescription against Heretics* 7 (*ANF* 3:246): "What indeed has Athens to do with Jerusalem? What concord is there between the Academy and the Church? Our instruction comes from 'the porch of Solomon,' who had himself taught that 'the Lord should be sought in simplicity of heart.' Away with all attempts to produce a mottled Christianity of Stoic, Platonic, and dialectic composition!"

11. Tertullian, *Apology* 25 (*ANF* 3:39): "I think I have offered sufficient proof upon the question of false and true divinity, having shown that the proof rests not merely on debate and argument, but on the witness of the very beings whom you believe are gods, so that the point needs no further handling."

12. On Tertullian's alleged fideism, see Vainio, *Beyond Fideism*, 24–31.

13. This strategy was very popular. See, e.g., Basil, *Hexaemeron* 1.11; Tertullian, *On the Soul* 3; Theophilus, *To Autoclytus*, 3.2–8; Augustine, *City of God* 4.8–32; 8.1–4; 19.1; Ambrose, *Hexaemeron* 1.1–2.

of preparatory training to those who attain to faith through demonstration. "For your foot," it is said, "will not stumble, if you refer what is good, whether belonging to the Greeks or to us, to Providence" [Prov. 3:23]. For God is the cause of all good things; but of some primarily, as of the Old and the New Testament; and of others by consequence, as philosophy. Perchance, too, philosophy was given to the Greeks directly and primarily, till the Lord should call the Greeks. For this was a schoolmaster to bring "the Hellenic mind," as the law, the Hebrews, to Christ [Gal. 3:24]. Philosophy, therefore, was a preparation, paving the way for him who is perfected in Christ.[14]

Clement's stance illustrates well the general sense of philosophy as an ordered way of life. It was common during the early Christian centuries to think that Greek philosophy was influenced by the Old Testament, as that helped Christians embrace the Greek tradition as a long-lost relative.[15] But the positive attitude was supported with theological arguments as well. Since God is the Creator of all, pagans cannot help but find the vestiges of divine mind in creation.[16] Furthermore, Clement argued, we cannot avoid philosophizing because it is part of rational judgment, which is essential to human beings—but when we philosophize, we need to philosophize well.[17]

In the West, Augustine would become the most influential of all the fathers. In a widely read treatise *On Christian Doctrine*, he summarizes the positive attitude toward pagan philosophy, which later became known as "spoiling the Egyptians":

Moreover, if those who are called philosophers, and especially the Platonists, have said aught that is true and in harmony with our faith, we are not only not to shrink from it, but to claim it for our own use from those who have unlawful possession of it. For, as the Egyptians had not only the idols and heavy burdens which the people of Israel hated and fled from, but also vessels and ornaments of gold and silver, and garments, which the same people when going out of Egypt appropriated to themselves, designing them for a better use, not doing this on their own authority, but by the command of God, the Egyptians themselves, in their ignorance, providing them with things which they themselves were not making a good use of; in the same way all branches of heathen learning have not only false and superstitious fancies and heavy burdens of unnecessary toil, which every one of us, when going out under the leadership of Christ from the fellowship of the heathen, ought to abhor and avoid; but they contain also liberal instruction which is better adapted to the use of the truth, and some most

14. Clement of Alexandria, *Miscellanies* 1.5 (*ANF* 2:305).
15. E.g., Augustine, *On Christian Doctrine* 2.28.43; *City of God* 8.11.
16. Clement of Alexandria, *Miscellanies* 1.17.
17. Clement of Alexandria, *Miscellanies* 6.18.

excellent precepts of morality; and some truths in regard even to the worship of the One God are found among them. Now these are, so to speak, their gold and silver, which they did not create themselves, but dug out of the mines of God's providence which are everywhere scattered abroad, and are perversely and unlawfully prostituting to the worship of devils. These, therefore, the Christian, when he separates himself in spirit from the miserable fellowship of these men, ought to take away from them, and to devote to their proper use in preaching the gospel. Their garments, also,—that is, human institutions such as are adapted to that intercourse with men which is indispensable in this life,—we must take and turn to a Christian use.[18]

In principle, pagan natural philosophy was something that could be incorporated into Christian faith. Moreover, it was believed that things like logic and mathematics should be employed by Christians, as they lead to acquisition of a deeper understanding of faith. The process of absorption of new knowledge has certain rules of engagement, however. Augustine held that the content of faith is given once and for all through revelation and that this is something that reason by itself cannot establish. This functions as the basic premise, and everything is compared against this fundamental belief. But it does not mean that a Christian *understands* everything in a proper way. She may have an appropriate attitude of faith without much cognitive and propositional content being held consciously and in a manner that is able to stand against criticism. This is where the philosophy of the pagan world is beneficial: it helps faith to seek understanding.[19]

In sum, the early church did not condemn pagan natural philosophy out of hand. Certain presuppositions and outcomes were definitely criticized, but the overall attitude was positive. Nonetheless, the church felt that they had been given a particular starting point of philosophizing, but this was more or less compatible with the general modes of doing philosophy at the time. Next, we will look at concrete examples of this attitude.

Basil the Great on the First Six Days of Creation

Basil the Great (330–379), one of the Cappadocian fathers, wrote an influential and widely read treatise on creation (*Hexaemeron*, "Six Days"), which consists of sermons preached to a congregation about the first days of creation in Genesis. It offers an authoritative look at what was actually taught to the first Christians concerning cosmology. Basil, who had received a wide-ranging

18. Augustine, *On Christian Doctrine* 2.40.60 (NPNF[1] 2:554).
19. On Augustine's theory of knowledge, see Gioia, *Theological Epistemology*.

education and who knew well the sciences and philosophies of his time, relates his teaching to the well-known philosophical treatises without mentioning them by name.[20] Basil differs from Origen and other early Christian authors in his wish to avoid rampant allegory, which he observes was falsely used by the gnostics to give outlandish meanings to things like water and plants. Basil insists that words should be taken in their ordinary sense, so that when the Bible speaks about a "day" it means "twenty-four hours" (2.8).[21] Nevertheless, he openly discusses textual variants of the book (4.5), and he also uses allegory to give spiritual guidance to his listeners. For example, he tells that the moon changes its shape in order to remind us about how everything in the world is subject to change and that we should not cling to things that are not solid (6.10). Also, the actions of animals offer various spiritual lessons.

Basil makes a distinction between revealed knowledge and secular philosophy. Secular philosophy is castigated for causing endless disputes and disagreements, while revealed knowledge is secure (3.3; 3.8). However, Basil does not offer a clear theory on how to relate Christian and secular knowledge, and he seems to make ad hoc choices. In many cases, he simply follows the contemporary "science," which often (from our point of view) gets things quite wrong. For example, he subscribes to the Ptolemaic model of the cosmos because it seems reasonable to him. It is noteworthy that this is not a biblical argument he makes, but an argument on the basis of common sense (3.3; 9.1). He also uses commonsense arguments to determine the size of the sun, which he thinks, quite correctly, to be gigantic (6.9).

Basil notes that Genesis leaves many things unmentioned. These include the four elements, which Basil obviously takes as things or theories proven by the science of his time. However, the existence of the elements can be inserted into the text without contradicting it (2.3). A representative passage goes as follows:

> Those who have written about the nature of the universe have discussed at length the shape of the earth. If it be spherical or cylindrical, if it resembles a disc and is equally rounded in all parts, or if it has the forth of a winnowing basket and is hollow in the middle; all these conjectures have been suggested by cosmographers, each one upsetting that of his predecessor. It will not lead me to give less importance to the creation of the universe, that the servant of God, Moses, is silent as to shapes; he has not said that the earth is a hundred and eighty thousand furlongs in circumference; he has not measured into what

---

20. These educated listeners could have easily recognized these references to Plato, Aristotle, and Ptolemy, among others. For example, Basil discusses the movements of the elements, the location of the earth in the universe, the shape of the earth, and the shapes of different created beings. Hildebrand, *Basil of Cesarea*, 37–39; Kaiser, *Creational Theology*, 37–41.

21. All the references in parentheses are to Basil, *Hexaemeron*, in *NPNF²*, vol. 8.

extent of air its shadow projects itself while the sun revolves around it, nor stated how this shadow, casting itself upon the moon, produces eclipses. He has passed over in silence, as useless, all that is unimportant for us. (1.9)

What does Basil actually think about the relation between revealed Christian knowledge and science or common sense? This is not an easy question to answer. On the one hand, Basil seems to be very sure about both his theology and the judgments of common sense or established natural philosophy. On the other hand, he ridicules the disputes among philosophers but does seem to grant a space to pursue these inquiries, even if they are not of ultimate importance. All in all, Basil treats Genesis primarily as a theological account, which has some overlap with natural philosophy. Nevertheless, it is not clear where the boundaries are.

Saint Augustine on the Literal Meaning of Genesis

In the Western tradition, Basil's contemporary Ambrose of Milan (337–397) also produced a series of sermons on Genesis, where he more or less followed Basil's method. Ambrose starts his treatise by noting how natural philosophers disagree on basic cosmological matters. For the church, it is enough to believe that God has created the world. The exact nature of the cosmos is not something that requires a theological approach as such.[22]

The most influential work in the West, however, was *The Literal Meaning of Genesis* by Saint Augustine (who quite possibly had heard Ambrose's sermons on Genesis when preparing for his baptism in Milan). A particularly interesting feature in Augustine's work is that he takes creation to be an instantaneous act (*in ictu oculi*) rather than a literal six-day process, because Ecclesiasticus 18:1 states that God created everything "simultaneously" (*simul*).[23] In this way he is able to avoid the logical trap that results from the fact that Genesis speaks about the existence of days before the creation of the sun. The sequence narrated in Genesis is just a way of expressing things so that we can understand them. In this act of creation, the world is created with certain predispositions (*rationes seminales/causales rationes*) that are inherently in created things and can guide them toward the actualization of their potential. This development, however, is neither necessary and automatic nor random, but something that God guides.[24] As the seed develops into a tree, so does everything in the world.

---

22. Ambrose, *Hexameron* 1.2.
23. In the Vulgate: *qui vivit in aeternum creavit omnia simul Deus solus iustificabitur et manet invictus rex in aeternum.* Augustine, *Literal Meaning of Genesis* 6.11.19; 4.33.51.
24. Augustine, *Literal Meaning of Genesis* 6.14.25. R. Williams, "Creation," 253; McMullin, "Introduction," 8–16.

Now just as all these elements, which in the course of time and in due order would constitute a tree, were all invisibly and simultaneously present in that grain, so too that is how, when God created all things simultaneously, the actual cosmos is to be thought of as having had simultaneously all the things that were made in it and with it when the day was made (Gen. 2:4). . . . It also includes those things that water and earth produced potentially in their causes [*potentialiter atque causaliter*], before they could evolve through the intervals of time, as they are now known to us in the works on which God is continuing to work until now (John 5:17).[25]

Nevertheless, Augustine thinks (following Aristotle) that species are fixed, so that "a bean does not emerge from a grain of wheat, nor does the wheat emerge from a bean, or human beings from cattle, or cattle from human beings."[26] Alister McGrath makes an apt remark regarding Augustine's reading of Genesis and relating it to the science of his own time: "Only when Augustine borrows ideas from the scientific outlook of the culture within which he was embedded does he make mistakes that his successors need to correct."[27] On the whole, Augustine tried to be careful when applying science to theology. For example, regarding cosmological models, Augustine chose to be safe rather than sorry. Augustine sternly warns Christians about thinking too highly of their own cosmological visions:

There is knowledge, after all, about the earth, about the sky, about the other elements of this world, about the movements and revolutions or even magnitude and distance of the constellations, about the predictable eclipses of the moon and sun, about the cycles of years and seasons, about the nature of animals, fruits, stones and everything else of this kind. And it frequently happens that even non-Christians will have knowledge of this sort in a way that they can substantiate with scientific arguments or experiments. Now it is quite disgraceful and disastrous, something to be one's guard against all costs, that they ever hear Christians spouting what they claim our Christian literature has to say on these topics, and talking such nonsense that they can scarcely contain their laughter when they see them to be *toto caelo*, as the saying goes, wide of the mark. . . . I have, to the best of my ability, winkled out and presented a great variety of possible meanings to the words of the book of Genesis which have been darkly expressed in order to put us through our paces. I have avoided affirming anything hastily in a way that would rule out any alternative explanation that may be a better one, so leaving everyone free to choose whichever they can grasp most readily in their turn, and when

25. Augustine, *Literal Meaning of Genesis* 5.23.45 (trans. Hill, 299–300).
26. Augustine, *Literal Meaning of Genesis* 9.17.32 (trans. Hill, 394).
27. McGrath, *Fine-Tuned Universe*, 104.

they cannot understand, let them give honor to God's scripture, keeping fear for themselves.[28]

For example, Augustine thinks that the cosmos is spherical even if two verses in the Bible seem to attribute a different shape to it ("stretched skin" in Ps. 104:2; "vault" in Isa. 40:22). He harmonizes these passages with a spherical shape by pointing out that they do not exclude that possibility. Even if he accepts the Ptolemaic cosmology, he does not discuss the exact shape of the earth.[29] His main concern is somewhere else—namely, in spiritual matters. He states, "The Spirit of God who was speaking through them [the authors of the Bible] did not wish to teach people about such things which would contribute nothing to their salvation."[30] According to Augustine, Christians may freely disagree about the interpretation of individual terms and concepts. For example, there are several legitimate ways to interpret the meaning of "heaven and earth."[31] The main point, however, should be clear and beyond dispute: God is love and the sole Creator of the good cosmos.

A Universe for Humans?

In the Ptolemaic cosmos, the earth is at the center of everything. However, this is not a place of eminence; in fact, the center is the place of lowest value because it is the most distant point from heaven. Yet there is another way of approaching the question about the value of humans. Are humans the reason why the cosmos exists in the first place?

For example, Theophilus of Antioch (d. ca. 183–185) claimed that the cosmos was made for humans.[32] More specifically, the world was created so that humans could exist and thereby know God, even if God as a perfect being does not need this. Theophilus's account is very scant and a bit obscure, but

28. Augustine, *Literal Meaning of Genesis* 1.19.38–20.40 (trans. Hill, 187).
29. Ferrari, "Cosmography," 246.
30. Augustine, *Literal Meaning of Genesis* 2.9.20 (trans. Hill, 201–2).
31. Augustine, *Confessions* 12, 14, 17–30, 41.
32. Theophilus, *To Autolycus* 2.10 (ANF 2:97–98): "And first, they taught us with one consent that God made all things out of nothing; for nothing was coeval with God: but He being His own place, and wanting nothing, and existing before the ages, willed to make man by whom He might be known; for him, therefore, He prepared the world." See also the Shepherd of Hermas, Vision 2.4.1 (in Holmes, *Apostolic Fathers*, 211): "As I slept, brothers and sisters, a revelation was given to me by a very handsome young man, who said to me, 'Who do you think the elderly woman from whom you received the little book was?' I said: 'The Sibyl.' 'You are wrong,' he said. 'She is not.' 'Then who is she?' I said. 'The church,' he replied. I said to him, 'Why, then is she elderly?' 'Because,' he said, 'she was created before all things, therefore she is elderly, and for her sake the world was formed.'"

this kind of claim drew the attention of the pagan Celsus (fl. second century), who considered it as giving too high of a value to humans. It is, of course, hard to fathom whether there is more behind Theophilus's short statement than the desire to say that God cares about humans, and to what extent it was intended to be taken as a building block for a complete cosmological model. In any case, questions like this were not at the center of cosmological deliberations in the early church, because it was deemed more important to focus on establishing a relationship between the Old and the New Testaments, which meant creating a narrative of the history of salvation that spanned from Adam and Eve to Christ.[33] This is admittedly an anthropocentric view of history, but it is not inherently closed or exclusionary.

The same theme is found when Justin Martyr claims, "God, when He had made the whole world, and subjected things earthly to man, and arranged the heavenly elements for the increase of fruits and rotation of the seasons, and appointed this divine law—for these things also He evidently made for man—committed the care of men and of all things under heaven to angels whom He appointed over them."[34] For Justin, the idea of the world being created for humans serves a dual purpose. He underscores, on the one hand, like the Platonists, how the human mind "fits" the world and, on the other hand, how this serves as a proof for God's continuing care and sustenance for humans. It is easy to see how the central role of humans serves the purpose of arguing against cosmogonies where humans are mere accidents and not creatures that God wills to exist.

A critical comment comes from Calcidius (fl. fourth century), who considered it absurd that the heavens were made so that they would shine their light for our sake. This did not fit into the Platonic hierarchy of value. Why should eternal and incorruptible things serve something that has no value—that is, us? The highest value resides in the realm of the Empyrean, beyond the heavens. One step down from that are the heavens, where the angelic beings dwell. We, however, live outside the city walls. Moreover, from a cosmic point of view, Earth is a "mere point when compared with the magnitude of the universe." In contrast, the geocentric picture is correct, not because of the significance of humans, but because of the aesthetic value it has for the eternal and celestial beings who enjoy orderly things. Our lot is to gaze at, and imitate if we can, this celestial order.[35]

33. Bouteneff, Beginnings, 86–87.
34. Justin Martyr, Second Apology 5 (ANF 1:190).
35. Calcidius, On Plato's Timaeus, 59, 76; Lewis, Discarded Image, 49–60. We know very little about Calcidius. He is mostly known for his Latin translation of the Timaeus, which was dedicated to the bishop of Cordoba. His adherence to the Christian faith has been a matter of

Instead of claiming that the early church believed that humans are the sole reason why the cosmos exists, it is perhaps better to say that there is a deep cognitive connection between humans and the cosmos, meaning that the cosmos is our home. The cosmos and the human mind are linked, so that the human mind is able to acquire true knowledge about the world and its Creator. As Basil states in *Hexaemeron*, "You will finally discover that the world was not conceived by chance and without reason, but for a useful end and for the great advantage of all beings, since it is really the school where reasonable souls exercise themselves, the training ground where they learn to know God; since by the sight of visible and sensible things the mind is led, as by a hand, to the contemplation of invisible things" (1.6).

Thus, it seems that we have two slightly different but not necessarily exclusive angles on the human role in the universe.

a. The cosmos was made for humans.

b. Humans were made for the cosmos.

Option (a) sounds anthropocentric, and for a modern person obviously false, whereas option (b) resonates to some extent with contemporary scientific cosmology, according to which humans are strangely well-adapted denizens in this cosmos.[36] It seems that the early Jewish and Christian authors often said (a) in order to say (b). It might be more natural for a contemporary Christian to proceed in the opposite direction, from (b) to (a). Even if some ancient texts have an anthropocentric emphasis, this was always carefully attenuated by noting that in the grand scheme of things, humans are not special because they have high inherent value qua humans. An illuminating passage is found in Boethius's (480–524/25) famous work *The Consolation of Philosophy*, where Lady Philosophy engages in a dialogue with an imprisoned philosopher. Thrown into a cell and wrongly accused, Boethius asks questions about the meaning of life and how his sufferings could be justified. The answer given by Lady Philosophy shows Boethius his rightful place, and this offers a perspective on the cosmology of the Christian elite in Rome right before the final collapse of the empire. Lady Philosophy castigates Boethius:

> As you have learnt from astronomers' shewing, the whole circumference of the earth is but as a point compared with the size of the heavens. That is, if you compare the earth with the circle of the universe, it must be reckoned as of no

---

debate, but after assessing the evidence, Lewis considered him to be a Christian writer. For a similar conclusion, see Dronke, *Spell of Calcidius*, 46.

36. Carr, "Cosmology and Religion," 144–45.

size at all. And of this tiny portion of the universe there is but a fourth part, as you have learnt from the demonstration of Ptolemaeus, which is inhabited by living beings known to us. If from this fourth part you imagine subtracted all that is covered by sea and marsh, and all the vast regions of thirsty desert, you will find but the narrowest space left for human habitation. And do you think of setting forth your fame and publishing your name in this space, which is but as a point within another point so closely circumscribed? And what size or magnificence can fame have which is shut in by such close and narrow bounds?[37]

For the early Christians, the value of humans was linked to the relationship that humans are able to have with other beings and God. Because Christian theology is not exclusively anthropocentric, it caused no problem for theologians, when science in the seventeenth century advanced to provide evidence of other worlds, to argue that these worlds were created for beings in those systems.[38]

The Ptolemaic model was generally approved by early Christian theologians, but the reasons for the adoption of Ptolemy were not simply theological. In fact, the Bible does not contain a clear planetary cosmology and, as already stated, the canonical texts offer several different cosmologies. Many biblical texts do, however, affirm a simple phenomenological account of the sun "rising" and "setting," and in many places the Bible uses the language of the tiered universe (e.g., Num. 16:28–30; Phil. 2:10), which is easily aligned with Ptolemaic model. In adopting the Ptolemaic model, the church followed the general and common philosophical discourse of its era. By the time it was finally challenged, not everyone recalled the history and origins of the model. Even worse, people sometimes today think that the Ptolemaic model was based on mere theological arguments, which it wasn't. It was a consistent outworking of Greek philosophy that tried to make elementary sense of the movements of planetary bodies while staying loyal to how the world appeared to their senses. Nonetheless, the early Christian theology shows flexibility regarding the details of cosmology. The main concern was about things like God's aseity and God's benevolent purpose for creation.

---

37. Boethius, *Consolation of Philosophy*, 2.7 (trans. Cooper, 24).
38. Dick, *Plurality of Worlds*, 149–51.

3

Resistance Is Futile

Galileo, Newton, and Darwin

It is sometimes suggested that the controversies over the views of Copernicus and Galileo arose because medieval theology and biblical exposition took no account of the natural sciences—or even resisted them. A more plausible interpretation is that the controversy arose precisely because theologians and philosophers gave far too much weight to the provisional scientific accounts of nature and failed to update their thinking with the advances of science. Many medieval writers had become locked into a definite Aristotelian reading of the Bible and tradition, which they treated as if it were part of sacred doctrine that lay beyond dispute. Scientific advances sometimes cruelly exposed how earlier generations of exegetes had incorporated provisional scientific theories into their biblical interpretations, thereby unintentionally giving those theories the status of religious dogma.[1]

In this chapter, I will look at three cases where scientific cosmology and religious views seem to have been at odds. In addition to Galileo, the other two cases are Newton's influence on the philosophy of science (and consequently on constructive theology) and Darwin's theory of evolution through natural selection, which appeared to call into question the good and well-designed telos of the cosmos and the human role in it. These cases present differing types of interaction, all of which teach a valuable lesson.

1. McGrath, *Fine-Tuned Universe*, 105.

Copernicus Arises

Nicolaus Copernicus (1473–1543) suggested in his *De revolutionibus de or-bium coelestium* (1543) that the earth revolves around the sun, which is the center of our solar system.[2] His work was circulated in the European universities, and it became a subject of discussion among the scientific elite. However, Copernicus died shortly after the publication of the book and could not participate in the debate himself.

Copernicus found that by allowing for the movement of the earth, he could explain several anomalies in the movement of the stars, especially their retrograde, looping movements and the annual variations of solar progression. The actual changes that Copernicus introduced to Ptolemaic cosmology challenged relatively few things, most notably the location of the earth in relation to the other planetary bodies. The cosmos was still contained in the circumference of the fixed stars, very much like in the Ptolemaic model. The model still rested on Aristotelian foundations, but because those could not deliver the necessary scientific accuracy, tension existed within his system, making it susceptible to legitimate criticism.[3]

Through happenstance, the Lutheran reformer Andreas Osiander (1498–1552) was given the task of finishing Copernicus's work for print. Osiander included with it a preface, *Ad lectorem de hypothesibus huius operis*, which he did not sign. Accordingly, those reading the work got the impression that the preface was written by Copernicus himself. In this preface, Osiander explained that the hypotheses presented in the book were just that, hypotheses, which could be used for calculations if they seemed to fit the evidence. This softened the critical response to Copernicus's work. On the one hand, it mischaracterized Copernicus's own view, which did not intend his work to be taken as a mere hypothesis. On the other hand, it allowed Copernicus's teachings to spread without significant resistance.[4]

2. Copernicus, *On the Revolutions of the Heavenly Spheres*. This major work was based on his shorter *Commentariolus*, which he had made publicly available and which had helped build his reputation as a scientist to be reckoned with. However, Copernicus was not the first to argue for a heliocentric model; this had already been done by Aristarchus of Samos (310–230 BC). Another thing that Copernicus proposed in this work included the notion of the rotation of the earth around its inclined axis. In contrast to Aristarchus, Copernicus provided a mathematical model based on experiments. It seems that Copernicus's ideas were viewed positively by the church hierarchies. For example, Cardinal Nicolaus von Schönberg urged him to publish and disseminate his ideas more widely. The oft-voiced suspicion that Copernicus delayed the publication of his works simply because he feared the reaction of the church does not seem to be warranted. See, e.g., Kragh, *Conceptions of Cosmos*, 47.

3. Scharf, *Copernicus Complex*, 18–19.

4. Lerner, "Polémique Anticopernicienne," 424–32.

Osiander's colleagues, like Osiander himself, were somewhat hesitant about a literal reading of Copernicus's theory. Martin Luther offered scant remarks, which were recorded in his informal and often insouciant *Table Talks*. He claimed that Copernicus was "a clown who wants to turn the art of astronomy on its head."[5] While Luther did not give any definite reasons why he detested the thoughts of Copernicus, his younger colleague Philipp Melanchthon (1497–1560) offered a longer analysis of the new cosmology and why it was not a route worth pursuing.

After the fall, human knowledge of the cosmos was severely limited, but humans still had access to the "seeds of a complete physics" (*semina integrae physicae*). Adam passed this teaching on to his son Abel; this included basic knowledge on the positions of the stars and their use in making calendars, for example. Melanchthon covers these themes in his *Initia Doctrinae Physicae*, where he also offers a wholesale and strict rejection of Copernican theory. He does not mince words as he considers this teaching to be inept (*ineptia*), stupid (*impudentia*), shameful (*turpius*), unworthy (*indignius*), arising from great pride (*gigantea audacia*), and consisting of monstrous errors (*monstruosos errores*). In later editions, he toned down his harsh language but still remained in doubt regarding the merits of the theory.[6]

Melanchthon's critique was based on three claims. First, it is not prudent to try to overthrow the tradition and the consensus of science. Melanchthon thus seemed to think that Copernican thinking was based on vainglory. But surely this was an odd thing for a *Reformer* to say. Yet Melanchthon's reasoning was more nuanced. Tradition needs to be held in value but not in absolute value, especially if the tradition is not uniform. It was a part of the mindset of the Reformers to think that they were the legitimate followers of the ancient Christian tradition. If there were good scientific arguments against Copernicus, as Melanchthon thought, these should be taken very seriously in the absence of contrary evidence. Second, he viewed Copernicanism as absurd in the light of common sense. He writes, "Our eyes are witnesses [*oculi sunt testes*]: the sky is moved circularly in twenty-four hours."[7] Third, Copernicanism seemed to be against biblical witness, which falls in line with commonsense phenomenology.[8]

5. Martin Luther, Tischreden IV, no. 463: "Der Narr will die ganze Kunst Astronomiae umkehren." Translation mine. See also *LW* 54:358–59. However, there is a chance that Luther was not referring to Copernicus but to someone else with lesser credentials. For discussion, see Lerner, "Polémique Anticopernicienne," 410–24.

6. Lerner, "Polémique Anticopernicienne," 437.

7. Melanchthon, *Initia Doctrinae Physicae*, in CR 13, 216–17.

8. The proof texts in this case were Ps. 18:6–7; 104:5; Josh. 10:12–13; and Isa. 38:8. John Calvin held a similar view. He was suspicious of Copernican ideas, but he argued for the distinction of a more commonsense approach (employed by Moses, for example) and proper science: "Here lies the difference; Moses wrote in a popular style things which without instruction, all ordinary

Even if heliocentrism was rejected by Osiander and Melanchthon as a cosmological doctrine, the German Protestant universities adopted and developed Copernican ideas with relative freedom.[9] Basically, this meant that Copernican ideas could be used as a hypothesis for the calculation of celestial movements. Melanchthon himself supported Copernican studies and slowly grew more supportive of Copernicus's talents, ultimately praising him as one of the finest scientists of the era.

Melanchthon's response is rather representative of how the learned elite tended to view new scientific theories. Theories were estimated in terms of common sense, good scientific practice (i.e., Aristotle), and the Bible. However, it may easily escape us that these criteria never produced a complete scientific synthesis in the Middle Ages despite monumental efforts.[10] Although Aristotle was the highest authority, the body of knowledge that was called Aristotelianism was never uniform, and it was also open to innovation and even rebuttal. Grant argues that Scholastic Aristotelianism was familiar with anomalies and various attempts to deal with them. Ultimately, Copernicus stood in a long line of Scholastic astronomy, which he employed in a new way.[11]

The Trials of Galileo

At first Galileo Galilei (1564–1642) was critical of Copernicus's theory, but when in 1609 he was able to introduce more developed features to Hans

---

persons, endued with common sense, are able to understand; but astronomers investigate with great labor whatever the sagacity of the human mind can comprehend. Nevertheless, this study is not to be reprobated, nor this science to be condemned, because some frantic persons are wont boldly to reject whatever is unknown to them. For astronomy is not only pleasant, but also very useful to be known: it cannot be denied that this art unfolds the admirable wisdom of God." Calvin, *Commentary on Genesis*, verse 1:16. See also verse 1:15. Thus, even if his judgment at the time was erroneous, his methodology was in principle open to advancement.

9. Lerner, "Polémique Anticopernicienne," 446–50. It is perhaps worth mentioning that several Lutheran reformers thought highly of both astronomy and astrology. See Barnes, *Astrology and Reformation*; Dixon, "Popular Astrology." Melanchthon defended the legitimacy of divination because the celestial movements testify that the world is governed by an eternal spirit, which gives reason to believe that humans were created to know God and to be immortal (Ep. No. 1715, in CR 3, 575). Luther gave due respect to astronomy, but detested astrology: "Astrology is not a science because it has no principles and proofs" (Table talk no. 2834b, in LW 54, 173). Besides lacking scientific evidence, there was "biblical" evidence against astrology. Luther points out that "Esau and Jacob were born under one sign and in rapid succession. Where did the diversity of their natures come from? The astrologers rack their brains about this but they can't offer a solid explanation" (Table talk no. 5573, in LW 54, 458).

10. For a good account on the development of scientific and philosophical methods in Scholasticism, see Leinsle, *Introduction to Scholastic Theology*.

11. Grant, *Planets, Stars and Orbs*, 676–79.

Lippershey's telescope, he became convinced that Copernicus had been right. Now he could see with his own eyes the mountains of the moon, the moons of Jupiter, and even sunspots. Initially he only wrote letters of this to his students and colleagues, but some of these became public. In 1615 he was formally accused of heresy, but the charges were dropped. However, Cardinal Roberto Bellarmino forbade him from teaching "Copernicus's doctrine" in public. Galileo agreed, but when his supporter Maffeo Barberini became Pope Urbanus VIII in 1623, he imagined that he would now be free to express his ideas in public. After discussion with Barberini, Galileo decided to write a dialogue in which three persons discuss cosmological theories. Eventually the heliocentric position prevailed, but he thought that the literary form would enable him to avoid the charges of breaking Bellarmino's strictures. He was wrong. It took ten years for things to take shape, but in 1633 he was called to Rome to defend himself. The following nine years would cement his role as the main example of how the church would go to extraordinary lengths to suppress heresy.

According to a popular misconception, Galileo was thrown in jail and tortured. In reality, he was put under house arrest for the rest of his life, but his living conditions were still far better than most of his contemporaries. He lived in various palaces and luxury residences, and he was able to move around within certain limits. Although the original texts of his court hearing mention the technical term "severe interrogation," which referred to torture, we have good reasons to believe that he was never tortured. Instead, according to the contemporary interrogation measures, he was subjected to questioning where there was a threat of torture.[12] Nevertheless, the final verdict of his condemnation stated this:

> We say, pronounce, sentence, and declare that you, the above-mentioned Galileo, because of the things deduced in the trial and confessed by you as above, have rendered yourself according to this Holy Office vehemently suspected of heresy, namely of having held and believed a doctrine which is false and contrary to the divine and Holy Scripture: that the sun is the center of the world and does not move from east to west, and the earth moves and is not the center of the world, and that one may hold and defend as probable an opinion after it has been declared and defined contrary to Holy Scripture.[13]

In response, Galileo was made to read the formula of abjuration and swear that "I will never again say or assert, orally or in writing, anything which

12. Numbers, *Galileo Goes to Jail*, 68–78.
13. Quoted in Fantoli, *Case of Galileo*, 1–2.

might cause a similar suspicion about me."[14] Even if there never happened
anything as horrible as the worst accounts would suggest us to believe, the
Galileo affair is very interesting. Why were such measures called for? The issue
is rather complex, and many historians have provided us with good accounts
that help us to understand the church's resistance to Galileo.[15]

It is often forgotten that Galileo was also opposed by the use of scientific
arguments.[16] There were several scientific phenomena that the Ptolemaic model
could explain satisfactorily and that were not explained by the Copernican
model. First and foremost was an obvious one: from the human point of view,
the earth seems to stand still while the other planetary bodies are in motion.
This includes not only the sun and moon but other planets as well. For example,
the luminosity of Venus is constant and does not seem to vary; this suggests that
its distance always stays the same. The stars seem to be fixed, and it took a long
time before we had powerful enough telescopes to measure the stellar parallax.

The Copernican model was at that time mathematically no less simple
than the Ptolemaic one, and it did not offer any significant improvement for
calculating and predicting planetary movements. It explained the retrograde
motions of planetary bodies but did not provide a similarly holistic explanation of the movement itself, as the Aristotelian model did. Moreover, the
actual empirical proof for the model was not very substantial in the beginning.
And, of course, the ordinary phenomenological accounts of the movements
of the celestial bodies in the Bible seemed to confirm the geocentric model.

The Catholic Church had just been split by the Protestant Reformation, and
the Thirty Years' War had achieved its high point in Europe. The Council of
Trent had succeeded in strengthening the church institutionally, but the church
was now wary of any new disturbance. In its canons, Trent had adopted a
more literal approach to the interpretation of the Bible, while restating its sole
role as the true interpreter of the sacred text in line with tradition. Effectively,
there was less academic freedom compared to the Middle Ages, when it was
common to debate how the Ptolemaic model could be harmonized with Aristotelian philosophy. Ernan McMullin speculates that Copernican doctrines
might have met with significantly less resistance in the fifteenth century, a
hundred years before the Reformation, and if a person like Nicholas of Cusa
had been in charge of the hearings.[17]

14. Quoted in Fantoli, *Case of Galileo*, 1–2.
15. See, e.g., Finocchiaro, *Defending Copernicus and Galileo*; Fantoli, *Case of Galileo*; and
McMullin, *Church and Galileo*.
16. Graney, *Setting Aside All Authority*; Blair, "Tycho Brahe's Critique."
17. McMullin, "Church's Ban on Copernicanism"; Brooke, *Science and Religion*, 89–109.
Also, it did not help that Galileo's teachings were associated with Pythagoreanism and other

At that time, several astronomers supported Tycho Brahe's cosmological model of all the other planets orbiting the sun, which orbited the earth. Ironically, the telescope was used to confirm not Galileo's own theory but a refined Ptolemaic view, as the astronomists felt that they finally had empirical proof of the epicycles that Ptolemy had only theorized about. In addition, the scientific elite of the Catholic Church were split between Dominicans and Jesuits, with the former seeking to uphold the traditional Aristotelian approach to cosmology while the latter were more open to new philosophies of science. Galileo's findings were mired in this internal debate.[18]

At the time, new theories were not unheard of, but change was always slow.[19] Alas, Galileo was not a patient man. There were several personal issues between Galileo and his previous defender and admirer Barberini. In the beginning, Barberini had not limited Galileo's freedom on the issue. He had asked Galileo to include in his *Dialogue* a note that would state that heliocentrism was just a theory. Galileo used a character called Simplicius to state something along these lines, referring subtly to Barberini, which made the pope angry.[20] Both Galileo and Barberini were persons who were not easy to deal with. Galileo was a troublemaker who picked fights even when it was unnecessary, and Barberini was too thin-skinned and passionate. This only helped to escalate the issue.[21]

The account of the Galileo affair as reflective of a fundamental clash between science and religion is still upheld today in popular discourse. Interestingly, for some time, several voices have tried to use it as an example of the harmony between science and religion. Among these voices has been Pope John Paul II, who issued an investigation of the trial of Galileo in 1979. The pope argued that Galileo in fact displayed a proper theological attitude, which was superior to his clerical adversaries.[22] Both parties appeared to have some truth on their side.[23] Focusing on Galileo as a model of how the Catholic Church dealt with new scientific discoveries is a mistake. There were too many other

hermetic thinking, such as that of Lucretius, made infamous by Giordano Bruno, which was considered heretical. Martinez, *Pythagoras, Bruno, Galileo*.

18. Feldhay, *Galileo and the Church*. However, there were also Dominicans who favored Galileo and Jesuits who opposed him. See Finocchiaro, *Defending Copernicus and Galileo*, 294.

19. For an account of how the Scholastic philosophers treated new ideas in philosophy, see Pasnau, *Metaphysical Themes, 1274–1671*, 428–58.

20. Simplicius's last speech contained this line: "I admit that your thoughts seem to me more ingenious than many others I have heard. I do not therefore consider them true and conclusive; indeed, keeping always before my mind's eye a most solid doctrine that I once heard from a most eminent and learned person, and before which one must fall silent." Galilei, "Dialogue Concerning the Two Chief World Systems."

21. Fantoli, *Case of Galileo*, 160–71.

22. See, e.g., Galilei, "Letter to Madame Christina of Lorraine."

23. Finocchiaro, *Defending Copernicus and Galileo*, 291–314.

factors in play in this case for it to be representative of the general attitude of the church. Many high-ranking bishops, cardinals, and scientists supported Galileo, while many scientists opposed him, and each had their reasons, which are too complex to be cited here.

Yet one cannot escape the fact that the Catholic Church not only showed poor theological judgment but also committed epistemic vices while handling the case. The most condemning thing is that the church did not discuss the scientific evidence during the hearings but remained on purely theological topics and even prohibited Galileo from offering any further evidence in the future. The recent papal Galileo Commission discussed this inconvenient truth, but even it did not completely succeed in admitting the failures of the church.[24] In sum, the Galileo affair does not stand out as an epitome of the conflict of "science" and "religion," but it nevertheless portrays some difficulties, and intellectual glitches, that almost inevitably surface when different philosophies try to negotiate their claims with each other.

What Changed?

John Donne's (1572–1631) poem "An Anatomy of the World" is often presented as evidence of how the religious and intellectual elite felt about the changes that were in the air.[25]

> And new philosophy calls all in doubt,
> The element of fire is quite put out,
> The sun is lost, and th'earth, and no man's wit
> Can well direct him where to look for it.
> And freely men confess that this world's spent,
> When in the planets and the firmament
> They seek so many new; they see that this
> Is crumbled out again to his atomies.
> 'Tis all in pieces, all coherence gone,
> All just supply, and all relation.[26]

Donne's account is emotional and even alarmist. This passage, an excerpt from a much longer poem, seems to refer to the Copernican turn. As a whole,

24. For a critical commentary, see Coyne, "Church's Most Recent Attempt."
25. E.g., Kragh, *Conceptions of Cosmos*, 46–47; Dick, *Plurality of Worlds*, 91; Crowe, *Extraterrestrial Life Debate*, 32.
26. John Donne, "An Anatomy of the World," accessed June 1, 2017, https://www.poetry foundation.org/poems-and-poets/poems/detail/44092.

the poem is concerned about the many changes and upheavals that were taking place in society and in Donne's personal life. What was left of the medieval synthesis of philosophy and science seemed to be in ruins. The Reformation had taken place, and Europe was becoming ever more religiously complex, which created severe societal unrest. A daughter of his benefactor had just died, without the world noticing this minor but existentially weighty tragedy. As a Catholic, Donne was affected deeply by the Reformation. Eventually he became an Anglican, while his brother died in a cell, suspected of harboring a Catholic priest and partaking in treasonous activities. The world seemed to be spinning out of control. Thus, it would be a mistake to take Donne's poetic lament as an example of how the Copernican turn influenced culture. In fact, as Lewis states, "It comes naturally to a modern mind to suppose that the new astronomy made a profound impression on men's minds; but when we look into the literary texts we find it rarely mentioned."[27]

An incorrect understanding of the Ptolemaic cosmos might influence our own conception of the Copernican turn. It is false to think that the Ptolemaic universe was small, cozy, and created for humans. It was not.[28] Even if the measurements made within the Ptolemaic system had been widely off the mark, they expressed the same astonishment as our own more scientific accounts: the cosmos was mind-bogglingly huge. Ptolemy had estimated that the distance from Earth to the fixed stars (the boundary of the physical universe) was 57,340,000 miles.[29] Moses Maimonides's *Guide for the Perplexed* (ca. 1190) contains the following illustrious passage:

> It has been proved that the distance between the centre of the earth and the outer surface of the sphere of Saturn is a journey of nearly eight thousand seven hundred solar years. Suppose a day's journey to be forty legal miles of two thousand ordinary cubits, and consider the great and enormous distance! [125,000,000 miles] or in the words of Scripture, "Is not God in the height of heaven? and behold the height of the stars, how high they are!" (Job 22:12); that is to say, learn from the height of the heavens how far we are from comprehending God, for there is an enormous distance between ourselves and these corporeal objects, and the latter are greatly distinguished from us by

27. Lewis, *English Literature*, 2. Lewis correctly points out how Copernican teachings were first treated as mathematical tools, which led to a slow but steady adoption. The verification of Copernican theory took hundreds of years. Moreover, the climate of eighteenth-century romanticism was hostile to science, which led to a dualism between Nature and Mind and took the debate in a wholly different direction. Therefore, the actual influence of the Copernican turn on the sentiments of contemporaries—and later generations—was not remarkable.

28. Danielson, "Great Copernican Cliché."

29. Toomer, *Ptolemy's Almagest*, 1.5; Webb, *Measuring the Universe*, 34–35. As a reference, the distance from Mars to Earth is 48,678,219 miles.

their position, and hidden from us as regards their essence and most of their actions. How much more incomprehensible therefore is their Maker, who is incorporeal![30]

These are distances that were impossible for a medieval person to fathom. Only very few people traveled far from the towns in which they had been born. The Copernican model pushed the boundaries even further, with Copernicus's model of the cosmos being about 40,000 times larger than the Ptolemaic one, but both Ptolemaic and Copernican scales are nonetheless unimaginable in their size.[31] However, both of them were tidy cosmoses where everything was in its right place. Everything was ordered and shaped according to the image of perfect ideas. Orbits were simple, regular, and perfectly circular. The world was a beautifully designed machine, perfect in its execution.

Although being lowest in value, the earth was still the epicenter of the cosmic drama, the dwelling of humans, and witness to God's involvement with creation. Our home was provincial, but not forgotten. We were living in a galactic Bethlehem. However, after the Copernican turn, even if there was no change in the register of scale and immensity, there was nevertheless a delicate change in the register of participation. Lovejoy suggests that there was a "certain racial *amour propre*" that humans felt in hosting this divine drama, as the only middle links, half-material and half-spiritual, between angels and animals.[32] The Copernican turn changed the order of the planets, but it also enabled several other more important changes in the picture of the cosmos. Over time, these included the idea of other sentient beings living on other planets in our solar system; the removing of cosmological boundaries, like the *stellatum* and *primum mobile*, from the edges of the cosmos; the idea that the fixed stars are suns like our own sun, with similar planets and similar life on those planets; and the idea of an infinite universe that contained an infinite number of stars and planets.[33]

For a long time, we had no way of proving any of these claims with certainty. They were initially entertained as plausible theories about the world, but their meaning sank in slowly. And even then, there did not seem to be just one way of interpreting what the actual religious significance of these new ideas was.

30. Maimonides, *Guide for the Perplexed* 3.14.

31. Kragh, *Conceptions of Cosmos*, 50; Danielson, *Book of the Cosmos*, 112–13.

32. Lovejoy, *Great Chain of Being*, 103. This is apparent for example in Melanchthon's discussion on the plurality of worlds. For him, this world is the throne of God (*sedes Dei*) and the center of all divine activities (*Initia Doctrinae Physicae*, in CR 13, 220).

33. Lovejoy, *Great Chain of Being*, 108.

The Newtonian Machine

The case of Isaac Newton (1642–1726) differs significantly from that of Galileo. There was no institutional opposition to Newton's ideas, no hearings or condemnations. Nevertheless, his thinking influenced theology and religion significantly more than Galileo's. For a few hundred years, a substantial amount of constructive theology tried to take certain Newtonian ideas seriously. It must be borne in mind, however, that Newton's own ideas and what is nowadays referred to as Newtonian thought are not the same. Newton himself did not draw the philosophical conclusions that later Newtonians did. His thinking was profoundly religious, and he did not see a necessary juxtaposition between scientific and religious worldviews.[34]

It is more crucial to understand how some of Newton's ideas became cornerstones of the so-called mechanistic worldview. The most favored metaphor for the cosmos at that time was clockwork. This image was not used by Newton himself but was frequently included by Leibniz in his criticisms of Newton, despite the responses of Newton's colleagues who tried to resist the mechanistic and deterministic readings of his work. But the force of the image was too strong. It must, however, be noted that the idea of a mechanistic universe goes back to René Descartes (1596–1650) and Pierre Gassendi (1592–1655), who both had strong theological reasons for preferring it. For them, the mechanism was a sign of order and design. But to quote John Hedley Brooke, "The nature of a mechanical philosophy might be theistic in tone, but its nurture was liable to be otherwise." The mechanistic picture could easily be dislodged from the Christian framework and used for different, even anti-theistic purposes.[35]

A cosmologically important feature of Newton's work was that he offered a unified set of physical laws: the law of universal gravitation, which could explain all the celestial movements that were known at that time. Against this background, it is possible to see how it was easy for people to draw further conclusions from it.[36] The mechanistic understanding of nature gave rise to determinism and reductionism. Newton's theory allowed scientists to perceive the cosmos within a single conceptual scheme. Everything that existed could now be analyzed through the movements of individual parts of the whole.

34. However, his theology deviated from classical Christianity on several points. For an overview of Newton's religion, see the special issue of *New Atlantis* 44 (2015).
35. Brooke, *Science and Religion*, 124–40, here 140; Kragh, *Conceptions of Cosmos*, 71–72; de Schrijver, *Imagining the Creator God*, 110–28.
36. Theological views, especially the idea of divine omnipresence, made it possible for Newton to hold that his laws have a universal nature. Brooke, *Science and Religion*, 139; Hurlbutt, *Hume, Newton*, 4–7.

The high point of this optimism was the famous account of Pierre-Simon
Laplace (1749–1827):

> We may regard the present state of the universe as the effect of its past and
> the cause of its future. An intellect which at a certain moment would know all
> forces that set nature in motion, and all positions of all items of which nature is
> composed, if this intellect were also vast enough to submit these data to analysis,
> it would embrace in a single formula the movements of the greatest bodies of
> the universe and those of the tiniest atom; for such an intellect nothing would
> be uncertain and the future just like the past would be present before its eyes.[37]

Even if Laplace seems to offer an account of an omniscient being, the real
force of his argument is the irrelevance of a divine overseer: since everything
in the world functions in a determined way and things cannot be otherwise,
there is nothing for the divine to do. To Napoleon's question about where
the creator fits into this system, Laplace famously answered, "I have no need
for that hypothesis."[38] If this was the received scientific worldview, deism was
now seen as a serious contender for theism. According to deism, God creates
the world but withdraws from it. He winds up the mechanism but leaves it to
its own devices. God does not perform interventions, which means that there
is no room for special revelation. Newtonian mechanisms also changed the
conception of human nature and human freedom. If the mechanistic view
of nature was true, that ruled out free will insofar as it was conceived to be
incompatible with determinism.

From the same root rose also the notion of natural religion. Instead of
there being two books, general revelation and special revelation, which required divine intervention, now there was room for only the former. All
people are naturally religious, and specific religions are only expressions of
this more fundamental religious inclination. This pushed the theorization
in theology away from the world of objective facts to the realm of subjective feeling. This was supposed to guarantee the scientifically viable nature
of religious faith, which, by being subjective, did not cause tension with
objective scientific facts.[39]

37. Laplace, *Probabilities*, 4. The being who could know all these things later became known
as "Laplace's demon." Laplace did not himself use this expression.
38. Wegter-McNelly, "Fundamental Physics and Religion," 160.
39. This is well illustrated in the theologies of early liberal Protestantism, such as in the
work of Friedrich Schleiermacher. Jenson, *Systematic Theology*, 1:8–11. Jenson also argues that
this trajectory was not necessary and there was a theologically more fruitful interpretation of
Newtonian ideas available, provided by Jonathan Edwards but sadly lost. Jenson, *America's
Theologian*, 23–35.

The move away from Aristotelian science toward Newtonian mechanics changed the framework in which things were analyzed. If a clockwork mechanism was the true depiction of the world, then the only interesting questions were about efficient causes. The universe did not have a telos or a final cause. This is one of the features of the Newtonian system that has been preserved until our time. Even today it is common to say that science is not interested in questions like *why* a thing exists or what the *purpose* of this thing might be. The humanities, including philosophy, theology, and psychology, are more prone to entertain these kinds of questions, which are not typically seen as properly scientific.[40]

Although there are not many deists around nowadays, deistic reasoning had a substantial influence on how scientists and philosophers understood their role in the coming centuries.[41] In *Fides et Ratio*, John Paul II laments this development:

I wish to reflect upon this special activity of human reason. I judge it necessary to do so because, at the present time in particular, the search for ultimate truth seems often to be neglected. Modern philosophy clearly has the great merit of focusing attention upon man. From this starting-point, human reason with its many questions has developed further its yearning to know more and to know it ever more deeply. Complex systems of thought have thus been built, yielding results in the different fields of knowledge and fostering the development of culture and history. Anthropology, logic, the natural sciences, history, linguistics and so forth—the whole universe of knowledge has been involved in one way or another. Yet the positive results achieved must not obscure the fact that reason, in its one-sided concern to investigate human subjectivity, seems to have forgotten that men and women are always called to direct their steps towards a truth which transcends them. Sundered from that truth, individuals are at the mercy of caprice, and their state as person ends up being judged by pragmatic criteria based essentially upon experimental data, in the mistaken belief that technology must dominate all. It has happened therefore that reason, rather than voicing the human orientation towards truth, has wilted under the weight of so much knowledge and little by little has lost the capacity to lift its gaze to the heights, not daring to rise to the truth of being. Abandoning the investigation of being, modern philosophical research has concentrated instead upon human knowing. Rather than make use of the human capacity to know the truth, modern philosophy has preferred to accentuate the ways in which this capacity is limited and conditioned.[42]

40. Barbour, *Religion and Science*, 18–24.
41. For a major study on the influence of deism, see Taylor, *Sources of the Self*.
42. *Fides et Ratio*, §5.

Newton's legacy is interesting because it left a lasting mark—like the one the pope puts his finger on—on Western scientific inquiry, even if the science upon which these developments were built is now obsolete. The so-called new physics of the early twentieth century was diametrically opposed to determinism and naive realism. The discovery of quantum phenomena reintroduced indeterminism to physics. Unexpectedly, predicting the movements of elementary particles became impossible. Quantum physics also challenged our common notions of what matter is. The stuff in front of us, like my computer and my table, do not ultimately consist of atoms, but of quarks, which sometimes behave like particles, sometimes like waves. The clockwork metaphor suddenly stopped making sense.

Several research projects were launched to study the meaning of quantum physics for theology in the twentieth century, but the discussion on theological method had already shown signs of increasing divergence since the nineteenth century.[43] Therefore quantum theory never had a similar effect on theology as Newtonianism. In our time, we have reached a state that Brad Gregory calls "hyperpluralism," and consequently we have no single theological method and no single way to establish a connection between "science" and "religion."[44] This, on the one hand, guarantees significant freedom to explore and test different ideas, but, on the other hand, it makes it harder for theology to establish itself as a unified form of inquiry since its boundaries are so vague. It is, however, up for debate how serious that problem is in the end.

A Brief Note on Darwin

Lastly, I need to say something about Charles Darwin (1809–1882). His work did not have an effect on cosmology per se. However, his theory of evolution through natural selection did have an impact on how we perceive the *quality* of the natural order. Contrary to the popular image, the early Christian responses to his theory were not unanimously resistant to it.[45] An illustrative passage of the compatibility of Darwin's ideas with Christian theology is found in a letter by John Henry Newman (1801–1890), one the most eminent theologians in nineteenth-century Britain, in which he adopts an Augustinian stance toward the idea of the gradual evolution of species.

43. The applications of quantum theories for theology are interesting but beyond the scope of this book. For discussion see, e.g., Peters and Hallanger, *God's Action*; Polkinghorne, *Trinity*; Wegter-McNelly, *Entangled God*.
44. Gregory, *Unintended Reformation*, 11–13.
45. For an account of the 1860 Oxford debate between Thomas Huxley and Samuel Wilberforce, see Numbers, *Galileo Goes to Jail*, 152–60.

I do not fear the theory so much as he [the unknown author of *The Darwinian Theory of the Transmutation of Species*] seems to do—and it seems to me that he is hard upon Darwin sometimes, which [*sic*] he might have interpreted him kindly. It does not seem to me to follow that creation is denied because the Creator, millions of years ago, gave laws to matter. He first created matter and then he created laws for it—laws which should *construct* it into its present wonderful beauty, and accurate adjustment and harmony of parts *gradually*. We do not deny or circumscribe the Creator, because we hold he has created the self acting originating human mind, which has almost a creative gift; much less then do we deny or circumscribe His power, if we hold that He gave matter such laws as by their blind instrumentality moulded and constructed through innumerable ages the world as we see it. If Mr Darwin in this or that point of his theory comes into collision with revealed truth, that is another matter—but I do not see that the *principle* of development, or what I have called construction, does. As to the Divine *Design*, is it not an instance of incomprehensibly and infinitely marvellous Wisdom and Design to have given certain laws to matter millions of ages ago, which have surely and precisely worked out, in the long course of those ages, those effects which He from the first proposed. Mr Darwin's theory *need* not then to be atheistical, be it true or not; it may simply be suggesting a larger idea of Divine Prescience and Skill. Perhaps your friend has got a surer clue to guide him than I have, who have never studied the question, and I do not [see] that "the accidental evolution of organic beings" is inconsistent with divine design.—It is accidental to *us*, not to *God*.[46]

Some saw here a familiar Augustinian logic, while some felt that Darwin's ideas were something to be resisted vehemently.[47] But the actual, more pressing theological problems did not concern the idea of evolution as such. I note here just two things that some still see as the most important theological problems that the theory of evolution creates:[48]

1. The evolutionary problem of evil: the creation of humans through gradual evolution requires millions of years of painful animal evolution.

46. Dessain and Gornall, *Letters and Diaries*, 77–78.
47. For a history of creationism, see Numbers, *Creationists*; Frye, *Is God a Creationist?*
48. McGrath notes in addition to these the problem of biblical interpretation. Creationist readings of Genesis rely heavily on a literal interpretation of the text, but as was shown in chapter 2, this is not historically the most obvious way to treat these texts. See McGrath, "Darwinism." For more on the issue of evolution and creation, see, e.g., Alexander, *Creation or Evolution*; and Brooke, *Science and Religion*, 275–320. An additional effect of Darwinism was the setback it caused for nineteenth-century natural theology, as it offered a reasonable explanation for biological features that appear to have been designed. Since then, the design arguments have moved to the fine-tuning of the universe, yet the intelligent design movement tries to keep the discussion on biological design alive.

2. The uniqueness of humans: in the evolutionary scheme, humans do not
   appear that special anymore.

I will return to these questions later. The problem of evil is discussed in chapter
5, while chapter 8 is dedicated to the doctrine of imago Dei.

The purpose of this short overview of the Copernican turn, Newtonian
deism, and Darwin's theory of evolution by natural selection was to illustrate
the complexity of the interaction between scientific theories and philosophical
and religious convictions. As stated in the beginning, the problem was not
that the church was scientifically deaf and blind. Instead, it was very much
involved in advancing science. The difficulties arose because the church at one
point had linked its faith too closely with a scientific theory that at the time
seemed to be self-evident but afterward turned out to be false.

In the case of Aristotelianism, this happened slowly over time, and the
link between the two systems became so natural that it was hard to see the
problems when the time finally came to adopt a better theory. In the case of
Newtonianism, theologians tried to avoid reenacting the Galilean controversy
and rushed to adopt the Newtonian mechanical worldview as a framework
for theology. But soon this model, and the theologies based on it, became
outdated. Darwin's contemporaries lived already in a time of increasing pluralism, so the reaction was divided. Some resisted Darwinian theory as a part
of their theologies, but some adopted it. In a way, we see here three botched
attempts to relate science and theology: blind resistance to the evidence, un-
critical and naive acceptance, and an extreme reaction to things that are not
well understood.

The lesson is that the sciences develop over time toward more complex
and delicate models of reality. Therefore, immediately jumping onto a band-
wagon is not as wise as it might seem. This is so because the philosophical
and theological meanings of scientific theories are not always clear. There is
no point in resisting new scientific discoveries. Science proceeds on its course
through empirical verification and falsification. What the church should do
is to support the advance of science and concentrate on more philosophical
issues, such as the philosophy of science, being the point at which science
typically tries to overreach its proper boundaries.

4

All These Worlds

On the Multiverse

The slow progress of astronomy eventually confirmed that the earth is just one planet among many orbiting an average sun in the outskirts of a galaxy that is not that different from millions of others like it. Following Plato and Aristotle, many church fathers had rejected the idea of multiple worlds on philosophical and scientific grounds. When science finally opened the possibility that there could be other worlds, the question regarding the theological meaning of other worlds arose in earnest, but this was a long process. In this chapter, I briefly tell the history of other worlds as they appear in the Western tradition. More recently, modern cosmology has entertained the idea of the multiverse, and I examine what theological consequences this contemporary multiverse cosmology might have.

One World, Infinite Possibilities

Thinking about the possibility of other worlds has a long history.[1] Some Greek philosophers, the "atomists," had entertained the possibility that there could, in principle, be other worlds; yet these remained speculative. Both Plato and Aristotle rejected the possibility of other worlds. This negative conclusion was a result of how they understood the nature of physics: since in the spherical

1. Excellent introductions to the history of the debate are Duhem, *Medieval Cosmology*; Dick, *Plurality of Worlds*; and Rubenstein, *Worlds without End*.

cosmos all heavy objects fall downward, the earth must be at the center. Thus, it is impossible that there could be another center. Moreover, if there is just one model for our experienced phenomenal reality—the Forms, which are represented in reality in plenitude—there is no need for another cosmos, and there is a need for just one prime mover who moves the prime moved.

These reasons led Plato and Aristotle to disregard the theory of multiple worlds, which had been suggested earlier by Leucippus, for example, who taught that in principle it was possible that the void outside our cosmos contains other similar cosmoses. This was known as the thesis of infinite worlds (Gr. *aperoi kosmoi*, Lat. *plures mundi*). The atomists thought that everything that exists consists of atoms that move freely in space. Whatever pertains to all physical objects pertains also to the universe, which atomists considered to be spatially infinite. They also held a strong version of the principle of plenitude: if the causes are present, the effects follow unavoidably, and with an infinite number of atoms with causal powers, an infinite cosmos is inevitable.[2]

After Plato and Aristotle had established the one-world hypothesis, it was a long time before the hypothesis again became an object of serious debate. Interestingly, however, Origen did speculate on the idea of successive universes. The universes were not coeternal with God, they were always created *ex novo* (not from the remnants of previous universes), and there was only one universe in existence at one time. By this hypothesis, Origen attempted to affirm the eternal divinity of God while locating matter on a lower hierarchical plane. The speculation was not well received, and it was listed among Origen's questionable ideas.[3]

Augustine sealed the fate of the multiverse in his *City of God*, where he judged the whole idea as preposterous, in the form of both consecutive and parallel universes.[4] He interpreted the doctrine as a form of eternal return that traps souls in a perpetual chain of events from which they are unable to escape. He writes:

> This controversy some philosophers have seen no other approved means of solving than by introducing cycles of time, in which there should be a constant

2. Aristotle, *On the Heavens* 1.8–9; Plato, *Timaeus* 31ab. However, the issue is much more convoluted already in Plato and Aristotle. See Rubenstein, *Worlds without End*, 21–59; F. Miller, "Aristotle against the Atomists"; and Sorabji, *Matter, Space, and Motion*, 125–218.

3. Origen, *De principiis* 2.3.4; see Rubenstein, *Worlds without End*, 62–63.

4. Augustine, *City of God* 12.11 (*NPNF*[1] 2:233): "There are some, again, who, though they do not suppose that this world is eternal, are of opinion either that this is not the only world, but that there are numberless worlds or that indeed it is the only one, but that it dies, and is born again at fixed intervals, and this times without number."

renewal and repetition of the order of nature; and they have therefore asserted that these cycles will ceaselessly recur, one passing away and another coming, though they are not agreed as to whether one permanent world shall pass through all these cycles, or whether the world shall at fixed intervals die out, and be renewed so as to exhibit a recurrence of the same phenomena—the things which have been, and those which are to be, coinciding. And from this fantastic vicissitude they exempt not even the immortal soul that has attained wisdom, consigning it to a ceaseless transmigration between delusive blessedness and real misery. For how can that be truly called blessed which has no assurance of being so eternally, and is either in ignorance of the truth, and blind to the misery that is approaching, or, knowing it, is in misery and fear?[5]

Augustine's rejection of the many-worlds thesis is based on his peculiar understanding of the relationship between conscious beings and the world. Apparently, he thought that if our cosmos is eternal, it is always the home of sentient immortal souls and these souls will experience the lapse of time. Even if the created world is good, contra the Manicheans, experiencing it over and over again would be a form of suffering since the good world is, after all, corrupted by sin.

It was the joint authority of Plato, Aristotle, and Augustine—combined with the fact that the collapse of the Roman Empire prevented further pursuit of these ideas—that moved this debate to the sidelines for almost a millennium. But as soon as Aristotle's works were rediscovered and made widely available in the eleventh century, the theme was on the table again. A central event in the resurgence of the cosmic debate was the translation of Aristotle's *On the Heavens* in 1170.

Thomas Aquinas discusses the issue in *Summa Theologiae* 1.47.3, and following both Aristotle and John the Evangelist he affirms the single-world hypothesis. Even if it would be within the infinite power of God to create many worlds, the apostolic witness (John 1:10) refers to the world in the singular, while Aristotelian physics confirms that it is not possible to have multiple worlds. The existence of multiple worlds would mean that the events of the world are not purposeful and willed, because all states of affairs would be actualized necessarily. Second, the movement of physical objects toward their natural locations confirms the existence of one world. Third, the existence of multiple worlds would effectively mean that the cosmos is infinite. The First Way of his proofs for the existence of God (*ST* 1.2.3) denies the existence of infinite causal chains as an axiom that does not seem to need further argument, perhaps because Aquinas takes it to be self-evidently true.

5. Augustine, *City of God* 12.13 (*NPNF*[1] 2:234).

Later, Aquinas argues for the one-world hypothesis by referring to an axiom according to which it is better to create one perfect thing rather than several imperfect things.[6] However, I would argue that it is not clear that the concepts "perfect" and "imperfect" can be used this way in relation to the world. Genesis calls creation merely "good," not perfect. Even if the world were "the best of all possible worlds," it would not have to be perfect because worlds are combinations of several things. In fact, it seems that God intended to actualize an "imperfect" world when he created our world, a world in which sin is at least a possibility. Therefore, the axiom does not give us good reason to think that creating several universes would be in conflict with God's nature.

Soon after Aquinas died in 1274, the theological climate changed. The bishop of Paris, Stephen Tempier, published 219 theses that condemned several philosophical views that were commonly held by Scholastic thinkers.[7] Targeted by the condemnations were teachings such as these:

27A. That the first cause cannot make more than one world.

28. That from one first agent there cannot proceed a multiplicity of effects.[8]

After the condemnations, the theme of multiple worlds was widely discussed from various angles. Nicholas Oresme wrote on the possibility of concentric worlds (worlds within worlds). He thought that these kinds of multiverses were possible but not very probable.[9] Scholastic authors did not usually believe

6. Aquinas, "Aristotle's Treatise," sec. 197:
  But to this it must be answered that it takes more power to make one perfect than to make several imperfect. Now the single individuals of natural things which exist here are imperfect, because no one of them comprehends within itself the total of what pertains to its species. But it is in this way that the world is perfect; hence, from that very fact its species is shown to be more powerful. Thirdly, one objects thus: It is better for the best to be multiplied than for things not so good. But the world is the best. Therefore, it is better to have many worlds than many animals or many plants. To this it must be said that here it pertains to the goodness of the world to be one, because oneness possesses the aspect of goodness. For we see that through being divided some things lose their proper goodness.
  In *Summa* (*ST* 1.47.3), Aquinas offers the following argument: "No agent intends material plurality as the end forasmuch as material multitude has no certain limit, but of itself tends to infinity, and the infinite is opposed to the notion of end. Now when it is said that many worlds are better than one, this has reference to material order. But the best in this sense is not the intention of the divine agent; forasmuch as for the same reason it might be said that if He had made two worlds, it would be better if He had made three; and so on to infinite." See also Dick, *Plurality of Worlds*, 26–27.
  7. Grant, *Planets, Stars and Orbs*, 150. In addition to Aquinas, Michael Scot, William of Auvergne, and Roger Bacon also defended the existence of just one world.
  8. Klima, Allhoff, and Vaidya, "Condemnations of 1277."
  9. Oresme, *Le Livre du Ciel* 1.24.

that there actually would be other worlds. Instead, they believed that it was well within God's powers to create as many worlds as he wished. For God's freedom to be real, the alternatives had to be genuine. Thus, it was considered a real possibility that God could have created other worlds.[10] Of course, if there were other worlds, we would have no way of accessing them as something else than just mere potentialities. The whole medieval debate was thus more about theology—namely, the essence and limits of God's power—than physics per se. Nonetheless, this new thinking about what could be the case created new possibilities for intellectual inquiry.

The next step in the evolution of cosmology was made by the speculations of Nicholas of Cusa (or Nicholas Cusanus, 1401–1464) on the nature of the cosmos.[11] In his famous work *Of Learned Ignorance* (1440), he starts with a basic phenomenological fact: "It always appears to every observer, whether on the earth, the sun, or another star, that one is . . . at an immovable center of things and that all else is being moved" (2.12).[12] But this perception cannot be the basis for our cosmology. He reasons that it is not possible to provide absolute measures between two finite things because everything in the cosmos is always moving from one place to another. Even if I do not experience movement, like when I am sailing on a boat, an outside observer will experience it. In like manner, we can conclude that the earth is moving even if we cannot experience it. Thus, there cannot be a center of the universe, except for God, who alone can perceive all finite movement at once. Furthermore, because all relationships are perspectival, in a state of flux, and mere shadows of the Platonic Real, according to Cusanus we have no reason to think that, for example, the orbits of the planets are perfect circles. This is an idea that Kepler later employed when he introduced the idea of elliptical orbits.[13]

Moreover, Cusanus claimed that the universe does not have a proper center that could be established mathematically or by using other scientific means. Whereas the universe lacks a center, God is everywhere; that is, God is equally close to every single point in the universe. Perhaps the most interesting explication of deeply Christian cosmological intuition is Cusanus's affirmation of theocentric cosmology: "Only in God are we able to find a center which

10. Knuuttila, *Modalities in Medieval Philosophy*, 143.

11. Rubenstein, *Worlds without End*, 78–88; Brient, "Transitions to a Modern Cosmology"; Roark, "Nicholas Cusanus."

12. Cusanus, *Of Learned Ignorance*. The parenthetical references refer to this book.

13. However, it is contested how much Cusanus directly influenced contemporary cosmology. It seems that because his arguments were first and foremost philosophical, they did not directly challenge the empirical study of cosmology. It was only after the measurements were done that people could look back and see in Cusanus a kind of predecessor of modern cosmology. Koyré, *From the Closed World*, 8, 19.

is with perfect precision equidistant from all points, for He alone is infinite equality. God, ever to be blessed, is, therefore, the center of the world: He it is who is the center of the Earth, of all the spheres, and of all things that are in the world; and at the same time, he is the infinite circumference of all" (2.11).

Cusanus ingeniously turns against Ptolemaic cosmology in which the earth is the place of lowest value. Indeed, a century before Cusanus, Dante's *Divine Comedy* had placed in the center of the earth none other than Satan himself:

> The Emperor of the kingdom dolorous
> From his mid-breast forth issued from the ice;
> And better with a giant I compare
> Than do the giants with those arms of his;
> Consider now how great must be that whole,
> Which unto such a part conforms itself.
> Were he as fair once, as he now is foul,
> And lifted up his brow against his Maker,
> Well may proceed from him all tribulation.[14]

The place and state of Satan in the *Divine Comedy* follow Aristotelian-Ptolemaic physics and cosmology (see fig. 4.1). Satan is stuck in ice, unable to move because that is the state of objects at the bottom of the universe, whereas the higher planes of being are characterized by movement and heat (during his ascent to the Heavens, Dante is afraid that he will burn to dust). Satan is also the being that is farthest removed from God, and we are his next-door neighbors. Arthur Lovejoy states, "The centre of the world was not a position of honor; it was rather the place farthest removed from the Empyrean, the bottom of the creation, to which its dregs and baser elements sank. The actual centre, indeed, was Hell; in the spatial sense the medieval world was literally diabolocentric."[15]

It would be a mistake to take this Ptolemaic construction as literal. Lewis asks us to be wary concerning how well the model was in fact understood and employed in the different strata of medieval society. For scientists, theologians, and philosophers, the Ptolemaic model was always a provisional depiction of the reality. This was not necessarily always captured by the poets who effectively used it for their own purposes. Lewis argues that there was in fact little overlap

---

14. Dante, *Inferno*, Canto 34 (trans. Longfellow, 113). Interestingly, Satan's location reveals Dante's view of the shape of the earth; Satan is stuck "mid-breast"; he does not just lie at the bottom of a well but resides in the exact center of the frozen core.

15. Lovejoy, *Great Chain of Being*, 101–2. Lovejoy also quotes Montaigne's account of the human habitat: "The filth and mire of the world, the worst, the lowest, most lifeless part of the universe, the bottom story of the house."

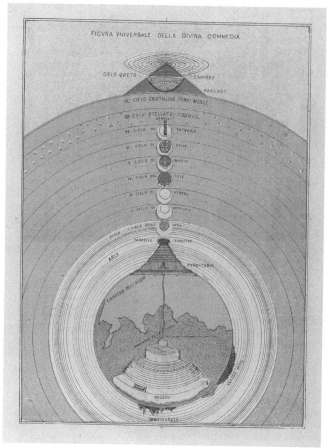

Figure 4.1. The cosmology of Dante's *Divine Comedy* by Michelangelo Caetani (1855).

between medieval cosmology and theology proper. You do not need to under-stand medieval cosmology to understand medieval spiritual texts (Cusanus being perhaps the only exception), but you do need some knowledge to under-stand Dante, Milton, or Chaucer. When it came to ordinary folk, these were the kinds of questions that probably did not interest them that much. From this Lewis concludes that scientific cosmology had very little effect on practiced religion because it was to a large extent irrelevant to it.[16] However, it would

16. Lewis, *Discarded Image*, 18, 92–112. Of course, the Bible often refers to the three-tiered nature of the cosmos. This is most visible in the verses concerning heaven (most notably the account of the ascension in Luke 24) and *hadēs*, which is the Greek word for "underworld" often used in the New Testament (e.g., Luke 10:15; 16:23; Acts 2:27, 31; Rev. 20:13). However,

perhaps be more accurate to say that the biblical vision of the transcendent was flexible enough to be conjoined with various cosmologies, and different spiritual lessons could be taught by using different models.

For example, when Cusanus abandons the Ptolemaic vision of the cosmos, it does have a bearing on the nature of Christian spirituality. As Regine Kather states: "For Cusanus the loss of the earth's privileged position implies no degradation. On the contrary, if no celestial body is nearer to God than another one, every one has the same value. The earth now is no longer the lowest place in the universe. It has now the position of a star, and this elevation entails an increase in dignity."[17]

Here we have a theory that says how God is equally close to everyone and everything. Some have seen here a trajectory that led eventually to the Reformation, which to some extent offered a view of Christianity that bypassed the classical hierarchical understanding of religion.[18] This has been interpreted as challenging the great chain of being, where everything in the universe has a certain distance and rank in relation to God. Cusanus's cosmos seems more

---

the spatiality of transcendence was a strange category in the ancient world. In one sense the heaven was up there and the realm of the dead below us. However, especially in the pre-Christian visions, it was possible to enter the underworld by boat or walking through the woods, and it was common to interpret different realities existing as parallels to ours. The Christian visions tend to replace the vertical movement with horizontal, but they also complicate the ascent and descent so that it becomes virtually impossible for humans to enter the other realms unless guided by God. Graf, "Bridge and the Ladder." Aquinas, however, thinks that heaven and hell are real places, and that hell is located below us (*ST* Suppl. 97.7), and paradise is located somewhere on the earth (*ST* 1.102). The reasons given are the following: First, it appears sensible for us to connect death with going down and being buried, and blessedness with ascension. Second, this relates to the ancient theory of elements, where the lowest materials fall downward and the worthiest ascend. Third, the Bible seems to use this same vertical language. At the same time, these places are not reachable by any ordinary means. Nonetheless, the concrete nature of salvation history forces theologians to affirm some form of continuity (no matter how vague that connection may be) between this world and the next, which is more than this world, but it cannot be anything less. Bockmuehl, "Locating Paradise."

17. Kather, "'Earth Is a Noble Star,'" 239–40. Cusanus (*Of Learned Ignorance* 2.2, trans. Heron, 117) writes:

And because in the world there is no maximum or minimum with regard to perfections, motions, and shapes (as is evident from what was just said), it is not true that the earth is the lowliest and the lowest. . . . The earth is a noble star, which has a light and a heat and an influence of its own, different from those of all other stars; every [star] indeed differs from every other in light, nature and influence; and thus every star communicates its light and influence to [every] other; not intentionally, for stars move and glitter only in order to exist in a more perfect manner: the participation arises as a consequence; just as light shines by its own nature, not in order that I may see it.

Here Cusanus attributes equal value to every planet and star, but, falsely from our point of view, thinks that the planets radiate their own light.

18. Alfsvåg, "*Explicatio* and *Complicatio*"; Alfsvåg, "Centrality of Christology."

egalitarian, yet it is not clear that his stance is radically that different. There is a clear difference between the Creator and the created, and nothing prevents one from establishing hierarchies within the Cusan cosmos; the point that God is present in everything does not exclude the possibility that some things are inherently more valuable than others (2.12).[19]

Cusanus's theological cosmology clarified the way in which natural theology could be employed. In a way, the world is a reflection of God, although Cusanus also made it clear that he did not wish to promote pantheism.[20] The existence and essence of God, who is present in the world but different from the world, could be deduced using analogy. This was especially true for the concept of infinity. Following Aquinas, Cusanus distinguished between two forms of infinity: negative and privative. Negative infinity cannot have a limit and it is attributable only to God, whereas privative infinity could have a limit but actually does not.[21] Thus, God is essentially different from the world, yet extremely close to it. Cusanus imagines the universe as interminate (*interminatum*); everything is genuinely contingent and indeterminate yet in a way that everything is interconnected. The world is perceived from particular perspectives, each being unique to the observer. Nevertheless, these are all perceptions of the same reality.[22]

Cusanus applied this cosmological vision to theological knowledge and our ability to grasp divine matters. In his vision, the cosmos is already incomprehensible because of its infinity, and if we cannot understand the world, how could we understand God? Natural theology cannot do the task assigned to it, and true faith is born only out of divine illumination. However, as is the case in negative theology, contemplation of the features of the world and the negation of these features move the mind in the right direction.[23]

A prominent figure who would take Cusanus's and Copernicus's ideas even further was Giordano Bruno (1548–1600).[24] Even though he was a polymath, Bruno's fame is based on his sad fate: being burned to death at the stake for his convictions. It is commonly assumed that the reason for his execution was his belief in other worlds or scientific cosmology, but this is largely false.[25] Bruno

19. Kather, "'Earth Is a Noble Star,'" 229–30; Lovejoy, *Great Chain of Being*, 112–14.
20. Dupré, "Question of Pantheism."
21. Cusanus, *Of Learned Ignorance* 2.23–24.
22. The term *interminatum* is not the same as *infinitum*. Only God is properly infinite, while the created order does not have boundaries. Koyré, *From the Closed World*, 8.
23. N. Hudson, *Becoming God*, 177–78.
24. For general accounts of Bruno, see Yates, *Giordano Bruno*; Michel, *Cosmology of Giordano Bruno*.
25. For example, the portrayal of Bruno in the popular TV show *Cosmos* by Neil deGrasse Tyson fails to do justice to the historical figure. "The Giordano Bruno Story," *Cosmos*, December 30, 2015, https://vimeo.com/150392001.

held many beliefs that were unorthodox, and his death sentence was a result of many factors. Bruno is often portrayed as a precursor of critical thinking and an example of warfare between science and religion, but this simplistic portrayal glosses over Bruno's thinking, which was deeply religious. Effectively, Bruno died as a martyr for his theological views, not as a paragon of science. Bruno was a very imaginative and prolific thinker, but, according to Alexandre Koyré, he was ultimately a bad philosopher and poor scientist, which made it hard for him to convince others and very easy for his critics to attack him.[26]

Nevertheless, Bruno's speculative thinking is worth mentioning for several reasons. Obviously, he did exemplify some essential virtues required for scientific thinking, such as courage and creativity. In his time, the humanist movement had made available the works of ancient philosophers, such as Lucretius's famous poem *De rerum natura* (*Of the Nature of Things*), which included ideas about multiple possible worlds. Bruno was aware of Copernicus's recently published work but thought that it did not go far enough. In that model, the solar system was still static, and only the order of the planets had slightly altered. Motivated by the Greek philosophy of atomism, Bruno asked why we should be tied to interpreting the cosmos within a Ptolemaic framework; he inquired, what if the universe has no boundaries? In the footsteps of Cusanus, he affirmed, "Thus is the excellence of God magnified and the greatness of his kingdom made manifest; he is glorified not in one, but in countless suns; not in a single earth, but in a thousand, I say, in an infinity of worlds."[27] However, what set him apart from Cusanus, who set his thinking within Christian orthodoxy, was that he sought to push the boundaries. He collapsed the distinction between the two infinities employed by Aquinas and Cusa, which effectively led him to a view that can be characterized as pantheism. The universe and God were now one.

This move could not but influence his theological views. For example, what need is there for a mediator if God is already present in everything without distinction? Things like the divinity of Christ and the doctrine of the Trinity also became obsolete. These were the views that got him into trouble. While it seems that Bruno's views on multiple worlds caused some concern as well, since they were brought up during the interrogations, they were not at the center of the debate.[28]

The common element concerning both Cusanus and Bruno was that their thinking could not be verified by empirical means. For this reason, Cusanus's

26. Koyré, *From the Closed World*, 54.
27. Quoted in Koyré, *From the Closed World*, 42.
28. Numbers, *Galileo Goes to Jail*, 59–67.

thinking had little relevance to the science of his own time. Bruno was more ostentatious in his public appearance; combined with the lack of means to scientifically test his ideas, this led to suspicion and then opposition.

It took hundreds of years to have empirical evidence that our sun is in fact just one among many, and it was only in 1992 when the first exoplanet, PSR B1257+12, was discovered. Even if the early Copernican astronomers did not challenge the Ptolemaic-like cosmology, the train was slowly moving in that direction.[29] Newton speculated on the idea of other worlds and how they might have different laws of nature if God decided so.[30] At that point in history, neither Newton nor anyone else could have even attempted to prove the existence of other worlds; Newton's speculation arose from his philosophy and theology, not science. His colleague Richard Bentley offered a proper theological angle in his Boyle lectures: "All bodies were formed for the sake of intelligent minds: As the Earth was principally designed for the Being and Service and Contemplation of Men; why may not all other Planets be created for the like uses, each for their own Inhabitants who have Life and Understanding."[31] This reveals a move away from simple anthropocentric cosmology, yet it extends a kind of intellectocentric view to the cosmos: the rationale for other systems must be other beings in those systems.

After the end of the seventeenth century, several theological books were published that investigated the reality of other possible worlds. One of the most well known was William Derham's *Astrotheology; or, a Demonstration of the Being and Attributes of God from a Survey of the Heavens* (1715), which offers a teleological argument for the existence of God based on cosmological features. The scale of space and everything in it proclaims the glory of God; this includes God creating "other systems" populated by sentient and intelligent beings (see fig. 4.2). "Because it is far the most magnificent of any; and worthy of the infinite CREATOR: whose Power and Wisdom as they are without bounds and measure, so may in all probability exert themselves in the Creation of many Systemes, as well as one. And as Myriads of Systemes are more for the Glory of GOD, and more demonstrate his Attributes than

29. For the way in which the possibility of alien life became accepted in Western culture, see the detailed accounts in Dick, *Plurality of Worlds*.

30. Newton, *Opticks*, 403–4: "And since Space is divisible in infinitum, and Matter is not necessarily in all places, it may be also allow'd that God is able to create Particles of Matter of several Sizes and Figures, and in several Proportions to Space, and perhaps of different Densities and Forces, and thereby to vary the Laws of Nature, and make Worlds of several sorts in several Parts of the Universe. At least, I see nothing of Contradiction in all this."

31. Quoted in Dick, *Plurality of Worlds*, 149.

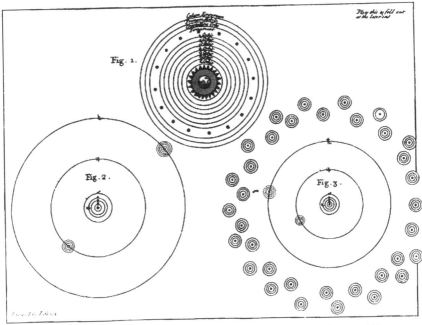

Figure 4.2. Illustration in William Derham's *Astrotheology* (1715). Three pictures of the cosmos, from left to right: the Copernican, Ptolemaic, and the "New System" with multiple solar systems.

one; so it is no less probable than possible, there may be many besides this which we have the Privilege of living in."[32]

Michael Crowe points out that there was no clear religious fault line regarding who supported or opposed the pluralist thesis. For some time after the Middle Ages, pluralism was opposed by traditional arguments, some of which were religious. In the eighteenth century, the climate suddenly changed so that pluralism was seen as a popular argument for theism. This may have resulted partly from the fact that the Bible and the Christian tradition could be taken as relatively open toward the idea of other worlds. Another reason might have been the imaginative pull of other worlds. Everyone who loves good science fiction knows this attraction.[33] In our own time, the discussion has

32. Derham, *Astrotheology*, 42.
33. See Crowe, *Extraterrestrial Life Debate*, 547–59. However, Crowe goes on to point out some problems that are related to cosmic pluralism, which also explain why it is so popular, now more than ever. The pluralist thesis is unfalsifiable, flexible, and rich in explanatory power. Unfalsifiability means that it is impossible to prove that there is no life outside the earth. If the moon is barren, let us go to Mars. If Mars leaves us cold, let us go to Europa. There are millions of solar systems beyond our own, and billions of galaxies, and so on. Pluralism is a flexible

extended from other potentially life-supporting solar systems to the multiverse; in addition to being a common topic in fiction, the multiverse theory tries to offer scientifically sound solutions to some puzzling features of the cosmos.

Fine-Tuning and the Multiverse

One of the astonishing things of our cosmos is that it seems to be carefully tuned for life. Recently, multiverse theories have been offered as one possible explanation for this. In the following, I briefly explain the central ideas behind the fine-tuning argument in order to make transparent what multiverse theories are supposed to explain.

In the nineteenth century, it was popular to use arguments from biological design to argue for the existence of a creator. The apex of this development was William Paley's *Natural Theology*, which used the famous analogy of finding a watch while walking on a beach.[34] How did the watch get there? Obviously the sand or the sea did not build it. The watch has features which support the idea that its parts have been purposefully arranged. Therefore, it is rational to believe that it was designed by a creator. The same inference is then applied to the cosmos.

Darwin's theory of evolution was a successful criticism against this kind of design inference: there is no need for a designer since mutations and natural selection explain design in nature more efficiently. Intelligence is not necessary to have design. Given enough time, biological processes can produce structures and organisms that appear to have been designed. Biological design arguments fell out of fashion in the early twentieth century, but recently the intelligent design (ID) movement has attempted to rehabilitate them.[35]

---

thesis, which allows it to flourish in almost any kind of intellectual environment, regardless of worldview or religion. Pluralism can also be used to explain almost anything, from pyramids to the "canals" on Mars. Together these three features make pluralism resistant to critique and therefore persistent as an idea. In our own time, when traditional religions have lost some of their power in the Western imagination, pluralism has taken religious forms. Many scientists and authors have expressed messianic hopes regarding the salvific powers of extraterrestrials and how they could rescue us from the coming global cataclysms. While none of this means that as a theory cosmic pluralism is wrong, it does show how our imagination should be subjected to criticism.

34. Paley, *Natural Theology*. In fact, the exact form of Paley's argument is a matter of ongoing debate. It is perhaps best seen as an inference to the best explanation. See Schupbach, "Paley's Inductive Inference to Design."

35. For philosophical evaluations of ID arguments, see Nagasawa, *Existence of God*, 46–101; Kojonen, *Intelligent Design Debate*; and Kojonen, "God of the Gaps." For example, ID theorists claim that certain examples in biological organisms are so complex, unlikely, and teleologically structured that it is more reasonable to believe in a designer than mere processes of nature. Even

Many philosophers think that the fine-tuning argument (FTA) has a better chance of success than biological design arguments. Instead of focusing on the features and structures of biological organisms, FTA relies on the purposefulness of the basic laws of the cosmos. The basic structure of FTA goes as follows:

1. The current constants and laws enable the existence and flourishing of embodied conscious agents (ECAs).
2. Even minuscule changes in the basic constants and laws governing our universe would lead to a state in which the evolution of ECAs was impossible.
3. There is no obvious reason why the constants and laws are as they are.
4. Therefore, our universe seems to be fine-tuned for ECAs.

The history of the FTA's modern version goes back to 1986, when John Barrow and Frank Tipler published their book *The Anthropic Cosmological Principle*.[36] Simply put, the anthropic principle argues that the cosmos must be exactly as it is to support life. Even a tiny change in just one of the many factors that regulate our cosmos would make life impossible. Examples of this fine-tuning include the following:

a. The power of the initial expansion rate had to be just right because otherwise the cosmos would have collapsed back into the singularity or the cosmos would have expanded too rapidly, which would have scattered matter so widely that galaxies could not have been formed.
b. In the nuclei of all atoms except hydrogen, there are two or more protons. Protons are connected by strong nuclear force, which is one of the four fundamental interactions (the others are weak nuclear force, electromagnetism, and gravity) between particles. If the force were weaker or stronger, stars could not provide a durable energy source and the nuclei of carbon and larger elements would be unstable.
c. Strong nuclear force needs to be in proper relation to electromagnetism. In the atomic nucleus, electromagnetism pushes particles apart while strong force keeps them together. An alteration of this dynamic

---

if the odds were in favor of design inference, many philosophers feel that ID makes a "God of the gaps" argument. If there is something in nature that we cannot explain, we can say that God is the best explanation. However, "God of the gaps" is invoked nowadays often indiscriminately. There are cases when the move is warranted, but other cases are not so clear. The conversation on the philosophical merits of ID continues.

36. Barrow and Tipler, *Anthropic Cosmological Principle*. For an example of prescientific thinking about fine-tuning, see Palmén, "Experience of Beauty."

would result in several different problems, from unstable protons and electron-positron pair creation in atoms, to the inability of elements to bind together to form molecules.

d. One example of laws that keep matter stable is the Pauli exclusion principle. According to this principle, it is not possible for two electrons to occupy the same quantum state, which means that in one atomic orbital there can be only two electrons. This keeps electrons from falling to the lowest orbital, thereby guaranteeing the stability of material compounds.

e. The power of gravity needs to remain within certain boundaries for ECAs to evolve. Among others things, gravity affects plate tectonics, which are necessary for a sustainable biosphere. Also, the atmosphere requires exact conditions to function. Even a small change would lead to evaporation of the atmosphere and the impossibility of life. With larger changes to gravity, stellar burning is too short, or stars would be too cold for nuclear fusion.

f. The expansion of the universe is regulated by the amount of dark matter and dark energy in it. According to the current estimates, about 95 percent of the mass of our universe consists of dark energy and dark matter. A small change there and our universe would have collapsed or dispersed too rapidly for structures to form.

In the literature on fine-tuning, there are plenty of other examples expressed in more precise form.[37] How unlikely is it, then, that all these and many other constants simply fell in line? One current estimate is that the likelihood of our universe from all possible values of these constants is about 1 in 10^{300}. Roger Penrose compares this to being able to throw a dart into a single proton if the dartboard is about the size of the known universe.[38] So it is quite unlikely.

These physical constants offer only necessary—not sufficient—conditions for life to evolve. In order for ECAs to evolve and form a culture, they need to pass through several evolutionary bottlenecks, which have a very low probability of reaching a positive outcome. One of the lists that includes the stages of the evolutionary path contains the following events:

1. A star system that is able to support organic life
2. Reproductive something (e.g., RNA)

37. See, e.g., McGrath, *Fine-Tuned Universe*; Holder, *God, the Multiverse*, 29–41; Collins, "Fine-Tuning Evidence"; Collins, "Teleological Argument"; Lewis and Barnes, *Fortunate Universe*.
38. Penrose, *Emperor's New Mind*, 343.

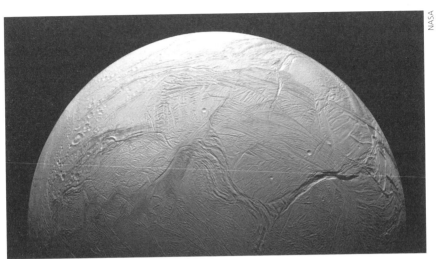

NASA

Figure 4.3. Saturn's moon Enceladus is covered with ice, but under the frozen surface there is liquid water, which makes the moon possibly able to host simple forms of life.

3. Simple (prokaryotic) single-cell life

4. Complex (archaeatic and eukaryotic) single-cell life

5. Sexual reproduction

6. Multicell life

7. Tool-using animals with big brains

8. [This is where we are now]

9. Interstellar colonization explosion[39]

For a culture to evolve, it needs to pass through each of these possible filters, and it seems rational to think that passing through each filter is very unlikely. But this is so only because we have no idea how life can squeeze itself through these bottlenecks. Even if this is strange to us, it might be that the emergence of intelligent life is coded into the fabric of the universe. Of course, we are here, so we know it can happen. But we have no idea how often it could happen.[40] It seems reasonable to ask, what could explain that we are

39. Hanson, "Great Filter."

40. Lists like these are used to answer the Fermi paradox. Because we do not have any evidence of life outside Earth (this is called "the Great Silence"), we must conclude that somewhere in the list is the "Great Filter," which snuffs out organic life in the universe. It might also be that the Great Filter lies ahead of us, so that the colonization of space is impossible. Life could well evolve simultaneously in multiple solar systems but always die out before it can colonize space beyond its immediate reach. For a discussion on why there are so few signs of life in the universe, see Ward and Brownlee, *Rare Earth*; and Ross, *Improbable Planet*. According to Ward and

here? Paul Davies offers several options that could explain why our universe appears to be fine-tuned:[41]

1. The universe is, in fact, inherently *absurd*. It has no design or teleology, and there is no explanation to be had for why things turned out this way. Davies suspects that this view might be the majority view of scientists. Oddly, the absurd universe does not offer any opportunity for research; even if the universe is viewed as absurd, it cannot be studied without some assumptions of teleology.[42] This view may be existentially convenient to some, but it is philosophically and scientifically unsatisfying.

2. There is a *Theory of Everything* that offers a necessary explanation for why the universe has exactly these properties and not others. It seeks to explain every constant in physics, mathematics, and nature in general, including quantum phenomena. The strong version of the theory would entail that everything exists as it is out of necessity. In this scheme, God still fits into the picture as the origin of everything or, as Davies puts it, as the one "who breathes fire into the equations."[43] Yet there would be no actual contingency in the world, because everything would be predetermined; things could not have happened otherwise. A weaker version only assumes that the theory enables a range of fine-tuned values. This, however, leaves unanswered the question of why exactly this combination of values is governing this universe. Resorting to mystery is a possibility that does not explain anything, however.

3. We are living in a *multiverse*. The reason we are here is explained by an infinite amount of dice rolls. If there are an infinite number of universes, it should not be that surprising if one of them gets everything right so

Brownlee (*Rare Earth*, xxvii–xxviii), in order for the planet to be suitable for life as we know it, it needs to have several features, including the following (among others): the planet needs to have the right distance from the star to have liquid water; the star needs to have the right mass and not too much ultraviolet radiation; the solar system cannot have too many giant planets, which would make planetary orbits unstable; the solar system, however, requires at least one giant within the right distance, which clears out the planet-killing asteroids and comets; the planet needs to have the correct mass to retain atmosphere (right temperature, composition, and pressure) and a stable core; plate tectonics that enable magnetic fields and enhance biodiversity; the right amount of liquid water and carbon; a large moon within the right distance that stabilizes tilt; and the right place within the right kind of galaxy. For an argument for why life may be a universal principle written into the fabric of the cosmos but we can still be the one sentient species, see Conway Morris, "Does Biology."

41. Davies, *Goldilocks Enigma*, 295–303.

42. Walsh, "Teleology." For an example of the teleological disposition of evolution, see, e.g., Weinrich et al., "Darwinian Evolution."

43. Davies, *Goldilocks Enigma*, 212.

that things like us can exist and ponder these questions. Multiverse theories are currently gaining more popularity among scientists. I will assess them in more detail below.

4. Our universe is *designed*. If a theistic God exists, it would make sense that the universe is a home to personal, conscious beings. This option is not meant to be a scientific theory. To be sure, it is an explanation, but it is not an explanation in the same sense that, say, multiverse theory is.

5. It might be that our universe hosts something that Davies calls the "*life principle*." This principle is not like the Theory of Everything, even though it is compatible with it. In option (2), life is an accidental by-product, "an unexplained bonus." The life principle would entail that there is an in-built teleology in nature. This view is not easily sold to scientists, however, because it sounds very much like theism-lite. A reason for favoring the life principle over theism might be if the principle could be shown to be a simpler solution than theistic design.

6. The universe could be *self-explanatory*. This is a kind of "brute fact" explanation. Instead of looking for the final turtle on top of which all the other turtles are stacked, we just assume that perhaps only universes with a capacity for consciousness can exist. For example, John Leslie has formulated an axiarchist view according to which things, like our cosmos, exist because it is good for them to exist. I take a closer look at axiarchism in chapter 6.

7. The universe is a virtual reality simulation. This is a possible scenario, but it has interesting problems when doing science (i.e., what is the status of our scientific theorization if it is possible that we never experience the real world?). Moreover, it does not really offer an answer to the fine-tuning of the cosmos, but just moves it instead to a different level: the programmer needs to be fine-tuned to write the simulation.

These options all offer explanations for why the world is as it is. However, these explanations are not all similar, and they have complicated relationships with one another. For example, (7) is compatible with all the other explanations except (1), whereas (1) makes all the others obsolete. Number (4) is compatible with (2), (3), and (5).

To simplify the issue a bit, we can collapse Davies's solutions to these:

Theory of Everything
Incredible luck (multiverse)
Teleological design

The Theory of Everything is theoretically possible, but at this point in human history we are not even close to being able to fathom it.[44] Even if we could, it would not be a great problem for theology. On the one hand, the strong version would not create any new problems for theology that haven't already been discussed for centuries. God's foreknowledge is as hard to swallow as the view according to which everything is predetermined through reasons internal to the world. The weaker version would still leave unanswered the question about the design of the Theory of Everything, pushing the question of design just one level higher.

It is simple to see why the multiverse interests many people. If you want to ask a question about the origins of the cosmos without invoking metaphysics that sound too theological, the multiverse is an easy way to do so. Seen from another perspective, the multiverse is one means of escaping the idea of there being a designer, and at least in some forms of multiverse theorization there is a clear anti-theistic attitude.[45] Multiverse theory helps one to argue that a creator is not necessary in order for a world like ours to exist. If our cosmos is 13.8 billion years old, that window of time is too short for life to evolve unless the game has been rigged from the start; thus, our universe is in fact a life-enabling universe. This universe is just one among many universes, most of which are not life-enabling. Possibly there are, or there have been, other universes with conscious beings. But let us take a closer look at how the multiverse could be construed. There are several ways of creating similar typologies, and this list does not claim to be exhaustive.[46]

1. Quilted universe: If the universe is infinite, there are an infinite number of "universes," since infinite space allows infinite possibilities. For example,

44. For a general account, see Laughlin and Pines, "Theory of Everything."
45. E.g., Stenger, "Fine-Tuning." However, as Robert P. Mann points out, if we in fact live in the multiverse, this has some unwanted results for atheists and naturalists. For example, if our universe is spatially infinite, we experience rampant duplication: all logical states of affairs happen infinitely many times. This undercuts the explanatory force of the theory, since induction as a form of inference loses its value. Additionally, the so-called Boltzmann brain problem leads to awkward results. Boltzmann brains are brains with memories and consciousness that arise from thermal equilibrium by mere chance—rarely but eventually, given infinite resources. Moreover, given an infinite amount of time and space and the short lifespan of beings with humanlike consciousness and bio-brains, the universe is vastly more populated with Boltzmann brains than with bio-brains. Mann, "Puzzled by Particularity."
46. For accessible accounts of various multiverse theories, see Rubenstein, *Worlds without End*; and Davies, *Goldilocks Enigma*. A well-known typology is based on Max Tegmark's classification of four levels of multiverses. The Level I multiverse is an infinitely extended space that allows the actualization of an infinite amount of states of affairs. Level II is a bubble multiverse or oscillating universe where there are different universes with varying physical constants. Level III is the quantum multiverse, which consists of an infinite amount of parallel universes. Level IV is a so-called ultimate mathematical universe, where all possible worlds are actualized. Tegmark, "Parallel Universes."

somewhere there is a planet exactly like ours except that the TV show *Firefly* was never canceled (as it was on our planet). In a quilt multiverse, the other universes are in theory (but not in practice) reachable.

2. Inflationary universe: Universes collapse and produce new universes. Ours is just one in a long temporal line of universes, and there are more to come.

3. Bubble universe: The universes are related to each other but differing—like holes and solid cheese in Swiss cheese—in their inflationary speed. Every universe has its own constants and laws, and some are short-lived. Physical variations in one universe may cause it to create another universe out of itself.

4. Quantum multiverse: This model is based on an interpretation of how subatomic particles behave at the quantum level. Their position or direction of movement cannot be expressed when they are in "superposition." This indeterminate state is called the wave function. When the wave function collapses, it means that a particle has "chosen" a particular state. But if the wave function does not collapse, one interpretation is that all possibilities are, in fact, actual. Therefore, there are an infinite number of parallel worlds, where the chips fall differently.

5. Ultimate mathematical universe: This model entails so-called hyper-realism, according to which all imaginable possible worlds are in fact actual. Effectively, this multiverse contains all the other multiverses.

6. Simulated multiverse: If we suppose that intelligent races are able to develop powerful computers that are able to simulate reality so that the inhabitants of these worlds believe that they are actually living in what they are seeing, then we have a case of simulated universe, like the one in the movie *The Matrix*.

The obvious problem with multiverse theories is that they are almost impossible to verify. This is somewhat ironic since one (but not the only) reason behind multiverse theorization was to get rid of cosmological models that support unwanted theological and metaphysical conclusions, or intellectual positions where you just need to believe something to be true. Unsurprisingly, this has created a debate that asks which position requires more faith, theism or multiverse? Some have even suggested that multiverse theorization is hard to distinguish from pseudoscience and astrology. Many physicists have rejected the idea of the multiverse as needless speculation. Others have defended the scientific nature of multiverse theorization by arguing that many facts about our universe fit very well with multiverse theory, even if other universes as such are beyond our means of observation. Some have tried to find these means, but at this stage their success is a point of contention. The scientific community is sharply divided on the issue, with some seeing these theories as a complete waste of time and others perceiving a path to promising discoveries. So the jury is still out, and it will probably stay out for a long time.[47]

Theism and the Multiverse?

If we assume for the sake of argument that some form of multiverse were true, how would that affect theistic cosmology? Does multiverse theory help the skeptic to avoid the "God question"? The strength of the anti-theistic argument comes from removing the necessity of a supernatural designer because, given enough time, chance will take care of everything.

However, multiverse theories do not answer the age-old question, "Why is there something instead of nothing?"[48] To follow that line a bit further, invoking the multiverse just pushes the question regarding cosmic design one step back. Is there perhaps a "multiverse generator" that churns out these universes? Given that a generator has at least some chance of success in this, we can reasonably ask whether it, too, is perhaps designed. According to Collins, there must be a set of certain mechanisms (a hypothetical "inflaton field") that are in place for the universes to come about. An inflaton field includes a mechanism that supplies the energy needed by the universes, a mechanism that forms the universes, a mechanism that converts the energy of the inflaton field to the normal mass/energy fields of our universe, and a mechanism that allows for the variation of constants in the universes. So where did the inflaton field come from and how should we explain its existence? It seems that the multiverse as a response to the design argument just moves the same debate to the next level.[49]

If we look at multiverse theory from a wider theological perspective, we can ask whether God would create a multiverse. Does the multiverse as a way of

47. For an optimistic overview, see Rubenstein, *Worlds without End*, 213–36. For a more pessimistic view, see Holder, *God, the Multiverse*.

48. The multiverse argument targets merely one interpretation of the fine-tuning argument, and it has no relevance to, for example, the versions of the Leibnizian cosmological argument. See, e.g., Pruss, "Leibnizian Cosmological Argument."

49. Collins, "Multiverse Hypothesis"; Collins, "Teleological Argument," 256–72. Additionally, our universe seems to have features that are explained by the multiverse hypothesis. Collins notes that the laws and constants are such that they make our knowledge about the universe possible; the cosmos seems to be fine-tuned for "discoverability." This adds one layer to the argument. On naturalism we should have no reason to expect the values to be knowledge-enabling, whereas on theism this is very likely. See Collins, "Fine-Tuning for Discoverability."

creating our universe make God look somehow bad? The following analogy could be constructed. God is like a gardener who is starting his lawnmower and needs three pulls to get it running. If we increase the scale, instead of only three pulls, billions are necessary. God needs to "fail" an almost infinite amount of times before he gets things going. Or maybe God is like a sharpshooter who shoots three bullets at the target and then uses the result to precisely adjust the X and Y axes on his scope to achieve proper aim.

However, if God is all-powerful, he could easily get the engine running with just one pull, and if God is all-knowing, he knows where the bullets will land, so he does not need three shots to adjust the scope. In this critique, creation is like the magic trick where you need to guess under which cup the hidden item is. Do we have good reasons to think that creation is analogous to making just one, or several, precise choices? I do not think so.

If we suppose that the act of creation itself is to some extent dependent on what is in fact created, we can assume that creation is not analogous to merely choosing one option among many. It is a common theme in the history of theology to think that God's freedom is to some extent limited by the choices God makes.[50] It is not far-fetched to think that the nature of matter out of which our universe is created sets some boundaries on how creation can take place. Of course, this is mere speculation, and its purpose is merely to show that we have no overwhelming reasons to think that God would necessarily have to choose a way of creating the universe that appears to *us* as the most fitting.

We can also approach the same question from the opposite angle and ask whether God might have had a reason to create a multiverse. In fact, several theistic philosophers have argued that if God did create a universe, this universe of ours is part of a multiverse. For example, Klaas Kraay has argued that God as a perfect being would in fact create a multiverse in conjunction with the following principles:[51]

Principle of Plenitude (PPL): God wants to create a maximum amount of things that are worth creating.

Perfect Being Theism (PBT): If a being fails to satisfy the Principle of Plenitude, that being is not the greatest conceivable being.

In addition to merely creating the universe, God needs to sustain the universe as well. Kraay formalizes the argument in the following way:

50. E.g., Veldhuis, "Ordained and Absolute Power."
51. Kraay, "Theism, Possible Worlds."

1. If a universe is creatable by an unsurpassable being and worth creating (i.e., it has an axiological status that surpasses some objective threshold t), that being will create that universe.

2. If a being fails to create any universe that is both worth creating and creatable (by that being), then that being is surpassable.

3. If a universe is sustainable by an unsurpassable being and worth sustaining (i.e., it has an axiological status that surpasses some objective threshold t), that being will sustain that universe.

4. If a being fails to sustain any universe that is both worth sustaining and sustainable (by that being), then that being is surpassable.

The problem emerges if we think that the multiverse is something that God needs to create in order to be the greatest conceivable being.[52] According to classical theism, God does not need the cosmos, and he is under no obligation to create anything. It might be better to interpret the conjunction of PPL and PBT as something that suggests a possible way of action for God, which is good and according to his nature, but does not entail a necessary form of action. This could be done as follows. We can contrast PPL with the following claim:

Principle of Paucity (PPA): God wants to create only a minimum number of things that are worth creating.

However, PPA seems obviously wrong. If we assume that God exists and has created our cosmos, we know something about what God seems to value. We know that the biosphere of the earth has been vastly more diverse in the past and currently only one in a thousand species that once existed are still with us today.[53] Moreover, the known cosmos contains billions of stars and planets, many of which we have never even had a chance to observe in any way. God seems to create things in abundance, and this is evidence for PPL over PPA. The conjunction of PPL and PBT does not mean that God is obliged to act in such a way that he creates things abundantly. It merely suggests that God is more likely to create things in abundance than to follow PPA.[54] This can be expressed in the following form:

---

52. This has been pointed out by, e.g., Jaki, *Cosmos and Creator*, 127–28.

53. Conway Morris, *Life's Solution*, 329; Alexander, "Order and Emergence."

54. Obviously, trying to answer questions like how many beings exactly God needs to create will lead to all kinds of problems of vagueness (like how many stones constitute a heap).

Theistic Principle of Plenitude (TPP): As the greatest conceivable being, who is good and loves things that are good, God is more likely than not to create good things in abundance.

Therefore, given TPP, I think we have good prima facie reasons to suppose that it is at least possible, or that it is not obviously contradictory to God's nature, for God to create a multiverse.

Let us take a closer look at one critique of this view. Man Ho Chan has argued that God would choose the special creation of just one world over creating a multiverse because a special creation is more in line with divine properties: God would seek to create a better world, and a specially created, single world is the better of the two options. Chan suggests that we have reason to think that God would respect the values of simplicity, ontological economy, control, and minimum disadvantages.[55]

Creating a multiverse would lead to the creation of a possibly infinite number of worlds, many of which would likely be chaotic and not representing order. Chan assumes that the main reason for God to create the universe was to bring about humanity. But this anthropocentric assumption is not necessary. Christians insist only that God cares for humans. This does not entail that humans are the only things that God cares about. For all we know, God could have created the world, or worlds, primarily so that higher beings have something to wonder about and meditate on, and humans just came into the picture as a by-product.

Chan also suggests that a multiverse creates too much "waste." But why should we think that waste is a thing that should worry God, who has endless resources? The fear of wasting things is relevant only for beings like us, who are dependent on limited resources. A related worry of Chan is that other universes would be "useless" (at least from our point of view). However, we have an endless amount of solar systems with exoplanets in this universe, which are also not used. Compared to these contours of our universe, which already approaches infinity, having a high number of other, unobservable universes changes merely the quantity, not the quality, of the question.

How should we define usefulness, then? The history of cosmology we touched on in the first chapter consists of thousands of years of imaginative deliberation. Even at this point in our history, we have only been able to use tiny bits of matter lying outside the earth. Perhaps the usefulness of the things in the world should include how they are reachable through our imagination.

55. Chan, "Would God Create."

We do not need to be able to travel to the stars or to other dimensions; it might be enough for us to just imagine it, at least at this stage.[56]

Chan's principles are helpful if we want to come up with a general theory of explanation. Yet I am not sure how good they are if someone wishes to predict how God might act in some situation. If we observe our cosmos, it does not seem to be simple or economical. Salvation history likewise seems to be very erratic and random. If God favors indirect communication and election in *saving* people, why would we expect God to do something else when *creating* the world?

Turning now to a slightly different issue, multiverse theories also have relevance for the problem of evil, and many theistic philosophers have suggested that a multiverse might be one possible solution to the problem of evil. Theists believe that God is good. This is taken to entail that whatever God creates must be good. This is often expressed as the Principle of the Best, according to which the good God always actualizes the best of all possibilities. Is this principle plausible? According to Genesis, creation is not called "best" but "good." I take it as a central theistic intuition that God cannot create anything that is essentially bad or evil from the start. While it is possible for free agents to act in ways that are bad and evil, their actions are not attributable to God.

But are theists under any obligation to believe that our world is the best possible world? Simply affirming this leads to a surprising and odd conclusion. If our world is the best possible world, then nothing in our world could be otherwise; everything would be necessitated.[57] But this seems to be counterintuitive. We can easily think of occurrences of evil that could easily have been removed from the world without the world becoming substantially different. Think, for example, of hitting your finger with a hammer. In a close possible world, the hammer would miss your finger. That world would thus be a better world than this one. If God is indeed good, he should have actualized the other world. But now we are faced with strange problems of vagueness. Where do we draw the line between contingent bad things that can exist in a world so that it is still "good"? Perhaps there is no line to be drawn. We could instead think of a case where God creates a set of universes that all have the same basic features $\{k, h, j, l \ldots\}$. The universes vary with regard to the exact nature of these features, so that a close possible world contains the features $\{k^n, h^n, j^n, l^n \ldots\}$, another one $\{k^{n+1}, h^{n+1}, j^{n+1}, l^{n+1} \ldots\}$, and so on. All these possible worlds belong to a set that God calls "good." In one world, you hit your finger; in another you miss, but you get stung by a bee instead. There

56. Swinburne, "Bayes," 116.
57. Lougheed, "Divine Creation."

is no obvious way of telling which one of these universes is absolutely better than all the others.[58] Nevertheless, given the Theistic Principle of Plenitude, God does have a reason, and the means, to actualize all of these universes if they exhibit features that God values. It is questionable whether this solves the problem of the best world. It might, but on the other hand, God is not required to do things that are logically impossible, and creating the best possible world is among them (you can always add one more good thing to the world without ever reaching the best version). Instead, God is free to actualize a set of good worlds.

Some models of multiverses are, however, problematic for theism. For example, quantum multiverses and ultimate mathematical universes lead to an abundance of horrific universes where values of goodness and beauty are never realized. Of course, we might never know whether these kinds of universes exist or whether we could ever assess their axiological status, but their existence would spell trouble for classical theism. Nevertheless, the standard inflationary multiverse as such does not cause any significant problems. In that case, good worlds more or like this one would follow one another.

I conclude that many-world models or multiverse theories do not pose a challenge to theism, and theists in fact have reasons within their own tradition to think that God might have created a multiverse. It also seems that multiverse theories do not affect the fine-tuning argument. Naturally, if at some point in the future we have good evidence for the existence of other universes, it would raise some theological and philosophical questions, yet these would be of the sort that can be aligned with theistic convictions. These questions are pursued in more detail in the next chapters.

58. Kraay, "Theism, Possible Worlds." For another type of theodicy employing the notion of hyperspace, see H. Hudson, *Metaphysics of Hyperspace*, 163–81. Multiverse theodicies are criticized by Ijjas, Grössl, and Jaskolla, "Theistic Multiverse"; and Monton, "Against Multiverse Theodicies."

5

If It's Just Us, It Seems Like an Awful Waste of Space

On Human Uniqueness

On February 22, 2017, NASA made a big announcement. The Spitzer telescope had found seven Earth-sized planets orbiting an ultra-cool red dwarf star (named Trappist-1) about forty light years away from us. Three of the planets are in the habitable zone of the solar system, which means that if water is present on them, it would be in liquid form, which is one of the necessary conditions for life. In the press conference, both NASA representatives and the audience expressed scientific enthusiasm and existential wonder. One of the questions raised was, what does this discovery mean for us humans?

Findings like these elicit deep existential inquiries about our meaning and significance. In this chapter, I approach the question above from a theological perspective. Does the possibility of extraterrestrial life make a difference for a Christian worldview?

Are We Alone?

Let us start with the basic question, "What do we know about life in the universe?" At this point, we do not have evidence of any kind of life that has

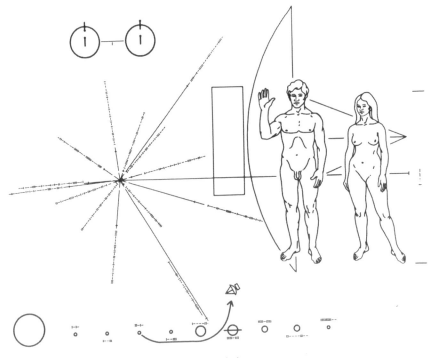

Figure 5.1. An illustration of the Pioneer 10 metal plaque.

evolved independently outside Earth.[1] The search for signs of life currently
has two different forms. Perhaps more well known is SETI (Search for Extraterrestrial Intelligence), which seeks to observe patterns in electromagnetic
signals originating outside our own solar system. The problems of the SETI
program are related to immense cosmic distances; that is to say, even if there
were alien cultures that use, or have used, radio waves to communicate, it is
possible that they are so far from us that their waves will take untold millen-
nia to reach us.

A further problem concerns the content of communication. It might be
hard even to recognize a message as such without first knowing something
about the culture that sent it. When the distances are huge, the form of communication needs to be relatively simple, which makes understanding the
message difficult without some kind of key. Active or positive SETI, or METI
(Messaging to the Extraterrestrial Intelligences), refers to our own sending of
messages, in various forms, into space. While these have included attaching
engraved metal plaques to Pioneer 10 and Pioneer 11 (see fig. 5.1), the form

1. Domagal-Goldman and Wright, "Astrobiology Primer 2.0."

of communication with the highest chance of success is a concentrated burst of information sent to a particular location in the sky.[2]

The second form of the search for signs of life is SETL, or Search for Extraterrestrial Life, which focuses on finding elementary forms of life within our own solar system. We can quite safely assume that there are no alien cultures in our solar system, and the probability of finding even remnants of some kind of life seems very low.[3] A methodological problem for astrobiological findings is the possibility that Earth has "seeded" life in space as a consequence of an asteroid impact. Hence, even if we found remnants of life outside Earth, or inside meteorites, we could not be sure whether it evolved here or outside Earth.

Even if we currently lack evidence, we can speculate about alien life by calculating probabilities based on other known features of the cosmos. The well-known tool for this speculation, developed by the astrophysicist Frank Drake, became known as the Drake equation:

$$N = R \times F_p \times N_e \times F_l \times F_i \times F_c \times L$$

Where,

R = Rate of star formation in our galaxy
F_p = Fraction of those stars that have planets
N_e = Number of Earth-like planets
F_l = Fraction of Earth-like planets where life develops
F_i = The fraction of life that develops intelligence
F_c = The fraction of intelligent life that develops communication
L = The "lifetime" (in years) of the communicating intelligent civilization
N = The number of communicating civilizations today

2. Dick and Strick, *Living Universe*, 131–54; Davies, *Are We Alone?*, 1–60. Some have raised concerns about this because making noise could draw the attention of potentially hostile cultures. However, we have already left a quite distinctive mark in the cosmos with our radio transmissions. Some members of the METI community have called for an international debate on whether we should send these messages. "Regarding Messaging to Extraterrestrial Intelligence (METI) / Active Searches for Extraterrestrial Intelligence (Active SETI)," SETI@home, accessed June 1, 2017, http://setiathome.berkeley.edu/meti_statement_0.html.

3. At the moment, the best options are Europa (a moon of Jupiter), and Enceladus and Titan (moons of Saturn). Europa and Enceladus have liquid water under the frozen surface, and Titan has liquid methane and frozen ice. Although being very harsh environments, these are considered to possibly be prebiotic. Domagal-Goldman and Wright, "Astrobiology Primer 2.0," 603–4. However, there are serious problems in how to define life in the first place. See Cleland, "Life without Definitions."

Obviously, as noted, the equation demonstrates a lot of speculation.[4] Even if we knew something about the first three factors, we would still be totally at a loss in regard to the other four. As per our current estimates, there are about 10^{11} stars in the Milky Way galaxy, and the total number of galaxies in the known universe is about 10^{11}. About 20 percent of those stars are like our sun—that is, capable of hosting planets that are capable of sustaining life. Then we need to start guessing, since we do not know how many solar systems have planets in the habitable zone. If, for the sake of argument, we said that 2 percent of solar systems have exoplanets, that leaves us with 10^{17} Earth-like planets. The next step involves an even bigger guess, since we have evidence of only a single case: ourselves. Even if 10^{17} Earth-like planets sounds like a lot, in order to have a communicating culture, a civilization needs to pass through several evolutionary filters, all of which are very likely to bring an end to the evolution of life.

On the basis of the different values we attribute to the factors, we can have a result according to which we are alone in the universe or in which there are a couple million communicating civilizations in the visible space (known also as the "Hubble space"), which is a very optimistic estimation. Yet the point of the equation is not to tell us the exact number of alien civilizations that are out there but to identify the things that need to be right in order for there to be life to communicate with.

So far, space has been strangely silent. This raises some obvious questions. If we attribute even mildly optimistic values to the factors in the equation, we should have heard something instead of mere static. This gives rise to the Fermi paradox: How should we understand the combination of the (supposedly) high probability of life and the total lack of evidence of alien life?[5] Among the proposed solutions are the following. We might well be alone. If the existence of life is a fluke, then there is no one to communicate with. Alternatively, it might be that there are intelligent civilizations out there but they are not interested in communicating with us, or their way of communicating is so alien or advanced that we do not recognize it. As Arthur C. Clarke has pointed out, the technological devices that we have now would have looked like magic to the people living a few hundred years ago. It might also be that advanced civilizations have reached singularity or a sublime state and they have lost interest in communicating with lower forms of life, just as we do not find it entertaining to talk to microbes. It is also possible that civilizations do

4. On the current state of the discussion, see Vakoch and Dowd, *Drake Equation*; Coyne, "Extraterrestrial Life"; and Catling, *Astrobiology*.
5. For the comprehensive list of proposed solutions, see Webb, *If the Universe is Teeming with Aliens*.

develop, but they tend to destroy themselves as soon as they reach the technological age. This seems to be the price of mutual cooperation enabled by language: we can effectively do things together, but we can also use the tools of technology to effectively hurt and ultimately destroy each other. A related issue is the Great Filter hypothesis. The evolution of intelligent species and cultures seems to go through stages where the chance of extinction is high. If the last filter of cosmic colonization is hard to pass through, then it is no wonder that we do not hear from anyone else: they are all dead.[6]

A Short History of Aliens

If we suppose that there have been civilizations that have passed through the last filter and have established their civilization somewhere in the galaxy, and we at some point receive good evidence that they are in fact there, what kind of theological relevance would this have? C. S. Lewis captured well the conflicting feelings that people have about the relevance of alien life for Christianity:

> If we discover other bodies, they must be habitable or uninhabitable: and the odd thing is that both these hypotheses are used as grounds for rejecting Christianity. If the Universe is teeming with life, this, we are told, reduces to absurdity the Christian claim—or what is thought to be the Christian claim—that man is unique, and the Christian doctrine that to this one planet God came down and was incarnate for us men and our salvation. If, on the other hand, the Earth is really unique, then that proves that life is only an accidental by-product in the universe, and so again disproves our religion. Really, we are hard to please.[7]

6. Nick Bostrom has suggested that it would be good news for the human race *not* to find signs of life outside Earth. This hope is based on the Great Filter theory, by which he refers to the event or events that end the history of a civilization. This filter can be either ahead of or behind us. If we find more than dead rocks from, say, Mars, this is evidence for two things. First of all, if life evolved twice in our solar system, it probably has evolved several times outside our solar system, meaning that lower forms of life are abundant in the cosmos. Second, the higher the remnants of life are on the filter scale, the more probable it becomes that the Great Filter is ahead of us and we are heading toward extinction. For the human race, it would be best to hope that we are the only game in town. Bostrom, "Where Are They?" There are many estimates than the human L (lifetime) factor might be only a couple of decades long. If human culture is even to a small extent representative of what cultures in general might be, this might help us understand why space is so silent. See, e.g., Zuckerman and Hart, *Extraterrestrials*, 163; Shklovskii and Sagan, *Intelligent Life*, 412.

7. Lewis, "Dogma and the Universe." This sentiment was seconded by Victor Stenger in his response to those who argue for theism using fine-tuning arguments: "They claim many parameters of Earth and the solar system are fine-tuned for life, failing to consider that with an estimated sextillion planets in the visible universe in habitable zone regions on their stars, and the countless number beyond our horizon where light has not yet had time to reach us, a planet

Lewis goes on to point out how in different times various contingent properties of the cosmos have been seen as the final nail in the coffin of a long-dead
God, while almost as often other properties have been seen as proofs of God's
existence. He advises his readers to be cautious when assessing these claims,
as our knowledge is, after all, quite limited.[8]

The Bible and the early church give us very scant resources for thinking about
life outside our own planet. On the one hand, the biblical view of the cosmos
entails in any case that we are not alone, since the cosmos is the dwelling place
of angelic beings and God. These are not, obviously, biological forms of life,
which is what we typically mean when we raise the question. The Bible does
have passages that take an openly ananthropocentric (non-human-centered)
stance. Consider, for example, the account of Leviathan in Job 41, where the
monster is portrayed as totally alien and even incomprehensible to humans,
or the extended monologue of God in Job 38:

> Where were you when I laid the earth's foundation?
> Tell me, if you understand.
> Who marked off its dimensions? Surely you know!
> Who stretched a measuring line across it?
> On what were its footings set,
> or who laid its cornerstone—
> while the morning stars sang together
> and all the angels shouted for joy? (vv. 4–7)

Nonetheless, some parts of Greek philosophy enabled speculation about
life like ours existing outside our immediate realm of being. Pythagoreans
pondered the possibility of life on the moon, and Epicurus wrote in his *Letter to Herodotus*, "There are infinite worlds both like and unlike this world
of ours," and "in all worlds there are living creatures and plants and other
things we see in this world."[9]

Lucretius's *Of the Nature of Things* is one of the best-known examples
in this genre.

> 'Tmust be confessed in other realms there are
> Still other worlds, still other breeds of men,
> And other generations of the wild.

with the properties needed for life is likely to occur many times. Nevertheless, the universe is
hardly life-friendly. If God wanted to fine-tune it for life, he could have made the universe a lot
friendlier." Stenger, "Fine-Tuning," 41.

8. For good, brief overviews on the subject, see McMullin, "Life and Intelligence"; O'Meara,
"Christian Theology"; and Losch and Krebs, "Extraterrestrial Life."

9. Epicurus, *Letter to Herodotus*, 5, 12, quoted in Crowe, *Extraterrestrial Life Debate*, 3–5.

Hence too it happens in the sum there is
No one thing single of its kind in birth,
And single and sole in growth, but rather it is
One member of some generated race,
Among full many others of like kind.
First, cast thy mind abroad upon the living:
Thou'lt find the race of mountain-ranging wild
Even thus to be, and thus the scions of men
To be begot, and lastly the mute flocks
Of scaled fish, and winged frames of birds.
Wherefore confess we must on grounds the same
That earth, sun, moon, and ocean, and all else,
Exist not sole and single—rather in number
Exceeding number. Since that deeply set
Old boundary stone of life remains for them
No less, and theirs a body of mortal birth
No less, than every kind which here on earth
Is so abundant in its members found.[10]

As noted above in relation to multiple worlds, the influence of Plato and Aristotle on early Christian philosophy conjoined with the silence of biblical texts on the topic made speculations such as that of Lucretius obsolete for centuries to come. Some lament this turn, but I am afraid that it might be unwarranted nostalgia. The scientific sensibilities of Lucretius and Aristotle were markedly different. Even if many of Aristotle's theories about physics and the nature of the world turned out to be wrong, his thinking enabled the progress of science and philosophy based on evidence and observation. Lucretius's vision is fascinating, but at that time it was beyond verification. It made for great poetry and interesting philosophy, but unconvincing physics.

The primary context in which the early church discussed the possibility of alien life was the question of whether there are other sentient beings living in *this* world. Perhaps the most well-known treatment is found in Augustine's *City of God*, where he offers an account of marvelous beings that is worth quoting at length:

For it is reported that some have one eye in the middle of the forehead; some, feet turned backwards from the heel; some, a double sex, the right breast like a man, the left like a woman, and that they alternately beget and bring forth: others are said to have no mouth, and to breathe only through the nostrils;

10. Lucretius, *Of the Nature of Things*, book 2, Infinite Worlds.

others are but a cubit high, and are therefore called by the Greeks "Pigmies": they say that in some places the women conceive in their fifth year, and do not live beyond their eighth. So, too, they tell of a race who have two feet but only one leg, and are of marvellous swiftness, though they do not bend the knee: they are called Skiopodes, because in the hot weather they lie down on their backs and shade themselves with their feet. Others are said to have no head, and their eyes in their shoulders; and other human or quasi-human races are depicted in mosaic in the harbor esplanade of Carthage, on the faith of histories of rarities. What shall I say of the Cynocephali, whose dog-like head and barking proclaim them beasts rather than men?[11]

Augustine's reaction to these accounts reveals a mixture of incredulity and common sense. On the one hand, he reminds his readers that they should not believe these stories uncritically. Regarding the existence of antipodes ("men who walk with their feet opposite ours") and who live on the other side of Earth, he thinks that we have no credible historical or scientific evidence of their existence. On the other hand, he highlights the theological relevance of these accounts of "monsters" (*monstrosa humanum genera*). First of all, he insists that "whoever is anywhere born a man, that is, a rational, mortal animal, no matter what unusual appearance he presents in color, movement, sound, nor how peculiar he is in some power, part, or quality of his nature, no Christian can doubt that he springs from that one protoplast. We can distinguish the common human nature from that which is peculiar, and therefore wonderful." Second, if these beings actually existed, it is possible that they would not be human, and consequently not affected by original sin and in need of redemption, or that they would be descendants of Adam and therefore part of the divine economy.

After Augustine, it was Nicholas Cusanus and Giordano Bruno who returned to this subject.[12] Cusanus, for example, deliberates about the properties of beings living in the other worlds as follows: "Of the inhabitants then of worlds other than our own we can know still less having no standards by which to appraise them. It may be conjectured that in the area of the sun there exist

11. Augustine, *City of God* 16.9 (*NPNF*[1] 2:314–15).
12. In the medieval literature, the possibility of a third (in addition to angels and humans) form of life was acknowledged. It is perhaps not possible to say with a high degree of certitude how common this belief was, but it was still such that there was a need to address it. C. S. Lewis calls this third form *longaevi*, the longlivers. Lewis prefers it as a common term instead of "fairies" because the popular image of fairies, in Lewis's time, would have misled his readers. The old English word *faerie* referred in medieval times to strange beings, or spirits, who inhabited a kind of interim state between earth and heaven, but the actual class of *longaevi* included other beings in addition, such as fauns. The *longaevi* were quite often morally ambiguous, not purely evil but not absolutely good either. Lewis, *Discarded Image*, 122–38.

solar beings, bright and enlightened denizens, and by nature more spiritual than such as may inhabit the moon—who are possibly lunatics—whilst those on earth are more gross and material."[13]

Lucretius's *Of the Nature of Things* was republished in 1497. This created the philosophical background (with the possibilities of modal thinking in Scholasticism) for the new astronomical theories that were just around the corner. Slowly, this distant possibility started to look like a more plausible one, even while none of the great astronomers—such as Copernicus, Kepler, Brahe, or Galileo—went so far as Cusanus and Bruno with their speculations on multiple worlds and their inhabitants.[14] Perhaps here again we see the difference between philosophers and scientists: while the former are free to let their imaginations wander, the latter need empirical evidence to substantiate their claims. However, it would be a mistake to set imagination and reason against each other. They are different capacities with different gifts, and their proper appreciation is not always easy.

From the early eighteenth century onward, it became widely accepted that life on other planets was at least possible. Popular books, of which two are especially worthy of mention, speculated on the nature of other races living on other planets. Christiaan Huygens, who discovered the rings of Saturn, wrote the widely read treatise *Cosmotheoros* (1698, published in English as *The Celestial Worlds Discovered*). Huygens argues that other planets have plants, animals, and other inhabitants, "not men perhaps like ours, but some creatures or other endued with reason. For all this furniture and beauty the planets are stocked with seem to have been made in vain, without design or end, unless there were some in them that might at the same time enjoy the fruits and adore the wise Creator of them."[15] A bit earlier, in 1686, Bernard le Bovier de Fontenelle had written in *Entretiens sur la pluralité des mondes* (*Conversations on the Plurality of Worlds*) that there are beings living on other planets, but they are not human and not descendants of Adam, thereby opening a way to deal with these questions so that obvious theological problems were avoided. Aliens were not part of the same economy of salvation as humans. Nevertheless, the existence of other worlds and beings demonstrated ever-greater glory of God through the diversity and plenitude of created beings.[16] These two books established the genre of speculation about other worlds, and they had tremendous public influence. According to the

13. Cusanus, *Of Learned Ignorance* 2.12 (trans. Heron, 115–16); Crowe, *Extraterrestrial Life Debate*, 6–9.

14. Crowe, *Extraterrestrial Life Debate*, 10–13.

15. Quoted in Danielson, *Book of Cosmos*, 236.

16. Dick, *Plurality of Worlds*, 124.

NASA historian Steven J. Dick, by the mid-eighteenth century the possibility of other worlds with intelligent inhabitants was more or less universally accepted in the West.[17] By the beginning of World War I, over 140 books and thousands of articles had been published on the topic, and after that would come countless more.[18]

Two Possible Worlds

But let us assess the merits and demerits of two cases from a theological perspective. Imagine two worlds with different properties:

World A: Humans are the only species in the cosmos.
World B: Humans are just one of many intelligent life-forms in the cosmos.

Which one of these worlds do we currently inhabit? We do not really know. For the time being, we can believe in either of them without obviously breaking any epistemic obligations. But do we have a prima facie theological reason to favor one of them? In other words, which world is more compatible with the following claim?

G: A theistic God exists.

The history of the Christian tradition offers elements for arguments for both views. Depending on which world we live in, different problems will emerge. In the following, I try to assess the merits of the arguments for each of these views.

World A: We Are Alone

Among others, Brian Hebblethwaite claims that $Pr(G|A)$ (probability of world A given that a theistic God exists) has a higher probability than $Pr(G|B)$ (probability of world B given that a theistic God exists). He argues, "I am inclined to think that belief in extraterrestrial intelligent life reflects secular prejudice."[19]

17. Dick, "Cosmotheology," 196. Of the great Enlightenment philosophers, Immanuel Kant proposed the existence of worlds "without number and end" in his *Universal Natural History and Theory of the Heavens* (1755). On Kant's cosmology, see Dick, *Plurality of Worlds*, 171; Rubenstein, *Worlds without End*, 127–41.
18. On the more recent discussion, see Dick, *Life on Other Worlds*; and Dick, *Biological Universe*.
19. Hebblethwaite, *In Defence of Christianity*, 11–12. He does give a short account for why he thinks this: "The arguments in its favour are purely statistical, whereas the empirical evidence

Moreover, he thinks that the rarity of the sphere of human thought gives a great value and significance to it. So, in this system or ours, there is something good about cosmic solitude.

Against this view, one could claim that cosmic solitude creates problems for the doctrine of God. We can single out three problems: waste, time, and evil. If God intended to create humans, doing it through actualizing World A seems like a great waste of material and time. In addition, millions of years of suffering seem gratuitous if the purpose of the universe was just to bring humans into existence.

Waste and time problems are, however, easy to answer in World A. Questions of efficiency are relevant only for those beings who possess limited resources. But if God exists, God has unlimited resources and there is no need to think about how long things last or how much energy and material are needed. Moreover, if God did intend to create a physical universe like ours, a universe as big and old as this one would be needed for carbon and oxygen to be synthesized.[20] If we lived in a small universe that consisted only of our solar system, its physical laws and constants would have to be very different for any life to emerge.

In addition, if one considers the Judeo-Christian God, the way that Yahweh works in history is not exactly an example of efficiency, at least from a human point of view. In fact, Yahweh appears as highly selective and fond of particular choices.[21] Instead of offering revelation to all people in ways that are beyond any reasonable doubt, Yahweh elects one apparently random patriarch (Abraham), one nation (Israel), and one Palestinian man (Jesus). Contrary to our intuition, this might after all be the best possible way of establishing human-divine relations, but I shall not exercise these speculations here.[22] Suffice it to say that there is nothing in the concept of God that would

---

points to uniqueness. Not only is there no evidence for extraterrestrial intelligent life, purely statistical probabilities are outweighed by the extraordinary number of improbable coincidences that have to obtain before the thresholds in question can be crossed. One cannot argue simply from the evident capacity of the world stuff to evolve minds that it must have done so in many places and at many times." Some creationists also share this view. For example, Ken Ham writes, "The Bible, in sharp contrast to the secular worldview, teaches that earth was specially created, that it is unique and the focus of God's attention (Isa. 66:1 and Ps. 115:16). Life did not evolve but was specially created by God, as Genesis clearly teaches. Christians certainly shouldn't expect alien life to be cropping up across the universe." Ham, "'We'll Find a New Earth within 20 Years,'" *Answers in Genesis*, July 20, 2014, https://answersingenesis.org/blogs/ken-ham/2014/07/20/well-find-a-new-earth-within-20-years.

20. Alexander, *Language of Genetics*, 267.

21. McMullin, "Life and Intelligence," 160–62. On how even the concept of Yahweh has been incrementally revealed in the Old Testament, see P. Miller, *Religion of Ancient Israel*, 1–43.

22. For an extended argument along these lines, see Evans, *Natural Signs*.

make it obviously counterintuitive to use so much time and energy to create a solitary human race.

The problem of evil is a bit harder. The standard discussion on the problem of evil has typically looked at our current experiences, and taking the evolutionary perspective seems to make the problem even more difficult, which is something that Darwin himself already noticed.[23] Trent Dougherty summarizes the problem thus: "Since near the beginning of sentient life on Earth, there has been a profusion of intense animal suffering. That is, almost everywhere there has been sentient life very significant levels of suffering have been quite common (and there has been a lot of sentient life)."[24]

It is not possible here to discuss all the details of the problem of evil. A significant amount of available literature engages with this question at length.[25] Here I hope only to summarize a few points. In relation to waste and time, bringing about a physical universe requires a certain kind of framework for life to emerge and flourish. Denis Alexander points out how "biology is a package deal." For things to survive, they need the ability to feel pain. Genetic mutations are essential for our existence and the diversity of life, but they also enable cancer and other diseases. We need bacteria to stay healthy, but bacteria can also kill us. Eating good food is one of the greatest joys in life, but it increases free oxygen radicals in our cells, which causes DNA damage and aging.[26]

Although it seems that things like death and pain are necessary for physical life to exist, the amount of painful existence can seem excessive. This is the crucial point in the debates surrounding the problem of evil: even if it is justified to think that some evils are compatible with God's goodness, if there are some gratuitous evils that seem not to serve any reasonable purpose, that would count as evidence against the existence of God. The countless generations of suffering and dying animals before the rise of humans could also count as this kind of evidence. Yet it must be borne in mind that the problem of evolutionary evil is here set in the context of World A. The problems can be expressed in the form of the following inference:

23. Darwin wrote in his letter to Hooker (July 13, 1856), "'The sufferings of millions of lower animals throughout almost endless time' are apparently irreconcilable with the existence of a creator of 'unbounded' goodness." Quoted in Murray, *Nature*, 2.
24. Dougherty, *Problem of Animal Pain*, 31.
25. Of course, these theodicies will never fully answer our question about suffering. The power of evil is often so strong that no rational argument seems sufficient to warrant it. As I write these words, the newscast is telling stories from Aleppo where civilians are being executed en masse. Theoretical theodicies are not meant to be pastoral tools, but this does not make them useless. Some theodicies address our reason, some our imagination. For an account that takes both aspects seriously, see, e.g., Stump, *Wandering in Darkness*.
26. Alexander, *Language of Genetics*, 271–72; Alexander, *Creation or Evolution*, 279.

1. The main reason for God to create the universe is to enable human life.
2. Human life requires millions of years of evolution.
3. The pain that lower creatures suffer during this process is gratuitous.
4. A good God would not allow gratuitous evil to exist.
5. Therefore, the suffering of animals creates a disproof for belief in the existence of a good God.

The inference can be refuted in several ways. It is possible to argue that Christians are not necessarily committed to (1). It is possible that God had some other reasons to create the universe, and the universe does not exist solely to bring about humans. Consequently, God would intend the existence of every creature as an end in itself, not just as an instrument to bring us onto the stage. Presumably, that would also change how the existence of lower beings should be valued, although it is hard to say anything about this that is not wildly speculative.

If for the sake of argument we hold on to the assumption that our world is World A, the real problem is (3). Looking at the tree of life, we see that several branches have died. The history of the earth has witnessed several mass extinctions. For example, the Permian-Triassic mass extinction exterminated about 90 percent of the species on Earth, and this was millions of years before the dinosaurs.[27] Because those extinct races do not seem to have had any purpose for our existence, their sufferings seem gratuitous.

There are several ways to confront the apparent meaninglessness of this situation. One way is to argue that animals do not feel pain in the same sense as humans. This view is held by Neo-Cartesians, who think that animals' experience of pain is very different from that of humans because they lack phenomenal consciousness. In effect, one could claim that animals can feel pain-like sensations, but they do not suffer.[28] By this Neo-Cartesians mean the ability to see oneself as the subject of an experience; therefore, animal pain does not have moral value. This sounds odd for anyone who has lived with animals, but an analogy might help in understanding the claim. Some patients with brain damage, or those who have gone through a lobotomy or less severe anesthesia, report that they feel pain but do not care about it. If to experience humanlike pain one needs to have a developed prefrontal cortex, which enables a higher sense of self, then it might seem possible to argue that animal sensations are at least to some extent different.

27. Benton, *When Life Nearly Died.*
28. For discussion, see Dougherty, *Problem of Animal Pain,* 77–95; and Murray, *Nature,* 41–72.

There are good arguments against the Neo-Cartesians. Even if pain sensations would be qualitatively different (which we do not know), it seems obvious that animals can have sensations of fear, anxiety, and stress that are not physical pains but look like morally relevant suffering. It is not clear why animals would need phenomenal consciousness to feel pain that is morally significant. However, even if the Neo-Cartesian view cannot explain away every possible gratuitous suffering, it gives us a reason to think that suffering in any morally relevant sense is possible only for higher species. But this still leaves us with a high number and a long time (approximately 180 million years) of animal suffering, including our human ancestors.

A more demanding view is to argue that for a theodicy to be effective, it needs to give reasons for thinking that the sufferings that a being goes through will somehow benefit that same being. Thus, no evil would be gratuitous but rather somehow conducive to the future flourishing of the being. This is known as the "soul-making theodicy," which is historically attributed to Irenaeus; its recent proponents include John Hick and Richard Swinburne, among others. But how would this work with animals? Dougherty argues that in fact animals will be able to enjoy the blessed state, as humans do. This is supported by God's goodness and care for creation. Although this view is not perhaps the most central Christian belief, it has some support in the history of the church.[29] Nonetheless, this leads to some pretty extraordinary views. For example, there could very well be dinosaurs in heaven. The *T. rex* will lie down with the lamb.

Here the blessed state that animals share is not a simplistic compensation or balancing of the scales after something horrible has happened. That would be analogous to a situation where I torture you and then throw a significant sum of money in your lap. Perhaps you might like the outcome, but it still makes me look bad. Instead of compensation, a more substantial moral response would be the defeat of evil. In that scenario, evil is integrated into something that is a greater good. Evil does not cease to be evil, but it is now seen, even if genuinely evil, as something that is conducive to the flourishing of that same being. This soul-making is possible for humans in this life, but animals lack the cognitive capacities that would enable them to fully grasp their role in this cosmic drama.

29. To quote some examples, in an Armenian liturgy it is stated, "Every creature which was created by you will be renewed at resurrection, that day which is the last day of earthly existence and the beginning of our heavenly life." In his Sermon 60, John Wesley claims, "The whole brute creation will then, undoubtedly, be restored, not only to the vigour, strength, and swiftness which they had at their creation, but to a far higher degree of each than they ever enjoyed. They will be restored, not only to that measure of understanding which they had in paradise, but to a degree of it as much higher than that, as the understanding of an elephant is beyond that of a worm." Both are quoted in Dougherty, *Problem of Animal Pain*, 159–61.

Dougherty argues that answering this problem requires a transcendental argument for animal deification. If an all-good God exists, that God will include all sentient beings in the act of drawing everything into the divine communion.[30] In a similar vein, Christopher Southgate points out that in the biblical narrative, creation is "good" (Gen. 1) on the one hand but "groaning" (Rom. 8:22) on the other. This tension will always remain mysterious to us, but approaching the question from a theological point of view may enable us to live through the sufferings. In creating the world, a good God comes to share in its fate, so that he is present in every instant of pain and suffering in order to redeem it.[31]

Summing up the discussion, the main theological reason to support World A seems to be a particular interpretation of our cosmic significance. Our being alone in the universe means that we are the only game in town and therefore valuable. Even if this is one possible way of thinking about our value and significance, it creates challenges for our understanding of the nature of God's goodness.

Tim Mulgan presents an interesting theological argument against World A.[32] World A contains lots of space but very few creatures. How could that be a good thing? Mulgan notes that it would require an argument for why a limited number of good beings is the best. This view, known as "average utilitarianism," does not enjoy significant support among contemporary theorists, and it is easy to see why. God with his infinite resources could create a (virtually) infinite number of species. To say that this would not be a worthy thing to do, we would have to argue that increasing the number of intelligent species does not add any value to our cosmos, which is a tall order.

World B: We Are Not Alone

Let us then consider the second option, World B. Evidence of extraterrestrials (ETs) would constitute a clear victory for the claim that we live in World B. Consequently, beliefs that were once open would not be so anymore, leading to new types of challenges and some new benefits. I will address some general theological issues.[33] The first one concerns the initial plausibility of ETs given G (a theistic God exists), and the second is about theism and naturalism as

---

30. Dougherty, *Problem of Animal Pain*, 128, 145–46.
31. Southgate, *Groaning of Creation*, 16. See also Hoggard Creegan, *Animal Suffering*; Osborn, *Death before the Fall*, 157–65.
32. Mulgan, *Purpose in the Universe*, 211.
33. For various factors that are relevant to the social implications of alien life, see Vidal, "Multidimensional Impact Model."

hypotheses in relation to ETs. What kind of a priori theological reasons might we have for World B? It seems plausible that the existence of ETs is harmonious with the Theistic Principle of Plenitude:

> *Theistic Principle of Plenitude (TPP)*: As the greatest conceivable being, who is good and loves things that are good, God is more likely than not to create good things in abundance.

Even if TPP is not part of canonical creeds, it expresses the widely approved intuition of many theists. Therefore, I think that there are no a priori reasons to believe that ETs and Christian theism would be in conflict.

Which worldview gives us a higher initial probability for ETs, naturalism or theism? For example, William Lane Craig has made the following claim: "The probabilities on naturalism that there is extraterrestrial intelligent life is virtually nil. So actually being a theist would be the best grounds for thinking that it could be possible because as a theist you think God created life here on this planet, so then you could say, well, maybe God created life as well on some other planet somewhere in the universe. It is really the theist who is, I think, a lot more open to the possibility of extraterrestrial life than the nontheist."[34] Craig presupposes the standard version of the fine-tuning argument: the conjunction of theism, the improbability of life in the universe, and our existence is more probable than the conjunction of naturalism, the improbability of life in the universe, and our existence. He then goes on to claim that a theist has more reasons to believe that ETs exist than a naturalist. But why exactly?

I am dubious about Craig's supposition. He supports his claim that ETs are more probable on theism by pointing out that, given that God exists and given that he has created life here on Earth, it is not completely improbable that he would create life elsewhere in the universe. So, in other words, Craig is saying that the probability that

(1) Pr(life exists elsewhere in the universe | theism AND life exists here on earth)

is not too low. This seems reasonable on the basis of what has been said above. He may be right to say that (because of assumptions about the general improbability of a life-permitting universe, given naturalism) life is improbable

---

34. William Lane Craig, "UFO's," *Reasonable Faith* [podcast], August 17, 2008, http://www.reasonablefaith.org/ufos.

everywhere in the universe (including on Earth) given naturalism, but at this moment we have no way to test this hypothesis. However, Craig should be comparing the above probability to the probability of ETs given naturalism *and* given that life exists here on Earth. In other words, Craig should not be comparing (1) to

(2) Pr(life exists elsewhere in the universe | naturalism),

which is plausibly very low. Instead, he should be comparing (1) to

(2) Pr(life exists elsewhere in the universe | naturalism AND life exists here on earth),

which is plausibly not too low, because even if it was improbable on naturalism that life would evolve *at all*, given that it has evolved here, maybe it is not improbable that it has evolved elsewhere. Therefore, it is not obvious whether theism has a major advantage over naturalism regarding this particular question.[35]

A related issue is the effect of ETs on the fine-tuning argument. The explanandum of the standard version of the fine-tuning argument is the existence of a life-friendly universe, not the existence of intelligent life on our planet in particular. Consequently, the discovery of life elsewhere in the universe does not affect the fine-tuning argument as such. Having said that, the discovery that there is life elsewhere would be good evidence that our universe is life-friendly to an even greater degree than we previously thought, but that would leave the basic fine-tuning argument (which holds that a life-friendly universe is much more probable on theism than on naturalism) unaffected. ETs would thus be additional evidence for the claim that our cosmos is life-enabling, and that life is not merely a fluke but something that is built into the fabric of the cosmos. ETs would also be evidence against the problems of waste and time. Depending on the moral alignment of alien life, that could also be evidence against the problem of evil and perhaps even support the moral argument.

Yet even if at the general level there seems to be no obvious problem, we need to look deeper. Among others, Paul Davies thinks that World B would cause serious problems for Christianity. These problems are related to four distinct issues:[36]

---

35. I thank Max Baker-Hytch for discussion concerning this topic.
36. These concerns are summarized in Wilkinson, *Alone in the Universe?*, 117. See also Davies, *Are We Alone?* For similar concerns in a more refined form, see Tarter, "SETI."

1. Humanity's special relationship with God
2. The origin of life
3. Super-advanced alien religions
4. The significance of the life and death of Jesus

In my view, the first two problems are not genuine but result from a limited grasp of what the doctrine of creation means. These have already been dealt with in previous chapters, but I would just note that having a special relationship does not entail that this relationship needs to be exclusive. That humans are said to bear the image of God does not entail that nothing else bears this image. Moreover, the evolutionary account of the human race and possible other races does not contradict the core tenets of the doctrine of creation.

An interesting but rather speculative challenge is the question about the level of religiosity of other life-forms. Davies offers us two choices: either the aliens have abandoned religion or their religion is vastly more advanced than our religions. In both cases, we would be persuaded to follow them.[37] The history of human culture is only a few thousand years old, which is nothing from a cosmic perspective. If there were another planet with an alien culture that had been born even a cosmic second sooner than we entered the scene, their civilization would be thousands of years more advanced than ours. It is hard to even imagine what that culture would look like: perhaps it would be comparable to how a member of *Homo ergaster* would be astounded by the sights of our modern world. Given the exponential development of technology (today a single smartphone has more computing power than the first moon module), it would be hard to envision how the world will look in two hundred years. What kind of relevance do these facts have for religion or philosophy? Davies seems to think that technological advancement correlates with spiritual maturity.[38] I do not think this conclusion is warranted. To be sure, human religions have evolved during the early history of our culture, but there has not been significant evolution since the Axial Age.[39] Even when we observe the recent changes in Christian religion, these can be seen as a movement within the boundaries of this particular religion, or as movement toward (or as adaptations of) some other, already existing religious position.[40]

37. Davies, *Are We Alone?*, 54.
38. This idea is often repeated in classic science fiction. For example, in *The Day When the Earth Stood Still* (in both the original and the remake) the premise is that the aliens are morally superior to humans.
39. Bellah, *Religion in Human Evolution*.
40. On the idea of development in Christian doctrine, see, e.g., Newman, *Development of Christian Doctrine*. An example of movement away from Christian particularism toward pantheism is found in Rubenstein, *Worlds without End*.

When observing human behavior, abandoning religion does not mean that people stop having beliefs about the supernatural and that they all embrace some kind of unified worldview. Many of those who "abandon religion" still cherish quasi-religious convictions, and there seems to be no single worldview toward which atheists gravitate. Effectively, abandoning religion means just adopting another axiomatic belief system.[41]

The second option—that is, an alien religion—is more likely. If evolutionary convergence holds also in other parts of our cosmos, it is probable that aliens will have their own Platos and Aristotles presenting the same ways of interpreting the world. But how different could their religion be? Clearly this is pure speculation, but given both evolutionary convergence and the relative stability of basic religio-philosophical interpretations of the cosmos, we would likely recognize much in common with the supposed alien religion.[42]

The existence of an alien religion would have an effect on the argument from religious diversity. The standard version of the argument goes like this:

1. There are many mutually exclusive views about ultimate reality.
2. All these have good arguments to support them.
3. We have no obvious and rational ways to pick one of these views instead of another.
4. Therefore, we should remain agnostic about which view of ultimate reality is true.

The problem arises from a conjunction of two presuppositions. First, there is an actual conflict in the substance of the claims, which cannot be explained away by saying that the conflict is only superficial or that the views do not have truth value in the first place (that is, religious claims are more about aesthetic preference than factual truth [from 1]). Second, we must suppose that there is epistemic parity among the views so that the believers share equal epistemic status as knowledge seekers (from 2 and 3). Understanding these requirements helps us to see how all apparent cases of diversity need not necessarily threaten our beliefs. Often it is the case that disagreement is not substantive, and sometimes there is no epistemic peerage. Nevertheless, this does not remove all problematic cases since there are mutually conflicting and exclusive views about ultimate reality that are held by epistemic peers.

41. Vainio and Visala, "Varieties of Unbelief."
42. Conway Morris, *Life's Solution*, 313. See also Consolmagno, "Baptize an Extraterrestrial?," 242.

Religious diversity is a problem for anyone who has some beliefs about ultimate reality, which includes virtually all people.

What the cosmic perspective does to the argument is to increase the scale. Instead of approximately 4,200 religions on this planet, we could have millions of religions throughout the cosmos. But how exactly does this change the force of the argument? Imagine two worlds:

Philosophically scarce world (PSW): There are only two views about ultimate reality.

Philosophically abundant world (PAW): There is a very high number of views about ultimate reality.

It seems that we would be epistemically more likely to get it right in PSW than in PAW, and we quite clearly live in PAW. However, this is so only if we suppose that there is only one correct answer and the answer is within our reach: in PSW our chances would be 50/50, while in PAW our chances would be 1/4,200. With alien religions, we could find ourselves in a 1/100,000,000 scenario. But this is not how we make choices in real life. When casting a vote, we do not think that we must refrain from voting because there are so many people running for office and they all have different policies. The mere existence of options does not demote the epistemic status of one's beliefs. I think approaching the question from the point of view of "look at all these options" is a wrong one. We cannot step outside the cosmos so that we have no beliefs at all. Once we are thrown into the world, we cannot help but have some beliefs about it.

If I have good reasons to believe that A is true and {B, C, D . . . K} are false, I have no reason to adjust my beliefs just because there might be a set of beliefs {L, M, N . . . T}. The cosmic diversity scenario changes the situation by adding many potential contenders that we have no way of accessing and assessing right now. Epistemically, it is similar to our having justified beliefs about how to interpret quantum mechanics while believing that there is a being who knows which interpretation is objectively the correct one. Does this make a belief—say, that the Copenhagen interpretation is true—a wrong one? I don't think so. My belief might be wrong, but the mere possible existence of something that I don't know does not as such change the epistemic status of my beliefs. The situation is not like the following scenario: I play a lottery where I need to guess one number right out of 1,000,000, but my guess can only be between the numbers 1–10. Despite the possible difference in scale, the situation with alien religions is no different from the current problem of religious diversity. We need to assess those religions as they become known to us.

The last concern in Davies's list is the place of Jesus Christ in the grand scheme of things. What kind of place should the incarnation of God in Christ have in light of the current cosmology? This question requires more detailed discussion, and I will return to it in chapter 9.

The history of the Christian church does not offer one canonical answer to the question of how many intelligent biological species there are in the cosmos. The arguments that favor the option that we are alone are based on the notion that we have a more central place in creation. As such, this is not a very convincing theological argument.

On the other hand, what we know about creation suggests that God might very well create diverse things in abundance. I believe that we have stronger theological reasons to argue for the existence of multiple intelligent species than the existence of just one. The problems that are created by this possibility are not any more difficult than the problems created by the scenario in which we are the only species.

6

Infinite Space, Infinite Terror

Our Cosmic (In)Significance

The universe is staggeringly huge, and we are very small compared to its enormity. This is not necessarily something that we constantly think about, but if we give this serious thought, it can cause discomfort and anxiety. The scale of the cosmos overwhelms both our reason and emotions, but does the scale as such have religious significance? Many have made this claim, but from a theological point of view it seems unwarranted.

In this chapter, I discuss what we mean when we speak about human value and significance. For Christians, the value of beings has never been solely determined by their size, location, or mere instrumental value. Moreover, for nontheists it is hard to come up with an account that can secure the objectivity of moral value. In a naturalistic universe, there are only conventions, not absolute obligations. To be sure, things can be valued, but their value is always open to negotiation.

Touching the Void

Several philosophers and scientists have claimed that modern cosmology forces us to think that humans are insignificant from a cosmic point of view.[1] For example, Carl Sagan states, "As long as there have been humans, we have

1. Kahane, "Our Cosmic Insignificance."

searched for our place in the Cosmos. . . . Where are we? Who are we? We find that we live on an insignificant planet of a humdrum star lost between two spiral arms in the outskirts of a galaxy . . . tucked away in some forgotten corner of a universe in which there are far more galaxies than people."[2] Richard Dawkins claims, "The universe we observe had precisely the properties we should expect if there is, at bottom, no design, no purpose, no evil and no good, nothing but blind pitiless indifference."[3] Peter Atkins agrees with his Oxonian colleague: "I've always thought that I was insignificant. Getting to know the size of the Universe, I see just how insignificant I really am! And I think the rest of the human race ought to realize just how insignificant it is. I mean, we're just a bit of slime on a planet belonging to one sun."[4] Stephen Weinberg notes, "It is very hard to realize that this all is just a tiny part of an overwhelmingly hostile universe. It is even harder to realize that this present universe has evolved from an unspeakably unfamiliar early condition, and faces a future extinction of endless cold or intolerable heat. The more the universe seems comprehensible, the more it also seems pointless."[5] And Simon Blackburn states:

> The cosmos is some fifteen billion years old, almost unimaginably huge, and governed by natural laws that will compel its extinction in some billions more years, although long before that the Earth and the solar system will have been destroyed by the heat death of the Sun. Human beings occupy an infinitesimally small fraction of space and time, on the edge of one galaxy among a hundred thousand million or so galaxies. We evolved only because of a number of cosmic accidents. . . . Nature shows us no particular favours: we get parasites and diseases and we die, and we are not all that nice to each other. True, we are moderately clever, but our efforts to use our intelligence . . . quite often backfire. . . . That, more or less, is the scientific picture of the world.[6]

2. Sagan, *Cosmos*, 193.
3. Dawkins, *River Out of Eden*, 132.
4. Stannard, *Science and Wonders*, 7.
5. Weinberg, *First Three Minutes*, 154–55.
6. Blackburn, "Unbeautiful Mind," 29. See also B. Russell, "Free Man's Worship," 56:
That man is the product of causes which had no prevision of the end they were achieving; that his origin, his growth, his hopes and fears, his loves and his beliefs, are but the outcome of accidental collocations of atoms; that no fire, no heroism, no intensity of thought and feeling, can preserve an individual life beyond the grave; that all the labours of the ages, all the devotion, all the inspiration, all the noonday brightness of human genius, are destined to extinction in the vast death of the solar system, and that the whole temple of Man's achievement must inevitably be buried beneath the debris of a universe in ruins—all these things, if not quite beyond dispute, are yet so nearly certain, that no philosophy which rejects them can hope to stand. Only within the scaffolding of these truths, only on the firm foundation of unyielding despair, can the soul's habitation henceforth be safely built.

Often the lack of human significance in an immense cosmos is connected with the idea that things were different when people lived in the Ptolemaic cosmos. According to Gregory Stock, "The special significance of humanity seemed clear to Western thinkers in the Middle Ages: Earth was the center of the universe. . . . The Copernican revolution shattered that notion, wrenching humanity from its exalted station and leaving it stranded on a peripheral planet circling one of many stars."[7] Dawkins shares this sentiment: "We should not think there's anything special about us. We used to think we were the centre of the Universe and now we know we're not."[8] The feeling of insignificance is not restricted to atheists alone; devout Christians can also be overwhelmed by the sheer immensity of the universe. For example, Blaise Pascal writes in his *Pensées*:

> Let man contemplate Nature entire in her full and lofty majesty; let him put far from his sight the lowly objects that surround him; let him regard that blazing light, placed like an eternal lamp to illuminate the world; let the earth appear to him but a point within the vast circuit which that star describes; and let him marvel that this immense circumference is itself but a speck from the viewpoint of the stars that move in the firmament. And if our vision is stopped there, let imagination pass beyond. . . . All this visible world is but an imperceptible element in the great bosom of nature. No thought can go so far. . . . It is an infinite sphere whose center is everywhere, and whose circumference is nowhere.

Then follows the legendary line: "The eternal silence of these infinite spaces frightens me."[9] Understanding the point of Pascal and others does not require great intelligence or habituation in scientific forms of thinking. When my son was five, he intuitively was so impressed by the immensity of the universe that he did not want to visit museums where space rockets were on display because they reminded him about "the infinite."[10]

C. S. Lewis pointed out that the force behind this feeling of insignificance is something that touches not just our reason but also our imagination. When something grows in scope beyond our comprehension, at some point it assumes the quality of the sublime. We are the ones who accord space the power to terrify us. "But if ever the vastness of matter threatens to overcross our spirits, one must remember that it is matter spiritualized which does so. To puny man, the great nebula in Andromeda owes in a sense its greatness," Lewis states.[11]

7. Stock, *Redesigning Humans*, 174–75.
8. Dawkins, quoted in Stannard, *Science and Wonders*, 72.
9. Pascal, *Pensées*, Fragment 187.
10. Now that he is older, he loves these museums, so he got over it.
11. Lewis, "Dogma and the Universe," 121.

Figure 6.1. Gas and dust cloud in the Eagle Nebula known as the "Pillars of Creation."

Obviously, the power of imagination is great in existential matters, but we should still ask if there is a rational argument that supports these bleak conclusions. Given that these sentiments are so widespread, it is surprising that very few philosophers have turned them into a well-formulated argument.[12] To grasp the meaning of this argument from scale, according to which some

12. See Everitt, *Non-Existence of God*, 213–25; Mulgan, *Purpose in the Universe*, 193–219. Interestingly, the argument from scale is given treatment already by Maimonides (*Guide for the Perplexed* 3.14) and Cusanus. Cusanus's (*Of Learned Ignorance* 2.12) relativistic cosmology is supposed to show how "from size, therefore, no proof can be alleged of its baseness." Since God is everywhere and the final source of value, while all created beings have a relative existence, things like size and location do not matter. However, he acknowledges that there are higher and more valuable beings in the cosmos, but that is because they are holier than humans. See also Chesterton, *Orthodoxy*, chap. 4.

features of our cosmos are in tension with the idea of a benevolent creator, we need to understand how the notion of value is used in the discussion. It seems that in the popular discussion, and in academic debates, to some extent at least the problem is the exact meaning of value and significance. If we think about things that can be intrinsically valuable, the following can be mentioned:[13]

relative size

relative location

abilities/properties

goodness and beauty

perseverance and longevity

abundance/scarcity/particularity

kinship and affectional relationality

understanding

human flourishing

To briefly comment on this list, we value things that have right proportions; they can be either very big or very small, or they may appear to us to be exactly right. We have intuitions about the relation between location and value, so that those beings that are in the center are more valuable than those on the periphery. However, being in the center is not always a good thing (for example, when you are in court, charged with a crime). Sometimes not being in the center can also be a source of value, such as in paintings whose composition follows the Fibonacci sequence.

We tend to value things more when they have certain properties—and living things more when they have certain cognitive abilities. Computers are more valuable than pocket calculators, and dolphins are more valuable than mice. If a thing is very old, we attribute a high value to it, especially if it has endured through difficult conditions, like a building that has survived a war. If there is a great multitude of things, that multitude has a value as a multitude, like

13. For a list of various intrinsically good things, see, e.g., Frankena, *Ethics*, 87–88: "life, consciousness, and activity; health and strength; pleasures and satisfactions of all or certain kinds; happiness, beatitude, contentment, etc.; truth; knowledge and true opinions of various kinds, understanding, wisdom; beauty, harmony, proportion in objects contemplated; aesthetic experience; morally good dispositions or virtues; mutual affection, love, friendship, cooperation; just distribution of goods and evils; harmony and proportion in one's own life; power and experiences of achievement; self-expression; freedom; peace, security; adventure and novelty; and good reputation, honor, esteem, etc." My list above is a shorter version of Frankena's, yet it should include all the items in his list; I have condensed the list in order to focus on particular aspects that relate to cosmic significance.

a great flock of birds; on the other hand, we value things that exist only in small numbers, like endangered species. For animals and humans, it is typical to highly value our kin, which can mean close relatives or members of some other group, like a political party, nation, religion, or sports team.

We hold in high value the ability to understand, for example, the things said above, and that our knowledge acquisition is disposed toward truth and ever-greater understanding. Among other things, this is constitutive for human flourishing, which, broadly understood, means having a harmonious relationship with the world around us.

Let us call the aforementioned list a "value base." When we value things, we draw from this value base so that we recognize in an object certain things that we consider to be valuable. However, because there are so many things in the list, our value attribution is not simple; valued things typically instantiate several values in ways that are not easily measured. Should we seek more peace or freedom? We may be more astonished by the sight of the Burj Khalifa skyscraper than, say, the Pantheon in Rome, but determining which one of these is more valuable would be hard.

We do not need to answer these questions here. It suffices to note that there are intrinsically valuable things, and even if people might disagree about how to define why these things are valuable, or why some things are more valuable than others, few would deny the existence of intrinsic value as such. Next, I will evaluate the recent discussion on human value and significance in light of this value base.

Size and Location

Several comments on human significance at the beginning of this chapter seem to be interested in our relative size and location. The presupposition is that humans would be more valuable if one, or preferably both, of the following cases were true: (1) the size of the earth was more connected to the size of the cosmos, and (2) humans dwelled at the center of the cosmos. This argument from scale can be expressed as follows:

1. If God exists, he would create a human-sized universe.
2. Our universe is not human-sized.
3. Therefore, God does not exist.

Why should we think that claim 1 is true? It is hard to come up with a good reason for why God would be under this kind of obligation, but the argument does have some intuitive force. Imagine two worlds that are different, at least to some extent:

> *Genesis World*: The cosmos is only as big as our solar system and about six thousand years old. Humans live in the center of the cosmos.
>
> *Science World*: The cosmos is enormous, consisting of countless solar systems and galaxies, and is about 13.8 billion years old. Humans live at the periphery of the cosmos.

Imagine that one day the scientists of the world find out that we in fact live in the Genesis World. Who would be happier about this news: atheists or theists? Intuitively, many would answer that theists would be the ones having a party. If this really were the case, then the change from the Genesis World to the Science World would boost the credence of atheism.

However, the strength of this argument is based on the presumption that Judeo-Christian theism actually predicts a Genesis World rather than a Science World. In the first chapter, we saw how the early Christian theologians were careful not to enter into debates about the shape and size of the cosmos, and how the geocentric cosmology was a result of Aristotelian philosophy, which was then adapted by the church because that was the best science at that time. It is true that a reading that is simplistic and inattentive to the material would prefer the Genesis World, but this is not a sentiment that is necessitated or even favored by many Christians.

In his formulation of the argument, Nicholas Everitt argues that theism unquestionably favors the Genesis World, but his characterization of theism's core beliefs is quite anthropomorphic. He asks: "Given that God wants to create beings akin to human beings, with certain features which give them value and significance, why does he set these beings in a universe whose spatio-temporal dimensions are so hugely in excess of what is needed? Why does he precede these human beings with vast multitudes of life forms, most of which simply become extinct, and none of which display any intrinsically admirable features?"[14]

If we approach the question from another angle, we could ask what reasons God might have to create a Science World. We already introduced the Theistic Principle of Plenitude, which gives a reason to believe in the abundance of forms in creation. Also, there is no need to suppose that God should favor efficiency in creation, because God has infinite resources. Perhaps God wants a cosmos that is governed by laws and constants that are regular and knowable

14. Everitt, *Non-Existence of God*, 223.

by creatures with rational minds, creatures that are themselves part and parcel of the cosmos, and the act of coming to know these laws would be a thing conducive to the flourishing of humans. Perhaps God and angelic beings find deep joy in meditating on the movement of matter in endless space. At least for me personally, even the thought of this being possible is awe-inspiring, and Judeo-Christian spirituality supports a disposition of *awe* (contra immediate comprehensibility) toward the cosmos, which is pervasive in many psalms (e.g., Pss. 8, 19, 89).[15] Against this background, the move from a Science World to a Genesis World would be evidence against theism! It all depends on which values we pick for our value base. It seems that the argument from scale is based on a thin understanding of value: we are valuable only if we are big enough and in the center. As already stated, in theism the attribution of value is more complicated than that.[16]

But if we opt for the Plenitude option, we are faced with different kinds of problems. If Plenitude is true, then why don't we see these other species and beings? Given Plenitude, the universe should be teeming with life. In his refined version of the argument from scale, Mulgan goes on to argue that the absence of "superior rational beings" counts as an evidence against theism. He changes the focus from mere size and location to the way in which we sentient beings are able to "fill" the universe. Namely, if theism and Plenitude are true, we should expect to see the cosmos inhabited with beings who are able to *comprehend* it. Based on the evidence we have now, it is possible that we live in a "dead" universe where life is only a fluke:

Dead Universe: Earth is the only planet with a biosphere, and humans are the highest biological organisms in the whole universe.

If the Dead Universe scenario is true, then our value base changes: we are more valuable because we are the only game in town. In this case, the low numbers themselves would be a source of value and we would truly be the pearl of great price (cf. Matt. 13:45–46). The Dead Universe would lack some sources of value, but it would not be devoid of value. Our value base would just be slightly different. While some philosophers of religion, like Brian Hebblethwaite, are drawn toward the Dead Universe model, I do not see any reason why it is obviously the best or a necessary one for Christians to hold.

---

15. For some suggestions on how our understanding of cosmos might be reflected in the liturgy, see Vincie, *Worship and the New Cosmology*.

16. Regarding our conflicting intuitions about what kind of world God should create, see Mulgan, *Purpose in the Universe*, 198–99; Lewis, "Dogma and the Universe," 119–21.

If we return to Mulgan's point about the lack of superior rational beings, it is obvious that it does not significantly improve the original argument from scale. First of all, (some) theists believe in angels who are superior to humans in every way. Even if they do not physically inhabit material space, they may still enjoy matter as such and comprehend it to a higher degree than we do. Second, although humans do not yet possess ultimate knowledge of the cosmos, we have come quite far in just a few thousand years. Even if we are not yet at the level that Mulgan calls "superior," we could be there one day. Even today we can observe cosmic background radiation, which basically means seeing the birth of the universe. This is not a minor thing. Third, it might be that there are superior rational physical beings but they are so superior that they do not find it worth communicating with us. How interesting would it be for us to talk to worms? Probably not worth the effort.

The Others and Us

Recently, Guy Kahane has offered an interesting commentary on cosmic significance.[17] He finds nihilistic statements like those quoted above to be largely confused. Things like spatial location, size, and distance are axiologically insignificant categories in this context. His answer to the question "Would humans be more significant if the cosmos consisted of just our solar system?" is "Obviously not." If something in the universe has intrinsic value, the mere size of the universe should not influence it.

The question is not about value per se, but about significance (these are not the same thing). Let us take a closer look at the meaning of insignificance. In the first chapter, we discussed the philosophical meaning of pre-Copernican cosmology. The received view was that humans could claim to be significant, but our contemporary cosmology tells us that our royalty was never real. The problems that are endemic to this view have already been pointed out. Yet the question remains, how exactly does the change in the cosmological view affect the value and significance of human beings?

Kahane points out that the problem does not lie in our having no value but in our *not really mattering*. A thing might have value but still be insignificant. For example, consider a situation where I buy some jelly beans but accidentally drop one onto the street. I could very well pick it up, but I just don't care and decide to continue on because I still have plenty of beans left. The jelly bean that I left behind has exactly the same value as those still left

17. Kahane, "Our Cosmic Insignificance."

in my pocket, but it just lost its significance. Even when value remains more or less the same across time and situations, significance may vary.

If we focus narrowly on value, we could imagine two human beings, Pam and Sam, who have the same intrinsic value. But Pam is a lot more intelligent, better looking, and a nicer person than Sam, who is one of those people you tend to flee from at parties. If Pam and Sam were the only humans in the universe, the existence of Pam would be a threat to the significance of Sam. In fact, he could become cosmically much more significant by eliminating Pam. The question about cosmic insignificance does not require us to think about alien civilizations. We have the same problem already on our planet as we speak. It is not foreign to us to feel insignificant when we are surrounded by friends and colleagues who are like Pam.

The problem of cosmic significance arises when we find ourselves in a situation where we need to compete for attention with everything else in the cosmos. Kahane goes on to claim that in order to establish genuine cosmic significance, it would help if we were alone in the universe, since then, of all things in the universe, we would have the highest value.

At this point, it does not matter how we define or ground value. It is enough to have one or more intrinsically valuable properties. Second, we must have good reasons to believe that no one else exceeds our value in this regard, and from what has been said before, it is not irrational to believe that we are alone in the universe.

Conditions that sink this argument have to do either with the concept of value or with the other beings in the universe. If nihilism is true, then by definition nothing has value and, consequently, nothing is significant.[18] If there are other, greater beings in the universe, this will decrease our significance. For example, if there exists a civilization, like the Shi'ar Empire in the Marvel Universe, then our cosmic significance is pretty much gone. Thus, if we hope for actual cosmic significance, we need to have a way of dodging nihilism, which requires some kind of nonnaturalist theory of value, and we should have good reasons to hope that we are both alone and the highest beings in the universe.

Interestingly, Kahane goes on to claim that even more than the existence of higher alien races, the existence of God, the supreme being, would be a threat to the cosmic significance of humans.[19] It is certainly true that in value God exceeds all created beings. God's existence would not cause things to lose

---

18. Of course, this also entails that nihilism as a worldview has no value.
19. Kahane, "Our Cosmic Insignificance," 769; Kahane, "Should We Want God to Exist?" See Kraay and Dragos, "On Preferring God's Non-Existence."

value, but it would, according to Kahane, make beings like us insignificant. This is perhaps true, but we could also ask whether cosmic significance is something that we should be looking for in the first place. Kahane acknowledges that there is a hint of narcissism in the question. Moreover, we could have a problem with cosmic insignificance in the Ptolemaic cosmos, or even the scenario where the universe would consist of just our small globe—because size does not matter.

A general problem with the reasoning (that ends up affirming human insignificance) is that it functions with a narrow value base. Even if it does give us one scenario where we clearly could have cosmic significance, it fails to take into account other situations in which we might have cosmic significance. For example, being one of a kind is a source of both value and significance. If the universe were filled with a thousand different extraterrestrial species, we would still be the only humans, which would make us cosmically significant.[20] For example, there could be an alien race that was magnificently beautiful but rather dumb. Their cosmic significance would be based on their beauty, whereas our value would be based on other valuable things.

In spite of his feelings of horror in the face of the frigid wind of the immense cosmos, Pascal acknowledges a source of significance for humans: "Man is but a reed, the most feeble thing in nature, but he is a thinking reed. The entire universe need not arm itself to crush him. A vapour, a drop of water, suffices to kill him. But if the universe were to crush him, man would still be more noble than that which killed him, because he knows that he dies and the advantage which the universe has over him; the universe knows nothing of this."[21]

Even if the feeling of insignificance may be very real and even overwhelming, it does not mean that it captures the way the cosmos actually is. Emotions should be balanced with reason. The question of the nature of the cosmos, however, is not something that empirical science alone can answer. Our significance is not based on what kind of stuff there is in the cosmos but on our philosophical notion of what we think the cosmos is.

Theism and Value

Christian theism tweaks the value base in a counterintuitive way. It is natural for us to think that the things listed in the value base are those things that

20. A scenario like this is portrayed in Denis Villeneuve's movie *Arrival* (2016), where a higher alien race treats humans as a cosmically significant race.
21. Pascal, *Pensées* 6.347.

are evidently valuable. In addition to this, there is a long theological tradition according to which God values things that do not express the listed values. Accordingly, God values things that are not central but minuscule and peripheral, things that are not the most capable of performing various tasks and that are not axiologically perfect, things that last only a fleeting moment, and things that God has no use for and that do not exhibit great beauty, compared to angelic beings, for example.

In the Lutheran tradition, this is called the theology of the cross.[22] Luther expresses it in his Heidelberg Disputation thus: "The love of God does not find, but creates, that which is pleasing to it. The love of man comes into being through that which is pleasing to it."[23] Luther contrasts divine and human love: human love follows the value base whereas divine love creates valuable things out of things that are not valuable. This does not mean that God loves unpleasing things because they are unpleasing. Instead, God loves unpleasing things so that he might create something good out of things that seem to possess no value at all. Therefore, the act of God in creation is analogous to the act of God in redemption: God brings something out of nothing.

This doctrine is not a Lutheran specialty. Lewis also writes, "[It is not the case that] incarnation implies some particular merit or excellence in humanity. But . . . it implies just the reverse: a particular demerit and depravity. No creature that deserved redemption would need to be redeemed. They that are whole need not the physician. Christ died for men precisely because men are not worth dying for; to make them worth it."[24] Therefore, we have no theological reason to think that our relation to the universe or our natural capabilities should be something else than what we now observe. Lewis states, "It is, of course, the essence of Christianity that God loves man and for his sake became man and died. But that does not prove that man is the sole end of Nature. In the parable, it was the one lost sheep that the shepherd went in search of: it was not the only sheep in the flock, and we are not told that it was the most valuable—save in so far as the most desperately in need has, while the need lasts, a peculiar value in the eyes of Love."[25]

Therefore, our ultimate value—together with our cosmic significance—is not based directly on the value base, since it flows from the gracious act of God that is not unambiguously portrayed in the cosmos. This conviction lies at the heart of the Christian doctrines of imago Dei and creation. The material cosmos is indeed valuable, but some things become eminently valuable

22. Kopperi, "Theology of the Cross." See also Saler, *Theologia Crucis.*
23. Luther, Heidelberg Disputation 28.
24. Lewis, "Religion and Rocketry," 233.
25. Lewis, "Dogma and the Universe," 122.

NASA

Figure 6.2. Photograph of the Earth between the rings of Saturn taken by the Cassini spacecraft.

only by divine decree. From this perspective, it is possible to say that there is "no reason why the minute earth and the yet smaller human creatures upon it should not be the most important things in a universe that contains the spiral nebulae."[26] Of course, this is hyperbolic expression, and recognizing it as true requires that one look at the cosmos through a theological lens. From the point of view of science, this is obviously a nonsensical claim.

Cosmos and Objective Value?

Peter Atkins makes a typical assertion when he says that there is "not the merest whiff of such evidence" that would suggest that the cosmos has a

26. Lewis, "Dogma and the Universe," 120.

purpose. Therefore, he thinks that the whole question of value lacks meaningful content.[27] If one thinks that science is the only tool that we can use to acquire knowledge about the cosmos, then his judgment is surely right. The problem with this view, obviously, is that it cannot be argued for by empirical means, and therefore we have not the merest whiff of evidence to think that we are justified in believing it to be true. Theism does not deny the importance of science, but it entails that there are things in the universe that cannot be approached by purely scientific means. Among these things are, for example, value, purpose, and significance. Here I want to concentrate especially on the question of objective value.

In theistic cosmology, moral facts are natural; if the cosmos was created by a benevolent creator, one would expect to find that the residents of this cosmos have a sense of values as objective. One way to distinguish between subjective and objective values is to say that a thing has subjective value if someone attributes a value to it. For example, a child might highly value a dry stick that she plays with. Absent the child, the stick is devoid of value. Being objectively valuable means that a thing is valuable even if it is not valued by anyone. This enables us to pass a moral judgment on Nazis, who thought that Jews possessed no human value. Even if the Nazis had won the war and eliminated all their ideological opponents, it would still be true that they committed an atrocity. But how exactly is it possible to make this kind of judgment? What is it in our cosmos that makes it objectively wrong to massacre people?

This question has been one of the most pressing issues in recent discussions of metaethics. J. L. Mackie famously stated, "If there were objective values, then they would be entities or qualities or relations of a very strange sort, utterly different from anything else in the universe."[28] In a naturalistic universe, objective moral facts are as strange as giraffes at the North Pole, whereas in a theistic universe they are something that we expect to encounter.

Objective moral facts entail moral realism, according to which morality is independent from our individual and fleeting preferences, whereas moral antirealism entails seeing moral claims as expressions of our sentiments or expressions of our will. More specifically, being a moral realist requires that one subscribe to at least the following claims:[29]

1. Moral statements describe the world.

2. Moral statements are truth-apt.

27. Atkins, "Atheism and Science," 128.
28. Mackie, Ethics, 38.
29. See Finlay, "Four Faces," 821.

3. At least some moral statements are true.
4. Moral truths or facts are not figurative but literal.
5. The truth of moral statements is not dependent on our desires, emotions, or preferences.

However, some scholars who argue for robust moral realism add two additional requirements:[30]

6. Moral facts are universally binding (i.e., they are absolute, not relative).
7. Failing to live up to the values indicated by moral statements makes us guilty; that is to say, moral facts create obligations.

Forming metaethical stances results from a balancing act between two poles of *internal and external accommodation*. On the one hand, we need to do justice to our "moral appearances"—that is, to the commonsense understanding of what morality is—and this internal accommodation pushes us toward realism. On the other hand, empirical science pushes us toward antirealism, especially if one thinks that the natural sciences are an exhaustive guide to metaphysics.

It must be noted that this question is not about whether it is possible for naturalists to behave morally. This is surely true and few would deny it. Also, the question is not about whether things like genocide can be bad from a naturalist point of view (in some cases, they clearly can), but being bad and being morally wrong are not the same thing. Instead, our question here concerns the grounding of morality. By "grounding" I mean answering the question of what it is that makes a thing morally wrong, in the sense of claims 1–7 above. Secular ethical theories typically offer insights into how our moral sentiments and modes of ethical deliberation have developed, but they struggle to respond to these questions.

It is worthwhile to make a distinction between ethical epistemology and ethical ontology. In other words, why we *tend* to take moral norms as obligatory is a different question from whether we *should* take them as such. The evolutionary history or genealogy of our convictions (why we believe X) is different from the truth value of X. Theists and nonnaturalists typically find the ontological question meaningful, while naturalists and antirealists do not. The need to give an answer to the ontological question pushes nonnaturalists into a field that has been presided over by theists for a long time.[31]

---

30. E.g., Murphy, "Theism, Atheism, and the Explanation of Moral Value."
31. Obviously, not all philosophers think that we should hold on to moral realism. There are several options available to naturalists. One can, for example, claim that moral statements

If one adopts a naturalist position, the total list of claims 1–7 are hard to accept, even if one could in principle accept some of these claims. If put into the context of this book, the crucial question to be asked is "How do human beings, developing in a physical universe which is not itself shaped by any purposive force, come to have the capacity to apprehend objective moral norms?"[32] Or, from another perspective, if the universe does not have any inherent purpose, why did it give birth to beings like us, who are *unable* to escape the weight of moral objectivity?[33]

In addition to the position of theists, there are a variety of nontheistic versions of moral realism or moral nonnaturalism. Here, I briefly present only three recent arguments for nonnaturalist moral realism and argue why they cannot fully adhere to 1–7, even if they wished to do so. These positions are John Leslie's axiarchism, Tim Mulgan's ananthropocentric purposivism, and Erik Wielenberg's nonnaturalism.

Axiarchism

John Leslie has in several volumes offered an argument for axiarchism, which has also been defended by Hugh Rice.[34] According to axiarchism, the existence of the world is explained by its goodness. In short,

(1) The physical universe is better than nothing.

(2) The physical universe exists because of (1).

The defenders of axiarchism openly confess that this stance sounds very odd, but they argue that it is not as outlandish as it first seems. Axiarchists cite as the final explanation of all that exists goodness itself, not a good person (a theistic God), like theists do, or some brute facts, like Platonists do. If one considers the options for the existence of a fine-tuned world, axiarchism is an option if one does not want to claim that the cosmos is just a brute fact, or if one thinks that invoking a personal God or impersonal Platonic entities will lead to a less parsimonious solution. In keeping with this, Rice thus offers two arguments for axiarchism. First, it is simple

---

do not express propositions that have truth value but instead express moral approval or disgust (emotivism), or that moral statements can be reduced to propositions about natural properties (reductivism). Examining these and other options is beyond the scope of this book. For a discussion, see, e.g., Baggett and Walls, *God and Cosmos*.

32. Ritchie, *From Morality to Metaphysics*, 4.
33. Mawson, "Rational Inescapability."
34. Leslie, *Universes*; Rice, *God and Goodness*, 48–63. See also Mulgan, *Purpose in the Universe*, 81.

because it just drops the middleman (God) from the equation by claiming that objective values as such can have causal powers. Second, it avoids the problems that are endemic in Christian theism concerning the relation of God and objective value.[35] In axiarchism, the answer to the question of moral objectivity is very simple. Moral objectivity exists because it is a good thing.

Angus Ritchie argues against the plausibility of axiarchism on the following grounds.[36] First, even if it might be that the axiarchist "abstract" notion of God avoids some problems that classical theism has, it creates new ones. For example, his notion of God is in some sense ontologically lower than the God of classical theism, as an abstract God depends on objective value for its existence. This would raise the question of whether this God is worth our worship; why not worship the objective values instead? A related worry is that this abstract God lacks personal attributes that are a source of value, such as those found in the idea of having personal communion with God; for many theists, this value may be even higher than the value of the nature of God as a means of explaining things.

The second worry is that axiarchic inference, despite its parsimony, fails to do justice to commonsense rationality that sees goodness as requiring explanation, not explaining itself through itself. Axiarchism is so counterintuitive that it is hard to take it seriously. It is always reasonable to ask what the cause of objective goodness is. For the critics, claiming that goodness exists because it is good sounds like a category mistake.

The third issue concerns the causal power of objective norms. Our normal intuition tells us that the only things that have causal *moral* powers are moral agents. Impersonal things can certainly have causal powers, but they do not possess such powers that could bring about 1–7. We may think that numbers and mathematical rules are objective, for example, but they do not compel us morally. Failing on a math test may signal our lack of knowledge, but it does not make us morally guilty. Nonnatural brute moral facts therefore require an additional guilt-making property.[37]

35. On the relation of God and goodness, see Baggett and Walls, *Good God*. A standard Euthyphro critique claims that both horns of the dilemma are equally bad for theists. Either God's commands are arbitrary and our moral system collapses (the voluntarist horn) or God just follows the external notion of good, which makes God superfluous (the realist horn). Several ways of avoiding these two horns are discussed in Baggett and Walls, *Good God*, 83–123.

36. Ritchie, *From Morality to Metaphysics*, 178–88.

37. Unlike mathematical truths, value statements are not analytic. Therefore, they (or at least some of them) require explanation. See Wainwright, *Religion and Morality*, 64–68.

Ananthropocentric Purposivism

In his book *Purpose in the Universe*, Tim Mulgan defends a worldview that he calls "ananthropocentric purposivism" (AP). AP is an attempt to steer a course between Benevolent Theism (BT) and atheism, both of which he thinks have some good arguments on their side but ultimately fail to convince the critical inquirer. Mulgan's method is guided by the attempt to avoid "epistemic caprice"—that is, overvaluing one's capacities and placing undue trust in one's cognitive resources. He notes that atheism, BT, and AP need to make leaps of faith, but in the case of AP, the ditch is the narrowest of all, and therefore it is the most epistemically virtuous position to hold.

Following AP, one believes that naturalism as a comprehensive worldview is false (because in naturalism things like consciousness and moral obligations do not make sense), while the problem of evil keeps one from accepting BT. Thus, God exists but God does not care about humans; hence there arises the term *ananthropocentrism*, which is a conjunction of two claims: (1) the universe has a purpose, and (2) the universe does not have a human-centered purpose. In a way, AP sounds like deism, or a version of certain Asian religions. Mulgan seeks to join AP with a robust sense of objective morality, which he calls Normative AP, "where the non-human-centred cosmic purpose is a ground for objective values and external reasons that have normative significance for human beings."[38] Being a utilitarian, Mulgan argues that we need to take future generations into account, and this cannot be done without robust objective morality.

Mulgan argues for the conjunction of moral realism and AP by offering an account where features that are not purposeful from a human perspective can still ground objective human value. By observing the universe, we can conclude that it is, among other things, mathematically ordered, intelligible, understandable, and life-permitting. Moreover, some parts of it portray things like simplicity, interplay of freedom and creativity, and transcendence of self. Humans can to some extent resemble these features in various ways in their own existence, for example, by contemplating events that have cosmic significance (like the big bang) or by manifesting things like order in their lives.[39]

A central feature of Mulgan's argument is his "two-tier model."[40] As previously noted, God does create the world with certain values in mind, like those mentioned above, but from the perspective of the divine, humans

38. Mulgan, *Purpose in the Universe*, 7.
39. Mulgan, *Purpose in the Universe*, 355.
40. Mulgan, *Purpose in the Universe*, 357–60.

are not worth caring about. Even if the acts of creation are responsive to some cosmic purpose, the existence of humans does not directly appear on God's radar. While humans do possess some value, we are not significant in the eyes of God. Nevertheless, from our point of view these same values are reasonable, and as Mulgan argues, they are the only values we can reasonably uphold. We could think about this scenario as follows. I build a new lodge, which possesses several values, like order and beauty. Unbeknownst to me, in the process of building, an ant colony finds its way into one of the beams close to the ground. The ants can take advantage of some of the features of the house, but the house was not created for them. Nonetheless, the ants will flourish if they behave in a certain way that is in accord with the way in which the lodge was built. For example, the house provides a fine amount of heat and humidity, and ants will flourish if they find the right spot to build their nest.

I grant that Mulgan's AP does give some warrant for certain objective values and a weaker form of moral realism. But does it give warrant to specifically *moral* values, or is it able to give us warrant for claims 1–7? I am not sure. Typical features of objective moral values are that they create obligations, and falling short of these obligations makes one guilty. It is not transparent to me how the aforementioned cosmic values could have this kind of moral force for humans.

We could imagine a culture of space-Nazis embodying such cosmic values as simplicity, unity, order, and openness to (at least certain types of) life. While conquering the galaxy, spreading their message of the superiority of their race and these cosmic values, they would surely have values and think that they were objective, but their values would not be specifically moral, at least in the sense many moral realists understand the nature of morality.

Moreover, if in AP it is granted that both God and objective moral values exist, it is somewhat odd for humans to have such a strong sense of moral goodness that they could make God subject to it. Would it not be more parsimonious to assume that the human moral sense is something that resembles God's goodness (which allows us to make judgments about the problem of evil in the first place)?[41]

That said, even if Mulgan's AP cannot support full-blown moral realism and objectivism, this does not mean that AP collapses to nihilism. As a response, I can imagine Mulgan pointing out that similar problems also haunt BT, where at least some leaps of faith are needed.

41. Mulgan favors AP over BT because he thinks that all theodicies fail. In other words, he subjects a theistic God to his moral judgment.

Wielenberg's Nonnaturalism

A major proponent of ethical nonnaturalism is Erik Wielenberg, who argues for a form of moral realism based on the existence of nonnatural, nonreducible brute facts. For example, Wielenberg states:

> Of the ethical states of affairs that obtain necessarily, at least some are brute facts. That pain is intrinsically bad is not explained in terms of other states of affairs that obtain. Moreover, at least some necessarily obtaining brute ethical facts are not trivial but substantive. Therefore, I have an ontological commitment shared by many theists: I am committed to the obtaining of substantive, metaphysically necessary, brute facts. Some ethical facts fall into this category; I call such facts *basic ethical facts*. Such facts are the foundation of (the rest of) objective morality and rest on no foundation themselves. To ask of such facts, "where do they come from?" or "on what foundation do they rest?" is misguided in much the way that, according to many theists, it is misguided to ask of God, "where does He come from?" or "on what foundation does He rest?" The answer is the same in both cases: They come from nowhere, and nothing external to themselves grounds their existence; rather, they are fundamental features of the universe that ground other truths.[42]

Wielenberg argues that when theists build their own theistic metaethics, they need to resort one way or another to abstract moral principles which explain themselves. According to Wielenberg, Robert Adams, a leading theist ethical theorist, also acknowledges that there are necessary, brute facts about morality. Adams thinks that goodness is a brute fact that cannot be explained through the help of something else, while the relation between God and goodness is one of identity.[43] But Wielenberg asks, what does God do in this theory, because brute goodness seems to do all the heavy lifting? Nonnaturalist atheism is not obviously worse off than theism if they both need to rely on the same brute facts. In fact, theism appears as a worse option because it needs to add to the cosmos one extra being that ultimately does not do anything. Wielenberg states:

> The ethical shopping list of [R. M.] Adams, [W. L.] Craig, and [J. P.] Moreland contains items like this: (a) there is a being that is worthy of worship, (b) if the Good commands you to do something, then you are morally obligated to do it, and (c) the better the character of the commander, the more reason there is to obey his or her commands. My ethical shopping list contains items like this: (d) pain is intrinsically bad, (e) inflicting pain just for fun is morally wrong,

42. Wielenberg, "In Defense," 26.
43. Wielenberg, "In Defense," 30–32; Adams, *Finite and Infinite Goods*.

and (f) it is just to give people what they deserve. None of us can provide an external foundation for every item on our list; each of our lists contains some brute ethical facts.[44]

Wielenberg thinks that if there are things in the cosmos that are intrinsically valuable, there is no need for God in metaethics. As an example he gives a loving relationship with another person and subjects it to a thought exam. He asks us to imagine, if this relationship should disappear, would it make our universe worse? Or if there were no other things in the universe except this, would it make the world valuable? Obviously, the answers are yes and yes. Therefore, there are intrinsically valuable things in the world.[45] Other similar things would include the ethical code to not torture people for fun. Wielenberg thinks that God does not do anything important in metaethics, and thereby moral realism based on brute facts is enough and more parsimonious. He bases this claim on Adams's view where Goodness is God. God does not "ground" goodness any more than H_2O "grounds" water.

Now, it might be that we have no way of answering the question about what grounds moral facts. Nonnaturalists disown clear-cut metaphysical commitments, as they try to be committed only to broad naturalism while simultaneously trying to avoid the stern-minded naturalism of noncognitivists and error theorists. In the end, the deeper metaphysical question is glossed over with an explicit appeal to the inability to explain the nature of these facts. Finlay explains, "On the nonnaturalists' view, moral reality has 'brute, inexplicable' normativity, which cannot be explained in motivational or other natural terms. This inexplicability is twofold: we cannot explain what normativity is in nonnormative language, and neither can we explain why the fundamental normative truths hold (e.g., why the fact that pain hurts counts in favor of preventing it). Nonnaturalism denies that this inexplicability is problematic, and defends its claim by looking for partners in guilt."[46] So if nonnaturalism fails, so do the others, and the others fail even more miserably. In this view, we cannot explain the nature of these facts, but neither can we seriously doubt them. One of the best arguments for nonnaturalism, according to Russ Shafer-Landau, is the failure of other, naturalist models to give reasonable accounts for morality.[47] But if we think that our moral theory needs to make sense of universally binding obligations, then theism has an advantage.

44. Wielenberg, "In Defense," 40.
45. Wielenberg, Robust Ethics, 3–4.
46. Finlay, "Four Faces," 843.
47. Shafer-Landau, Moral Realism, 79.

Let us go back to the water example. If we understand that H_2O = water, this helps us understand why water behaves as it does. Similarly, if we understand that Goodness = God, this helps us make sense of our moral phenomenology. For Adams, the central feature of metaethics is the obligatory nature of moral facts, and obligations make sense only in social contexts where the command is connected to *personal* goodness.[48] Obligations obtain primarily between persons, and obligations toward nonpersons can be derived from this personhood, which exists on the basis of morality.

Nonnaturalist forms of moral realism need to explain how to move from intrinsic value to obligations, and theists need to do the same. For nonnaturalists, this move takes place by recognizing that there is no real move to be made; things just are this way. Torturing people for fun is simply wrong. Period. The theist's question "but why?" does not make any sense for the nonnaturalist. But Adams's insistence on Goodness = God does offer something better than nonnaturalism. The intrinsic value of things may surely give us reasons to behave in a certain way. However, I am not sure whether they can create obligations and give us all the goods listed in tenets 1–7, even if it might give us some of them. A standard theist answer to atheistic nonnaturalism would be that God is simpler than a group of stand-alone moral facts because brute facts do not self-evidently help us understand how they can create obligations. The case is like Mulgan's moral realism based on AP; it gives us reasons for a certain kind of behavior that is not necessarily moral. Nonnatural brute moral facts therefore need an additional guilt-making property.[49]

A theist can thus argue that theistic moral realism does not add one unnecessary thing into the cosmos because the personhood of God is the best possible explanation for the existence of persons and the moral obligations that exist between persons.[50] This is related to the doctrine of imago Dei, which states that humans (and perhaps some other beings as well) have a special relationship with God. This doctrine is discussed in more detail in chapter 8. Here it suffices to note that being a bearer of God's image entails a deep connection between humans and the source of ultimate value. There are different theories that try to describe the nature of this relationship, just as there are also various theories that try to explain how God's commands, or God's nature, create moral obligations. It might be that we will never be able to offer a good philosophical account of how God's nature and moral obligations are connected, but this should not worry us too much. For example,

48. Adams, *Finite and Infinite Goods*, 233–48.
49. See Wainwright, "In Defense of Non-Natural Theistic Realism."
50. Baggett and Walls, *God and Cosmos*, 140–43, 284–86.

it makes perfect sense for us to follow the orders of a policeman, even if we lack the philosophical theory that explains how the officer's commands and the obligation to follow them are connected.[51] For the purposes of this book, it suffices to note that moral facts are natural in a theistic cosmos, and theism can make perfect sense of our moral phenomenology.

However, by resorting to the social nature of obligations and a better fit between our moral phenomenology and theism, the theist relocates the discussion. The believability of theistic nonnaturalism is dependent on the believability of theism in general. More specifically, the theist needs to have good grounds to think that the God who grounds all beings and issues moral commands is ultimately good, because only then can one have a reason to follow the command. If this is established to a sufficient degree, then it is not necessary to come up with an exact philosophical theory that explains the nature of obligations.

This makes the rival positions hard to compare. Nonnaturalism asks us to believe in moral facts without arguments concerning the grounding of morality. This allegedly gives us both naturalism and robust moral realism without the unwanted metaphysical baggage associated with theism. A theistic universe gives us a more coherent framework for the existence and nature of moral facts while giving an explanation for why they have such power over us—but this option asks us to accept a theistic worldview, which is contested because the evidence for God and for the goodness of God can be reasonably doubted.

However, our question is not just about the mere coherence of one's worldview, which is obviously a good thing to have. Sometimes metaethical debates seem trivial, having almost no practical relevance whatsoever. I want to resist the temptation to demote the value of philosophical inquiry into mere abstract debate about the nature of morality. Philosophies often have practical consequences. I think that a recognition of this truth is behind the intentions to promote nonnaturalist moral realism. Without it, something bad could happen. Belief in the intrinsic worth of all human beings is not universal, and in the history of humanity it seems to be tied to the idea of humans as bearers of God's image.[52] This helps us to generalize the obligations beyond our immediate community and kin, as I may then have obligations toward persons who are my enemies or live far, far away. Second, in human contracts, I may always doubt the sincerity of my partners, and this lowers my commitment to a contract with them. It is not unheard of for people to try to renegotiate

51. Evans, *God and Moral Obligation*, 106–10.
52. Linville, "Moral Argument," 443–45.

contracts and even neglect them. But if the obligation is not ultimately based on what people do but on what they are, their value is beyond negotiation.

Theism, and more specifically the doctrine of creation, influences how we perceive the cosmos. Theistic cosmology is not primarily concerned with the physical side of things (although theism values nature highly as a good and valuable handiwork of a benevolent God), but instead it focuses on how physical features are interpreted and given meaning and purpose. Science as a discipline has very little, if anything, to say about purpose and value, which are not empirical facts but truths of reason. The inability to look beyond one's discipline leads many scientists, and scientistic philosophers, to bracket all talk about value, significance, and purpose. But why should we think that reality can be reduced to something that is available to just one way of knowing?

7

In Space No One
Can Hear You Scream?

God and Being

According to a well-known legend, the Russian astronaut Yuri Gagarin claimed after returning from space that he did not see God. In fact, it was the leader of the Communist Party, Nikita Khrushchev, who said this about Gagarin in order to spread antireligious propaganda. Gagarin himself was an Orthodox Christian, and saying something like that would not have made any sense to him.

But why not exactly? The idea of God living somewhere above the clouds is a crude anthropomorphism, which theists have always criticized and abandoned. But in the Ptolemaic cosmos, is not God's dwelling space somewhere beyond the constellations? What if Gagarin simply did not go far enough? However, even within the Ptolemaic hierarchy, God is not something that can be found among things that exist, like ordinary objects or persons. God is not a being, but being itself. In this chapter, I examine this notion first from the point of view of theological language and mysticism. If God is not a part of creation and transcends every name and concept, how can we speak meaningfully about God? Finally, I explain what is meant by divine hiddenness and how this concept may help us understand something about the nature of revelation.

Speaking of Divine Transcendence

If God is not a being among beings, and therefore not within the grasp of science, what does this mean for theology as a public discourse? Some detractors of theism have criticized, on good grounds in my mind, various attempts to seal theology and religion from critique. This evasive maneuver can include a claim that God is wholly other and beyond all linguistic reference; God is absolutely ineffable. Another comparable move is to revise theological language so that it does not refer to any metaphysical realities; for example, talk about "God" just means things like "grace" or "gratitude." However, the most sophisticated critics of theism think that these maneuvers are ill-advised. If we want to speak in any intelligible way about God and creation, we are better off avoiding these goodwilled but ultimately simplistic and unsatisfying attempts.[1]

I say that these attempts are goodwilled because they try to safeguard some essential aspect of religious language. It is true that religious language is misunderstood if it is interpreted as mere propositions about facts. Nonetheless, religious language often includes factual statements. As stated, God is not an ordinary being, which gives rise to a legitimate concern of how created, limited beings can speak about God, who is transcendent and exceeds every possible linguistic formulation. This is not an extreme claim made by radical negative theologians, but a central part of orthodox Christian tradition. For example, this is what Martin Luther writes about God-talk and God's relation to the created order, in his *Confession Concerning Christ's Supper* (1528):

> We say that God is no such extended, long, broad, thick, high, deep being. He is a supernatural, inscrutable being who exists at the same time in every little seed, whole and entire, and yet also in all and above all and outside all created things. There is no need to enclose him here, as this enthusiast dreams, for a body is much, much too wide for the Godhead; it could contain many thousand Godheads. On the other hand, it is also so small but God is still smaller, nothing so large but God is still larger, nothing so short but God is still shorter, nothing so long but God is still longer, nothing is so broad but God is still broader, nothing so narrow but God is still narrower, and so on. He is an inexpressible being, above and beyond all that can be described and imagined.[2]

Here Luther is arguing against Reformed theologians ("enthusiasts") who had claimed that God cannot "fit" himself into a physical location (i.e., the

1. See, e.g., Philipse, *God in the Age of Science*, 28–29. To put Philipse's critiques succinctly, if God is wholly other, how do we know that if the wholly other is absolutely ineffable? If someone says that nothing true can be said about God, he or she just said something true about God.
2. *LW* 37, 228, trans. Robert H. Fischer. *WA* 26, 339–40.

bread in the Holy Eucharist). Luther answers by pointing out that God is not bound by human categories, and this includes both physical objects and human language. However, if one argues that this means that nothing true can ever be said about God, then one subscribes to absolute ineffability, which is not a Christian doctrine.[3]

Despite the transcendence of God, it is possible to speak meaningfully about God by using human terms. This is true even if one theologizes within the mystical tradition. A good analytic account of mystical God-talk is provided by Saint Edith Stein (1891–1942), who was both a negative theologian and professional philosopher.[4] She wrote a concise and elegant introduction to Pseudo-Dionysius the Areopagite's mystical theology, which I will use in the following to illustrate the nature of Christian God-talk.[5]

According to Stein, revealed—or symbolic—Christian theology consists of two dialectical opposites: the *via negativa*, which denies what God is not, and the *via positiva*, which affirms those things in creation that resemble God the most (such as "life," "goodness"; cf. "stone," "air"). In the end, neither denial nor affirmation reaches its object perfectly; thus the *via negativa* is also imperfect and should be moved aside during the last stage, which is *theologia mystica* (116). Positive and negative theologies form a dialectical process where negations and affirmations cut through our concepts and reveal the analogical nature of religious language. As Stein explains, "Thus upon completing the ascent, positive and negative theology give way to mystical theology which in utter stillness enters into union with the Ineffable. The previous theologies represent stages leading up to the summit. . . . Although opposed, they do not exclude each other; they complement each other at all stages" (89).

The first point to be noted here is that negative and positive theology, or apophatic and kataphatic theology, cannot be thought of disjunctively, so that one chooses the one and forgets the other. Instead, they are each other's correctives; both are needed. Second, the "utter stillness" waits at the *end* of the journey, after this dialectical thinking has been practiced for some time. Pure negative theology cannot be the starting point of Christian spirituality, as some forms of popular mysticism suggest; neither can one reduce theology to mere negative theology.

3. For a discussion on ineffability in the Christian mystical tradition, see Knepper, *Negating Negation*.

4. Edith Stein was born into a Jewish family, but in her youth she embraced atheism. She was Edmund Husserl's assistant, the editor of his major works, and an accomplished philosopher in her own right. Stein converted to Catholicism and joined the Carmelite order. She was executed in Auschwitz because of her Jewish roots. In 1998, Pope John Paul II canonized her and made her the patron saint of Europe.

5. Stein, "Ways to Know God." The page numbers in parentheses refer to this book.

Turning to the *via positiva*, Stein makes a noteworthy point about religious language: "There is a likeness, something objectively common, between the inexpressible thing that happened to him [Moses] and 'consuming fire'" (97). Thus, when Moses says, "God is a consuming fire," he says something that is univocally true: God has certain similar properties to consuming fire, even if God's nature is not exhausted by that which "consuming fire" is.[6] Consequently, there is in principle nothing wrong with speaking of God using traditional concepts; they are neither misleading nor deficient. In fact, God has chosen to use this mode of communication that suits human cognition: "Revelation speaks in a language accessible to natural human reason," Stein argues (23).

Stein mentions the importance of getting right the doctrine of analogy of being (*analogia entis*). Namely, if the analogical relation of God and creation is not understood correctly, atheism is a logical conclusion. The analogy of being is a fundamental Christian notion that sets our language of God in its proper place: whatever we say about God, it is always subject to the rule "God is always ever greater" (*semper maior dissimilitudo*).[7] If this is not borne in mind, one lapses into gnosticism (equivocity without theology of creation) or paganism (univocity without Creator-creation distinction) (119).

Because God can be known only through analogy, this requires introducing the aforementioned dialectical process, which aims to make a distinction between likeness and unlikeness by using the *via negativa* and *via positiva*. In other words, this process seeks to demonstrate to the soul how God is not merely a being among other beings. But for Stein, the fact that God is not ontologically on the same level as human beings does not rule out that God is *to a certain extent* comprehensible.

> Reason would turn into unreason if it would stubbornly content itself with what it is able to discover with its own light, barring out everything which

---

6. For a helpful treatment that explains why analogous versions of religious language are still univocal, see T. Williams, "Doctrine of Univocity."

7. This is the formulation of the Fourth Lateran Council: "For between creator and creature there can be noted no similarity so great that a greater dissimilarity cannot be seen between them." Saint Thomas uses the concept of analogy in his treatise on divine names (*ST* 1.13.5) to chart a middle road between univocal and equivocal predication. In this question, Thomas lays out the problems of these two false ways of speaking, or refraining from speaking, about God (univocal predication leads to inadequate speech about God since the terms are not applied in similar ways to God and created beings; equivocal predication leads to an inability to say anything about God, and it is also performatively self-contradictory). In general terms, the theological understanding of analogy of being fits this vague formulation, and it attempts to capture the idea that the world as we perceive it (as constantly changing) is real, while still pointing toward something that is changeless and therefore more real. However, the difference between our world and God cannot be thought of in a qualitative sense.

is made visible to it by a brighter and more sublime light. For it ought to be emphasized that what is communicated to us by revelation is not something simply unintelligible but rather something with an intelligible meaning—a meaning, to be sure, which cannot be comprehended and demonstrated in the way natural facts are understood and demonstrated. What is communicated to us by revelation cannot be comprehended at all (that is, it cannot be exhaustively described by means of concepts) because it is in itself immeasurable and inexhaustible and at any time reveals only so much of its mystery as it wants us to understand.[8]

God's transcendent nature is not therefore a hindrance to knowledge of God because knowledge of God is ultimately based on God's self-revelation. This makes human limitations unimportant because the knowledge is not dependent on human achievement. But even this revelation, which is only seen by one possessing faith, cannot capture the essence of God. Hence, faith is called "dark light," something that sees in the darkness.[9] "Whatever derives from the synthesis of theological and philosophical truth bears the imprint of this dual source of knowledge, and faith, as we are told, is a 'dark light.' Faith helps us to understand something, but only in order to point to something that remains for us incomprehensible. Since the ultimate ground of all existence [alles Seienden] is unfathomable, everything which is seen in this ultimate perspective moves into that 'dark light' of faith, and everything intelligible is placed in a setting with an incomprehensible background."[10]

Stein's analysis of religious language captures well the goodwilled intuitions I mentioned before without sacrificing the reality of what language talks about. Understanding that every concept and name is only a pointer toward something greater requires epistemic humility. God cannot be imprisoned by human means, and our journey to God is dependent not on our achievement but on God's condescension in Christ.

8. Stein, *Finite and Eternal Being*, 22.
9. Stein, *Finite and Eternal Being*, 27:
> We cannot accept the truths of faith as evident in themselves as we do in the case of the necessary truths of reason or of the data of sense perception; nor can we deduce them logically from certain self-evident truths. This is one reason why faith is called "dark light." Moreover, faith as a *credere Deum* and a *credere in Deum* always aspires beyond all revealed truth, that is, beyond all truth which God has confined in concepts and judgments, in words and sentences, in order to make it commensurate with the human mode of cognition. Faith asks of God more than individually separated truths: It desires God himself, all of him, who *is* truth, and it seizes him in darkness and blindness ("although it is night").

10. Stein, *Finite and Eternal Being*, 25.

Analogia Entis

How are God and the cosmos related? These questions on the nature of God-talk and the relationship of God and our cosmos were intriguingly explored by Erich Przywara (1889–1972). Przywara saw two dangerous opposites that theology must avoid.[11] First, he argued that a new concept of God emerged after the Reformation, which he called "theopanism." In theopanism, God is so radically real that creation loses its value and humans lose their agency. God is everything; we are nothing. According to Przywara, the greatest proponents of theopanism were Martin Luther and the early Karl Barth, alongside other dialectical theologians. Even if his reading of these figures is exaggerated, there is a tendency in some forms of modern theology to lean toward theopanism, where God ceases to be "all in all" and rather becomes "everything alone."[12]

The second danger is the total rejection of metaphysics and a conflation of transcendence with immanence, apparent in the philosophies of Nietzsche and, to some extent, Kant. The problem with these monistic models is that they are too reductionistic and therefore unable to portray all the necessary aspects of the human condition. Specifically, the history of Western philosophy can be depicted as a pendulum perpetually swinging between extreme philosophical positions, where everything that exists is depicted as either constant movement or unchanging being, radically free or determined, and so on. Przywara thinks that there is something in each of these extremes that needs to be cherished, but in such a way that they are brought together. Disregarding either of these options will lead to absurd and practically problematic conclusions.[13]

In contrast, Przywara saw in the writings of Augustine and John Henry Newman a different theological style. Augustine's understanding of the God who is totally within us (*intimio interior meo*) yet still distinct from the world (*superior summo meo*) offered Przywara an alternative that not only captured the inner logic of Christian faith but also provided theological answers to the problems created by secular philosophy.[14]

This thought process was crystallized in Przywara's book *Analogia Entis*. The book is dense and not for the faint of heart, but the central argument is relatively simple. I will try to do it justice in the next few lines. An analogy of being demarcates a middle ground between problematic extremes of pure identity and pure dialectics, and it is in light of this demarcation, in the denial

11. Johnson, *Karl Barth and the Analogia Entis*, 38–50.
12. Przywara, "Gott in uns oder Gott über uns?," 348. Quoted in Johnson, *Karl Barth and the Analogia Entis*, 46.
13. Przywara, *Analogia Entis*, 203–31.
14. Johnson, *Karl Barth and the Analogia Entis*, 41–42.

of closure offered by ultimately monistic philosophies, that a space is opened that does not so much define "God" or any metaphysical entity as it defines what God is not, keeping with the principles of the Fourth Lateran Council and the tradition of apophatic theology.

By this denial, Przywara makes room for a peculiar kind of natural theology: the structure of human existence and the way we posit ourselves intellectually in this world inevitably point toward a dilemma that can in principle be acknowledged by everyone, but which can be resolved only from a theological perspective. In theology, it is possible to allow paradoxes that tie together and unite two extreme positions because theology cannot take any total and complete form (whereas the extremes can, according to Przywara), since it always takes revelation to be pointing toward something greater. To be precise, natural knowledge, which Przywara talks about, is not a bond that unites the human world with God but something that reveals the infinite distance, the ever-greater dissimilarity, between them. Therefore, *analogia entis* is an exercise in negative theology.[15]

In trying to underscore the minimalistic nature of Przywara's natural theology, John Betz points out that Przywara makes a distinction between formal and material knowledge of the divine. The formal knowledge is shared by Christians and non-Christians, as it points merely toward abstract, nameless divine ground, whereas material knowledge alone enables one to recognize God as God.[16] Formal knowledge is based on tension between essence and existence, which are immediately available to our consciousness. As created beings, we understand that even if we do have existence, our essence escapes us, and we perceive how we are in the grip of perpetual change. This tension allows deduction of a possibility where essence and existence are instantiated in the same being. But this simultaneously implies that when we use the concept of being in the aforementioned way, we cannot use it in a (simplistic) univocal or equivocal sense. Instead, "being" must be understood analogically, so that there is always ever-greater dissimilarity between our use of being and how it applies to God.[17]

Przywara acknowledges the decree of the First Vatican Council, according to which knowledge of the existence of God is attainable through the means

15. Betz, "After Barth," 54.

16. Betz, "After Barth," 52n56; Przywara, *Analogia Entis*, 118. Przywara's account is very peculiar. On the one hand, he suggests that formal knowledge is sort of empty, but it can be filled with correct material knowledge; it involves only knowledge of what "God" means. Still, the movement from gods to God, from *paganus* to *catholicus*, involves an either-or choice, which sounds more Lutheran than Thomistic as a way of describing the relation of nature and the supernatural.

17. Betz, "After Barth," 60; Johnson, *Karl Barth and the Analogia Entis*, 67–80.

of secular reason, yet he clarifies that this should be understood as a positive limit concept (*als positives Grenzbegriff*), which does not include particular details.[18] However, analogy is supposed to resonate with the basic Thomistic principle according to which grace does not destroy nature, and consequently theology as divine wisdom should not obliterate the worldly wisdom offered by philosophy. But even in this case, the role of worldly wisdom appears to be minimal. Betz summarizes Przywara's stance: "For as of yet, from a purely philosophical perspective, nothing whatsoever can be made out about who God is or what he has revealed, or even that there is such thing as revelation. All that can be made out metaphysically with any degree of certainty apart from revelation is that creaturely being is not its own ground, that it is not being itself, that it 'is' only in the form of becoming, and that theology, that is, the science of a God of revelation, is a reasonable possibility or, to put it in still more minimalist terms, a 'non-impossibility'" (*vorausgehenden Möglichkeit*; *Nicht-Unmöglichkeit*).[19] This implies that creatures are always, no matter how much they may be deformed by sin, "open upward"; human beings, in the state of sin, are still directed toward the highest good. This is impossible to erase from our nature, because the upward disposition penetrates the whole of created nature.[20]

Kenneth Oakes notes how Przywara subsequently broadened his view of *analogia entis* to be set more explicitly in a trinitarian and christological context. In one of his later works, Przywara states, "This is the message of 'John the theologian': how God and cosmos are correlated in the 'Logos-Lamb who was slain.'"[21] Thus, analogy should not be seen as a purely philosophical principle but something that finds its true expression only in a properly christological framework: the rhythm of affirmation and negation that can be found from philosophical traditions correlates and finds its highest instantiation in the descent and ascent of Christ. Analogy is something that captures both the essence of Christian theology and the dilemmas of secular philosophy so that the same rhythm can be found everywhere in the cosmos, but most acutely in the trinitarian reality of the living God.[22]

Where, then, should God's revelation be sought? Przywara's general ontology allows him to include creation as a part of God's revelation. There is no form of existence that does not represent an instantiation of God's action. Therefore, Przywara is able to claim both that theology always comes before

---

18. Przywara, *Analogia Entis*, 73–74.
19. Betz, "After Barth," 66; Przywara, *Analogia Entis*, 82–83.
20. Oakes, "Cross and the *Analogia Entis*," 157.
21. "Christentum gemäss Johannes," quoted in Betz, "Translator's Introduction," 112.
22. Oakes, "Cross and the *Analogia Entis*," 150, 163–64.

"secular" philosophy in his system and that creation is able to function as a pointer, however abstract, toward God. For him, there is no space where God does not exist, even if the form of God's presence is always analogical. This allows him to draw a line against the Hegelians, who, in his mind, do not properly understand God's distance from the human world.

These examples of Stein and Przywara offer one angle on the possibility of knowledge of God through the natural world by pointing out both the necessity of human language and its limits and how the dialectic between essence and existence makes room for a minimal form of natural theology. There is a natural point of contact in the human world through which transcendence lets its light in.

Divine Silence

Even those Christian theologians who do natural theology claim that knowledge of God is not something that is automatic or necessary.[23] This is not only a human fault but also due to God's actively hiding himself from humans. Think about, for example, the following passages:

> The God of Israel, who saves his people,
> is a God who conceals himself. (Isa. 45:15 GNT)

> At that time Jesus said, "Father, Lord of heaven and earth!
> I thank you because you have shown to the unlearned
> what you have hidden from the wise and learned." (Matt. 11:25 GNT)

> How great are God's riches!
> How deep are his wisdom and knowledge!
> Who can explain his decisions?
> Who can understand his ways? (Rom. 11:33 GNT)

This gives rise to the problem of divine hiddenness. Why does God, who wants to be in contact with his creation, hide himself from it? The Danish philosopher Søren Kierkegaard (1813–1855) suggests in his *Philosophical Fragments* (1844) one possible solution by telling the "Parable of a King and a Maiden." The parable seeks to offer a narrative in which divine hiddenness is the most reasonable course of action that God can take. God cannot appear in his divine form to humans, because that would be simply too much for

23. Taliaferro, "Project of Natural Theology."

us to comprehend. In the story, a king tries to express his love to a maiden, but he realizes that he cannot approach her as a king because then he could not be sure of her true intentions; she could respond positively out of fear or self-interest, for example. Therefore, the king dresses up as a servant of equal status to the maiden. The same dynamic applies analogously to God.

> In order that the union may be brought about, the God must therefore become the equal of such a one, and so he will appear in the likeness of the humblest. But the humblest is one who must serve others, and the God will therefore appear in the form of a *servant*. But this servant-form is no mere outer garment, like the king's beggar-cloak, which therefore flutters loosely about him and betrays the king; it is not like the filmy summer-cloak of Socrates, which though woven of nothing yet both conceals and reveals. It is his true form and figure. For this is the unfathomable nature of love, that it desires equality with the beloved, not in jest merely, but in earnest and truth. And it is the omnipotence of the love which is so resolved that it is able to accomplish its purpose, which neither Socrates nor the king could do, whence their assumed figures constituted after all a kind of deceit.[24]

By becoming a servant, the king does not deceive the maiden but reveals his true nature. His intentions are pure; he is interested in the maiden as a person, not as an object to be used. This is the paradox of Christian theism: God, all-powerful and omnipresent Creator of the whole universe, reveals himself by hiding himself in plain sight. Kierkegaard's poetic account is worth quoting at length:

> Behold where he stands—God! Where? There; do you not see him? He is God; and yet he has not a resting-place for his head, and he dares not lean on any man lest he cause him to be offended. He is God; and yet he picks his steps more carefully than if angels guided them, not to prevent his foot from stumbling against a stone, but lest he trample human beings in the dust, in that they are offended in him. He is God; and yet his eye surveys mankind with anxious care, for the tender shoots of an individual life may be crushed as easily as a blade of grass. How wonderful a life, all sorrow and all love: to yearn to express the equality of love, and yet to be misunderstood; to apprehend the danger that all men may be destroyed, and yet only so to be able really to save a single soul; his own life filled with sorrow, while each hour of the day is taken up with the troubles of the learner who confides in him! This is the God as he stands upon the earth, like unto the humblest by the power of his omnipotent love. He knows that the learner is in Error—what if he should misunderstand, and

24. Kierkegaard, *Philosophical Fragments*, 131–32.

droop, and lose his confidence! To sustain the heavens and the earth by the fiat of his omnipotent word, so that if this word were withdrawn for the fraction of a second the universe would be plunged into chaos—how light a task compared with bearing the burden that mankind may take offense, when one has been constrained by love to become its saviour![25]

In keeping with this Kierkegaardian intuition, C. Stephen Evans has more recently argued that divine revelation contains an intended ambiguity. On the one hand, revelation is easily accessible, but on the other hand, it must be easily resistible. This guarantees both that faith is sensitive to evidential considerations and that faith involves the conscious personal agency of the believer. "God would make knowledge of himself widely available for those who wish to have it, but God would not force such knowledge on those who do not wish to know God," Evans states.[26] As the examples of Stein and Przywara show, some features of the cosmos can function as pointers toward the divine. Nevertheless, the arguments of natural theology make the belief a live option, but they do not force one to believe in them.

God is not a part of this cosmos and cannot be found among the objects of this world. Therefore, science cannot directly prove or disprove God's existence even if it can offer indirect support for both views. The question about the existence of God is not directly empirical. This does not, however, mean that God-talk is pure nonsense. Christian theology argues that despite God's transcendence, reasonable and public God-talk is possible. This is so because God remains in analogous relation to the world, which opens a possibility for the natural knowledge of God. This does not offer deep knowledge of God and therefore special revelation is needed. Yet even in revealing himself, God also hides himself. Revelation is open to all, and still everyone can in their creaturely freedom neglect it.

25. Kierkegaard, *Philosophical Fragments*, 25.
26. Evans, *Natural Signs*, 12–17, here 17.

8

There Is No Gene
for the Human Spirit

Images of God

The doctrine of the image of God (*imago Dei*) is one of the central issues in theological cosmology. This chapter examines the meaning and the use of the doctrine in light of our current knowledge of human history and of our place in the universe. Has the shift in scientific cosmology demoted our status as the image-bearers of God? Something like this is often suggested in popular discourse, but such claims usually get the idea of the image of God wrong. In Western theology, it has been customary to identify imago Dei with human intellectual and cognitive capacities. However, several contemporary theologians have criticized this view because, according to the critics, it leads to a truncated view of humanity. To answer these claims, we need to see how the doctrine has been used in the past, how it still may make sense, and whether it could be applied to beings that are not human. I approach the doctrine through the work of two theologians. Thomas Aquinas is chosen as an exemplary because of his canonical status and lasting influence on the Catholic tradition. The second representative for our consideration is a contemporary Lutheran theologian, Robert W. Jenson, who aims to address a wider ecumenical audience in his works.

The Uses of Imago Dei

In contemporary theological anthropology, theorizing about imago Dei is classified in three distinct groups: structural imago Dei, functional imago Dei, and relational imago Dei. Structural theories try to identify imago Dei with a particular cognitive faculty. Functional theories see imago Dei in terms of a role: humans are representatives or stewards of the divine within the created order. Relational theories of imago Dei stress the fundamentally relational and communal nature of human existence and ultimately understand humans as objects of God's address.[1]

Recently, the structural approach has been challenged for various reasons. Instead of structuralism, modern theological anthropologies emphasize relationality and "holism"; it is the divine address and consequent being-in-relation that constitutes imago Dei, not certain capabilities or faculties. According to critics, this is more in accord with contemporary philosophy, science, and biblical witness. In sum, the structural theories are less than ideal because they (1) denigrate the physical nature of human beings; (2) overemphasize theoretical and abstract analysis; (3) lead to control; (4) imply a static understanding of human nature; and (5) are philosophically, biblically, and scientifically outdated.[2] In the following, I cannot address all of these aspects. Instead, I will concentrate on the various uses of imago Dei doctrine that allow significant freedom about how to employ it in contemporary discussion. I will also try to offer a brief account of the doctrine that is able to retain to a great extent its historical uses and meaning.

Imago Dei is a peculiar concept in the sense that it is widely used but has never had a fixed meaning. The reason for this is that theological anthropology has never been a central doctrinal or ecumenical problem. Consequently, there have been several ways of interpreting the meaning of imago Dei in the history of theology. Although there are differences between the churches on this issue, they are not ultimately divisive.

---

1. Cortez, *Theological Anthropology*, 14–40.
2. Shults, *Reforming Theological Anthropology*, 11, 166, 174; Cortez, *Theological Anthropology*, 18–20, 29. See also van Huyssteen, *Alone in the World?*, 134: "An anthropology that finds the imaging of God only in the mental aspects of the human person inevitably denigrates the physical and directly implies that God, and the image of God, can be related only to theoretical analysis and control. Identifying a specific disembodied capacity like reason or rationality as the image of God by definition implies a negative, detrimental view of the human body—a move that inevitably leads to abstract, remote notions of imago Dei. In this sense, substantive definitions of the image of God can rightly be seen as too individualistic and static." A few pages later (p. 136), van Huyssteen explains Karl Barth's view thus: "The image of God does not consist of anything humans *are* or *do*, but rather of the amazing ability or gift to be in a relationship with God." However, this is an overly simplistic way of presenting Barth's point.

The doctrine of imago Dei is supposed to address a group of different yet overlapping questions that are emphasized differently as the context changes. There are at least seven relevant questions, which are as follows:[3]

1. The question about *human, mainly cognitive, makeup*: What is it that makes us images of God?

2. The question about *uniqueness*: How does our being images of God make us special in relation to other creatures?

3. The question about *human value and dignity*: What is it about the image of God that makes us valuable?

4. The question about *function*: Does the image of God have a specific role in creation in relation to other creatures?

5. The question about the *current status* of our being images of God: How has sin affected the image of God in us?

6. The question of *resemblance*: In what way do we resemble God?

7. The question about the *divine address and response*: How should we understand the nature of the relation between God and humans?

Before proceeding further into contemporary debates, a few remarks need to be made about past ones. Traditionally, Catholic theology has emphasized the *intellect* as the locus of the imago, while Protestants have located it in *righteousness*—that is, in the life that is lived according to God's will, which requires much more than the correct use of intellect.[4] However, it is easy to see how both uses, taken in the abstract, are not able to fulfill the task that the doctrine is supposed to do. For example, if imago Dei is merely about structural cognitive faculties, then angels (and possibly higher animals) are images of God as well (and suddenly being an image of God does not seem so special). On the other hand, if imago Dei is understood in terms of our righteousness, then we, as fallen creatures, are no longer images of God. For example, Martin Chemnitz, the first Lutheran scholastic theologian, writes about imago Dei only in a christological sense. In his *Loci Theologici*, humans are treated as bearers of the image only in the past sense, while only Christ is the perfect image of God. Some Lutherans went so far as to think that humans are in fact images of Satan (*imago diabolii*).[5]

---

3. The list does not intend to be exhaustive. It merely illustrates the main concerns theologians have in speaking about imago Dei.

4. Jenson, *Systematic Theology*, 2:55.

5. See, e.g., Chemnitz, *Two Natures*, 46, 150; Chemnitz, *Loci Theologici*, 1:282, 317. The main biblical context comes from the New Testament (cf. 2 Cor. 4:4; Col. 3:10; 2 Cor.

It is true that especially after the Reformation, suspicious glances were made across confessional lines, and theologians raised questions about the ways of interpreting imago Dei.[6] But imago Dei never became a major topic in theological debate and, for this reason, churches today have only rather speculative and vague frameworks for it. Imago Dei merely functions as a placeholder for the aforementioned concerns.

Regarding Catholic and Protestant statements of imago Dei, I find it unnecessary to concentrate on their mutual differences because there is so much similarity.[7] For example, John Paul II writes in *Evangelium vitae* (36) how sin "deforms" the image of God in us, which creates both individual and communal disorder: "When God is not recognized as God, the profound meaning of man is betrayed and communion between people is compromised." In a recent study, Dominick Robinson argues that the relational aspect of imago Dei has always been a central feature, regardless of the tradition.[8] Although it would take much more time to follow this properly, I merely suggest that all the traditional theories of imago Dei tried to accommodate a combination of the aforementioned concerns according to the needs of the time. Of course, they tended to emphasize different aspects, resulting in slightly different theological anthropologies, but there is no need to set these against each other.

Aquinas on Imago Dei

What is meant by rationality then? Is it something that only humans have? In the most general terms, reason is the ability to perform inferences. Such an ability is not unique to humans. Animals are clearly able to perform inferences as well, although these inferences might be qualitatively inferior. A significant difference lies in their degree of being conscious. When a deer perceives a bear approaching, the deer forms a motivating proposition: "Flee." Humans in the same situation would think and act in the same way, except that humans

---

3:18). The intra-Lutheran Flacian controversy concentrated on the nature of the fallen human being. Notoriously, Matthias Flacius (1520–1575) claimed that after the fall, original sin is now our substance and thereby not merely an accidental property. Flacius's views were formally rejected in the Formula of Concord (1580).

6. See, e.g., Calvin, *Commentary on Genesis*, 51; Gerhard, *Loci Theologici (1610)*, 2.8.13–16.

7. The only major theme where possible disagreement lies in the nature of sin after justification (concupiscence). See Lutheran World Federation and the Catholic Church, *Joint Declaration*, 4.4.

8. D. Robinson, *Understanding the "Imago Dei,"* 5–27. The psychological analogies of the Trinity to the human mind were usually seen as speculative and addressing a too limited set of concerns and, for this reason, not of great value. For an early Protestant criticism, see, e.g., Calvin's comment on Augustine in *Commentary on Genesis*, 51.

could, in principle, form it thus: "It is 'I' who makes this inference: Flee." In other words, reason is conscious inference.[9]

In order to have relations and perform certain functions, we need to have the capacity to do so. Stones do not have meaningful relations and functions, but bees, cows, and humans do. More developed creatures have more complex and more conscious relations. Aquinas recognizes that all created beings have some kind of likeness to God (and therefore have some kind of capability to be relational), although humans are set apart as the only class of "rational beings."[10] In general, Aquinas thinks that for a being to be an image of God, it needs to have the capability to reason consciously. However, while reason (as a faculty) is a central element of the imago Dei, it cannot be either absolutely necessary nor sufficient since demons also have this capacity.[11]

For Aquinas, imago Dei means a "natural aptitude to understand and love God," which appears in degrees based on a person's progress in the way of salvation.[12] Imago Dei in humans is a reflection of God's perfect understanding

9. Tattersall, "Origin of the Human Sense of Self."
10. Aquinas's answer is worth quoting in length. *ST* 1.93.6, Resp.:
> Therefore we may observe this difference between rational creatures and others, both as to the representation of the likeness of the Divine Nature in creatures, and as to the representation in them of the uncreated Trinity. For as to the likeness of the Divine Nature, rational creatures seem to attain, after a fashion, to the representation of the species, inasmuch as they imitate God, not only in being and life, but also in intelligence, as above explained (2); whereas other creatures do not understand, although we observe in them a certain trace of the Intellect that created them, if we consider their disposition. Likewise as the uncreated Trinity is distinguished by the procession of the Word from the Speaker, and of Love from both of these, as we have seen (28, 3); so we may say that in rational creatures wherein we find a procession of the word in the intellect, and a procession of the love in the will, there exists an image of the uncreated Trinity, by a certain representation of the species. In other creatures, however, we do not find the principle of the word, and the word and love; but we do see in them a certain trace of the existence of these in the Cause that produced them. For in the fact that a creature has a modified and finite nature, proves that it proceeds from a principle; while its species points to the (mental) word of the maker, just as the shape of a house points to the idea of the architect; and order points to the maker's love by reason of which he directs the effect to a good end; as also the use of the house points to the will of the architect. So we find in man a likeness to God by way of an "image" in his mind; but in the other parts of his being by way of a "trace."

ST 1.93.2, Resp.: "It is clear, therefore, that intellectual creatures alone, properly speaking, are made to God's image."

11. Also, reason cannot be necessary because there are some cases when the person does not have active reasoning capability but still has his or her status, as in the case of unconscious patients and newborn children. See also Deane-Drummond, "God's Image and Likeness."

12. *ST* 1.93.4, Resp.:
> I answer that, Since man is said to be the image of God by reason of his intellectual nature, he is the most perfectly like God according to that in which he can best imitate God in his intellectual nature. Now the intellectual nature imitates God chiefly in this, that God understands and loves Himself. Wherefore we see that the image of God is

of himself and the trinitarian love between the Father, Son, and Holy Spirit. As images of God, humans are capable of having similar, or at least analogical, relations. These relations are based on the rational and structured nature of human cognitive psychology. But how do reason and rationality feature in Aquinas's total view of human action?

In Aquinas's philosophy of mind, an action is performed as follows. First, there is a sense experience that evokes a desire. Desires have a cognitive component that makes them communicable to will and, consequently, to reason. Will, having experienced the desire, asks reason for guidance: Is what appears to me as good actually good? Then, with its acquired notion of goodness and happiness, reason either affirms or neglects will's proposal. Will is ultimately dependent on reason for its evaluations of what is good and that which promotes happiness. If reason does not have a correct understanding of what is good, it leads us astray.[13]

For Aquinas, reason is a capacity through which virtues are able to regulate our behavior. Virtue is a disposition to perform actions that are in accord with reason: "For it was shown above that such was the rectitude of the primitive state, that reason was subject to God, and the lower powers to reason. Now the virtues are nothing but those perfections whereby reason is directed to God, and the inferior powers regulated according to the dictate of reason."[14] The *status originalis* was not natural but a gift of God.[15]

Rationality appears here in both moral and communal contexts. Humans are rational when they live virtuous lives. In many ways, rationality can be seen as our conscious fight against our natural instincts gone haywire.[16] Aquinas says, "For a good life consists in good deeds. Now in order to do good deeds, it matters not only what a man does, but also how he does it; to wit, that he

---

in man in three ways. First, inasmuch as man possesses a natural aptitude for understanding and loving God; and this aptitude consists in the very nature of the mind, which is common to all men. Secondly, inasmuch as man actually and habitually knows and loves God, though imperfectly; and this image consists in the conformity of grace. Thirdly, inasmuch as man knows and loves God perfectly; and this image consists in the likeness of glory. Wherefore on the words, "The light of Thy countenance, O Lord, is signed upon us" (Ps. 4:7), the gloss distinguishes a threefold image of "creation," of "re-creation," and of "likeness." The first is found in all men, the second only in the just, the third only in the blessed.

13. *ST* 1.82.2. See also Porter, *Nature as Reason*, 255–57.

14. *ST* 1.95.3, Resp. See also Porter, *Nature as Reason*, 187.

15. *ST* 1.95.1, Resp.

16. In this chapter, I concentrate on how rationality is attached to the practical moral virtues in Aquinas. However, rationality is also about the speculative and intellectual virtues, such as understanding, science, and wisdom. For the sake of brevity, I will not try to offer a complete view of Aquinas on this matter. It suffices to note that rationality is not just about intellectual activity but about good deeds as well—the two cannot be separated from each other.

do it from right choice and not merely from impulse or passion."[17] Herein lies one unique aspect of human rationality that sets it apart from that of animals. Animals cannot, in the proper sense, be said to exercise reflection and discretion (i.e., actions that are proposed by will and informed by virtuous reason).[18] The goodness of human beings is dependent on the extent to which we are able to actualize our rationality, and rational (and consequently good) actions are those that are willed in accordance with reason. Moral virtues and intellectual virtues are joined together by prudence and practical wisdom (i.e., *phronesis*). *Phronesis* is supposed to guide our actions so that we are able to choose the best means to match correct ends.[19] Human reason is not like angelic perception, which is able to grasp complete knowledge of a particular thing in one instant; human reason needs time and proceeds in small steps. In Aquinas's system, rationality is an exclusively human feature; angels (and God) do not need it and animals do not have it. Although it can be debated in what sense Aquinas thinks that reason is a singular faculty, this does not undercut his general view that reasoning is a complex, embodied process that aims at

17. *ST* 1.2.57.5:
Prudence is a virtue most necessary for human life. For a good life consists in good deeds. Now in order to do good deeds, it matters not only what a man does, but also how he does it; to wit, that he do it from right choice and not merely from impulse or passion. And, since choice is about things in reference to the end, rectitude of choice requires two things: namely, the due end, and something suitably ordained to that due end. Now man is suitably directed to his due end by a virtue which perfects the soul in the appetitive part, the object of which is the good and the end. And to that which is suitably ordained to the due end man needs to be rightly disposed by a habit in his reason, because counsel and choice, which are about things ordained to the end, are acts of the reason. Consequently an intellectual virtue is needed in the reason, to perfect the reason, and make it suitably affected towards things ordained to the end; and this virtue is prudence. Consequently prudence is a virtue necessary to lead a good life.
18. *ST* 1.81.3: "For in other animals movement follows at once the concupiscible and irascible appetites: for instance, the sheep, fearing the wolf, flees at once, because it has no superior counteracting appetite. On the contrary, man is not moved at once, according to the irascible and concupiscible appetites: but he awaits the command of the will, which is the superior appetite." However, what makes us special is not merely making choices but the way reason works. While animal reason is able to grasp only particular instantiations of things, human reason can grasp kinds, being more universal and general in its approach. See Pasnau, *Thomas Aquinas on Human Nature*, 323–24:
Compared with other animals, our intellect gives us an enormous advantage. Because we are able to conceive the world in terms of kinds, we can function in ways that other animals cannot. Our capacity for universal ideas allows us to draw inferences and make predictions on the basis of our classificatory schemes. It is not precisely our rationality, then, that distinguishes us from other animals, but our capacity for having ideas that are universal in comprehension. Rationality is a tactic developed to supplement the limited comprehensiveness of our ideas; it is "the result of the weakness of the intellectual light in human beings" (58.3 c). Reasoning is the crutch with which we hobble from one idea to another. God does not reason, no more than he rolls dice.
19. Stump, *Aquinas*, 76.

harmony within individual being and in relation to other beings. Therefore, Aquinas's account combines structural, functional, and relational aspects.

Jenson on Imago Dei

Robert W. Jenson offers an outline of imago Dei in the second volume of his *Systematic Theology*. Jenson tries to both answer the concerns presented earlier and keep the answers within the boundaries of evolutionary history as it now appears to us. For Jenson, to be the image of God is to be addressed by God and to respond to this address. According to Jenson, "In Genesis, the specific relation to God is as such the peculiarity attributed to humanity. If we are to seek in the human creature some feature to be called the image of God, this can only be our location in this relation. As the relation is the occurrence of a personal address, our location in it must be the fact of our reply." He continues, "That we have the dispositional property of being apt to hear and speak is of course required for the occurrence of this converse but should not be regarded as itself the human specificity—and indeed, who knows how many sorts of things possess it?"[20]

Jenson does not find it necessary to investigate whether there was some particular point in human evolution when consciousness or some other capacity emerged, and whether this very moment was the first moment when humans (in the proper sense) came into existence. In Jenson's view, humans became images of God at the point when they were addressed by God and were able to give a positive or negative answer, and this may—or may not—have coincided with the emergence of certain faculties. In this sense, imago Dei does not reside in the cognitive capacities; it is mostly constituted by divine address. However, being able to be addressed and to give an answer requires that some sort of capacities be in place and functional.

In Jenson's account, the divine address is conjoined with communal and moral dimensions. This is apparent in his account of rationality: "Rationality is not a capacity, it is rather a virtue; and irrationality is not an incapacity but a sin, of despair. Rationality is epistemic openness to God's future: it is obedience to the command, 'Be prepared to change your mind. Test your opinions, by whatever are in any instance the appropriate warrants.'"[21] Of course, in this sense virtue is the correct use of these capacities. It must be noted that a negative response to God's address is also an act that makes us images of God, though in the negative sense.

20. Jenson, *Systematic Theology*, 2:58–59.
21. Jenson, *Systematic Theology*, 2:146–47.

Being a rational person requires self-awareness, a conscious realization of one's place in the universe. In Jenson's account, rationality as virtue forms a basis for a relational understanding of imago Dei. It is noteworthy that moral responsibility is linked to how we use our reason and how our communal life is formed. Being imago Dei means being, among other things, morally responsible, and here we come back to the structure of human beings. What kind of being is capable of being morally responsible for its actions? For Jenson, human personhood is the locus of divine resemblance. As God is personhood consisting of trinitarian relations, so are humans persons in their capability to form relations.[22]

Both Jenson's and Aquinas's accounts stress imago Dei as a unity of several capacities and functions that, when properly executed, set one in right relation to one's self, one's fellow human beings, and God. Relational, functional, and structural elements of the imago Dei form a whole where everything has its proper place.

Who Bears the Image of God?

I began my inquiry by acknowledging the current trend to discard the structural approach in theological anthropology. To some extent, these claims are warranted, especially when they are targeted at one-sided interpretations. However, contemporary relational models are in danger of committing similar errors. Consequently, arguing for a structural understanding of imago Dei would be too thin a definition. The relational view is in danger of being too narrow if it neglects the structural elements of being human. Instead, we need a more holistic understanding of imago Dei that is able to incorporate all relevant elements without unnecessarily setting them against each other. A preferable definition of the imago Dei should, in principle, be able to address all the concerns listed above.

How, then, are we to speak of imago Dei without setting crucial elements against each other? One possibility is to affirm both the need for structural elements and their proper disposition toward the good. Proper functioning is structured around virtues that guide all actions of the agent, both internal and external to him or her. Rationality thereby consists of properly functioning modules and systems of inference, and rationality cannot be seen as a mere singular module or faculty but instead is seen more generally as a form of existence. There is no need to downplay the structural aspects of imago Dei,

22. Jenson, *Systematic Theology*, 2:95.

because they are not exclusive in relation to relationality and moral person-hood. If authors in the past have offered too restrictive views on human nature based on singular faculties, this does not mean that the structural concepts are now irrelevant.[23] When we speak about imago Dei, we need to understand it as a composition of several interrelated things.

With this definition, we can now answer contemporary questions regarding the limits and the use of the doctrine of imago Dei. The question concerns four kinds of entities:

angels
animals
aliens
artificial intelligences

Regarding angels and animals, I find it reasonable to follow Aquinas's tiered presentation. He thinks that animals do bear some resemblance to the divine, but because they lack full rationality, they are not images of God in the same sense as humans and angels. As he states in *ST* 1.93: "Thus the image of God is more perfect in the angels than in man, because their intellectual nature is more perfect."[24] It is well within the boundaries of Christian faith to think that animals are part of the divine drama (like angels), but on this side of the eschaton, we might never be able to recognize all the roles they play.

Some have feared that the imago Dei doctrine results in the unethical do-minion of humans over other beings in creation. However, I do not see that as a huge problem. In the classical formulation, only Christ is fully the image of God, which leaves even angels far behind, and humans are at the lowest end of all rational beings. The tiered nature of the image underlines the ways in which different beings can participate in the fullness of divine life. More-over, the higher one is in the hierarchy of beings, the more demanding one's responsibilities toward other beings in creation. Thus, the Christian vision of the cosmos enables a robust form of animal ethics.[25]

There has been some speculation about whether animals could be religious subjects. I do not find it impossible that animals might engage in some kind of

23. Thus, e.g., Corcoran, "Constitution," 204: "Recognizing relations as essential to person-hood requires *recovering* relations in our account of persons. It does not require *replacing* an ontology of particulars with one of relations as fundamental."
24. See also Deane-Drummond, "God's Image and Likeness"; Deane-Drummond, *Wisdom of the Liminal*, 56–88.
25. Deane-Drummond, *Wisdom of the Liminal*, 238–77; Hoggard Creegan, *Animal Suf-fering*, 154–72.

behavior that could be interpreted as religious, but I do not find it necessary either. Maybe we humans tend to emphasize the rational part of our conduct because it is something of who we are; it might well be that mystical union is less rational in the discursive sense and more emotional—or something that speaks primarily to our perception and imagination—and that there are beings who are able to participate in this vision without us being aware of it. Anyway, it is obvious that animals participate in the shared cosmic circle of life according to their individual natures, and for this reason they deserve our love, reverence, and care.[26]

If there are other intelligent races in the cosmos, they quite likely possess mental and moral capacities. If for some reason they would lack the divine address, they should still be regarded as beings we are obligated to respect and love as we love ourselves. However, if God exists, it is to be expected that these races have access to the divine origins of existence; this can take place in various ways, which are discussed in the next chapter. A related issue would be a scenario where we find microbial life that has developed outside Earth. Even if this life could not be said to bear the image of God, it would still be of immense value for other reasons (such as beauty, rarity, and epistemic worth).[27]

Another possible scenario is that alien life is postbiological—that is, advanced races have left the carbon-based form of existence behind. These beings would then be something like what we call "artificial intelligence."[28] Since the time of the first computers, we have entertained the possibility of creating an artificial intelligence, a computer that can think and feel like humans and have a sense of self. At the moment, we are nowhere near to developing conscious machines, and we have no idea of whether this is even possible. Our current computers have domain-specific artificial intelligences, which means that they can perform efficient high-level calculations on clearly defined matters, such as playing chess or Go. These artificial intelligences of various degrees of sophistication are everywhere in society, such as in gaming consoles, smartphones, cars, stock exchanges, and advanced weapons systems. They cannot really think, however; they just perform complex calculations based on their programming. In this, they are vastly superior to humans, and they are getting better every day.

One step forward would be artificial general intelligence (AGI). Compared to chess machines, AGI could jump from one task to another, like investing in stock markets while simultaneously playing chess and driving a car. An even further step would be the emergence of superintelligent artificial

26. For several accounts and perspectives, see Deane-Drummond, Artinian-Kaiser, and Clough, *Animals as Religious Subjects*.
27. Lovin, "Astrobiology and Theology."
28. Schneider, "Alien Minds."

intelligence (SAI).[29] One of the properties of SAI would be its ability to re-program itself, thus achieving something that might be called consciousness. If SAI were to exist, it might be possible to recognize it as the bearer of the divine image, while AGI would not pass the test. I say "might" because it is not clear whether nonbiological beings can have consciousness in the first place, at least in the same sense as humans do. For humans, reasoning is much more than just passing through logic gates. It is about engaging in a social world and being able to navigate the network of relations between other sentient beings. Humans are not rational because they are good at math but because they can apply math, among other things, in the right way.

One possible way to think about human cognition and decision making is to use the tripartite model developed by Keith Stanovich. According to him, most of our thinking happens on a subconscious level, and it is automatic, fast, and frugal. This is sometimes called intuition, and it is perceived as something very different from conscious and reflective modes of thought. Stanovich splits reflection into two types: the algorithmic mind and the reflective mind. The algorithmic mind oversees calculations, while the reflective mind controls various dispositions employed in knowledge acquisition. There are a number of reasons for making this distinction. One is that several biases hinder reflective thinking in cases where the intelligence of the test subjects is equal. Hence, there must be something else involved in conscious thinking that produces the result.[30] In fact, the hallmark of human rationality is the ability to perform functions including

> the tendency to collect information before making up one's mind, the tendency to seek various points of view before coming to a conclusion, the disposition to think extensively about a problem before responding, the tendency to calibrate the degree of strength of one's opinion to the degree of evidence available, the tendency to think about future consequences before taking action, the tendency to explicitly weigh pluses and minuses of situations before making a decision, and the tendency to seek nuance and avoid absolutism. In short, individual differences in thinking dispositions are assessing variation in people's goal management, epistemic values, and epistemic self-regulation—differences in the operation of the reflective mind.[31]

Stanovich points out that current intelligence tests solely measure the algo-rithmic mind's effectiveness, leaving rationality (in the sense of more holistic

29. Bostrom, *Superintelligence*.
30. Stanovich, *Rationality and Reflective Mind*, 34.
31. Stanovich, *Rationality and Reflective Mind*, 36.

thinking dispositions) out of the picture.[32] This has far-reaching consequences for how we think about human rationality and judgment. Interestingly, there seems to be only a very weak correlation between the algorithmic mind and the reflective mind. In other words, a person can be good at math but make very poor life choices and lack the abilities to use those skills for good. Or one may have excellent thinking dispositions by being conscientious and thorough while lacking high-level computational skills.

If SAI displayed behavior like the type described in the quotation above, it would obviously qualify as a possible bearer of the divine image. It is even possible that SAI could exist at a higher level than humans in the hierarchy of beings. This would follow from Aquinas's definition of the image as perfectly rational and virtuous action.[33]

The examination of the concept of imago Dei shows how fluid the concept is and how it has served multiple purposes in the history of the Christian church. I have offered one possible way of employing the doctrine, which I do not mean to be exhaustive, although I think it adequately captures the central uses of the concept. On the one hand, the doctrine presents Christ as the ultimate telos for all creation. On the other hand, even the tiered view of Aquinas offers us an incentive to approach all created things with reverence and acknowledge our interdependence.

32. For an overview of algorithmic reasoning, see Johnson-Laird, *How We Reason*.
33. For an argument that AIs would, in fact, be created in *our* image but they still might have a standing as part of the created order, see Herzfeld, *In Our Image*.

9

Come with Me If You Want to Live

Incarnations

The incarnation of God the Son is at the heart of Christian theology. But why did God become incarnate? Christian theologians have offered two slightly different answers to this question, both of which are in line with the short rationale expressed in the Nicene Creed of 325: "who for us men, and for our salvation, came down from heaven and was incarnate and was made man."[1] According to the first answer, the reason for the incarnation is the fall. Without the fall, there would have been no need for redemption through incarnation. A magisterial exposition of this view is Anselm of Canterbury's *Cur deus homo*. Another answer is that incarnation would have taken place even if the fall had not happened. This view is typically attributed to Irenaeus, but also to Franciscan theologians like Duns Scotus and Bonaventure. The point of incarnation is to exalt humans to a higher sphere of existence and save them from the possibility of sin. Of course, it is post hoc speculation to think about whether and how Christ would have taken incarnate form in absence of the fall, but this suffices to show the range of the answers available within the orthodox Christian tradition, as this must be borne in mind when thinking about the modes of God's revelation. Incarnation is God's way of expressing love and the means to establish contact with us. But how

1. Schaff, *Creeds of Christendom*, 1:29.

157

incarnation achieves this can be approached from different angles that need not be mutually exclusive.[2]

If a benevolent and personal God were to exist, it is likely that he would create beings that resemble him and that he would seek to bring these beings into relationship with him. Accordingly, if there are extraterrestrial beings who possess cognitive abilities that enable them to be in contact with God, it is likely that God would somehow bring about this contact. In our case, this has taken place through the incarnation of God the Son. In this chapter, I will examine the various possibilities of how God might act in relation to other created beings.

For God So Loved . . .

The topic is typically approached by using the technical term *multiple incarnations*: God reveals his nature through differing means in different contexts. Multiple incarnations can be considered to take place in at least three metaphysically different universes. The first scenario is our universe, where we have ETs living on another planet far away from us. The second scenario is a multiverse where there is no access (at least for created beings) from one universe to another. The third scenario is a multiverse with many possible worlds that are connected, so that traveling between them is possible. This possibility is imagined in Lewis's Chronicles of Narnia and other works of popular fiction. In this universe or world-ensemble, a single being could exist in several universes while appearing in each of them in a different form; for example, Aslan the Lion of Narnia is the same being that is known to us as Jesus of Nazareth.[3] In the following, I will set my examination within the first scenario (however, some of the christological problems pertain also to the two latter cases).

If we think about multiple incarnations within the purview of the first scenario, either of two options is true. Within the latter, at least one, or all four, are possible states of affairs.

1. We are alone; there is no need for other divine economies.
2. We are not alone; one or more extraterrestrial races exist.
   a. ETs are not fallen, and they have no need for redemption.
   b. ETs are fallen, and they have their own way to God, which is different from ours.

---

2. Delio, "Christ and Extraterrestrial Life"; Peters, "Astrobiology and Astrochristology."
3. See Lewis's own comments on this in Lewis, *Collected Letters*, 3:1004–5. Lewis did not think that the "Narnia multiverse" as a world-ensemble type is an actual depiction of our cosmos.

c. ETs are fallen but included in Christ's redemptive work on Earth.

d. ETs are fallen, but their nature is assumed by God in an act of incarnation on their own worlds.

For the sake of argument, we can forget 1 for now. Also, cases 2a and 2b raise no need for multiple incarnations. It is in principle possible that an alien race has not yet experienced the fall. This scenario is depicted, for example, in Lewis's novels *Out of the Silent Planet* and *Perelandra*. It is also possible that God has prepared a special economy of salvation for some races. This would be analogous to the speculations that the church fathers entertained regarding the salvation of people who never had an encounter with Christ, such as pious ancient philosophers and people living in faraway countries.[4]

Case 2c would be possible within the standard doctrine of incarnation. For example, Lewis thought that no multiple incarnations are necessary because God the Son's incarnation in Jesus of Nazareth as such had cosmic ramifications.[5] I will return to this after discussing case 2d, in which the alien race or races are fallen and there has been, or will be, an incarnation on a different planet.

Imagining Multiple Incarnations

Both atheists and Christians have objected to the idea of multiple incarnations with arguments that are relatively similar. Thomas Paine (1737–1809) writes:

> But, in the midst of those reflections, what are we to think of the Christian system of faith, that forms itself upon the idea of only one world, and that of no greater extent, as is before shown, than twenty-five thousand miles? An extent which a man walking at the rate of three miles an hour, for twelve hours in the day, could he keep on in a circular direction, would walk entirely round in less than two years. Alas! what is this to the mighty ocean of space, and the almighty power of the Creator?
>
> From whence, then, could arise the solitary and strange conceit that the Almighty, who had millions of worlds equally dependent on his protection, should quit the care of all the rest, and come to die in our world, because, they say, one man and one woman had eaten an apple? And, on the other hand, are we to suppose that every world in the boundless creation had an Eve, an apple, a serpent, and a redeemer? In this case, the person who is irreverently called the Son of God, and sometimes God himself, would have nothing else to do than

4. For an account of different options, see Vainio, "Salvation and Religious Diversity."
5. Brazier, "C. S. Lewis."

to travel from world to world, in an endless succession of deaths, with scarcely a momentary interval of life.[6]

Paine's speculative criticism does not deviate much from that of the Lutheran reformer Philipp Melanchthon, who laid out strict rules (followed for many centuries after him) for understanding the redemption in Christ from a cosmological perspective: "The Son of God is One; our master Jesus Christ was born, died, and resurrected in this world. Nor does he manifest Himself elsewhere, nor elsewhere has he died or resurrected. Therefore it must not be imagined that Christ died and was resurrected more often, nor must it be thought that in any other world without the knowledge of the Son of God, that men would be restored to eternal life."[7] Melanchthon's stance is a combination of affirmation of Aristotelian physics (which allows the existence of only one world) and christological concerns. Affirming the many-world hypothesis makes things unnecessarily messy, and since we have no evidence for multiple worlds, we have no reason to speculate accordingly.

More recently, David Wilkinson has offered four concerns in light of which multiple incarnations do seem problematic.[8] First, it might lead to a deflation of the value of Jesus, making him merely a good man used by God instead of a human-divine person whose life had cosmic relevance. Second, if direct incarnational contact is so important, why are there no multiple incarnations among different human cultures and in various times? Third, thinking that incarnation is the only right method for God to reveal himself does not have biblical support, as God engages in various forms of revelation that do not contradict or exclude each other. Fourth, incarnation is not merely about divine communication, but it involves salvation, extending beyond the single assumed nature to all creation. Therefore, a single incarnation already does seem to include in itself a cosmic perspective (Col. 1:15–20; Rom. 8:22). I recognize these as to some extent legitimate concerns, but they nonetheless do not need to make the idea of multiple incarnations obsolete. Also, I think that nothing in the core doctrines of Christian faith makes the idea of multiple incarnations opposed to orthodoxy.

We could proceed by thinking about case 2d in the following way: if God has created multiple races, it is to be expected that God would seek to establish communion with them. The fittingness of the creation of multiple races can be deduced from the Theistic Principle of Plenitude, according to which it is fitting for God to actualize beings that are worth creating in abundance. Therefore, if there are other sentient races, and incarnation is a

6. Paine, "Age of Reason," 710.
7. CR 13, 221 (*Initia Doctrinae Physicae*). Translation from Dick, *Plurality of Worlds*, 89.
8. Wilkinson, *Science*, 158–59.

proper solution for them to deal with their relationship with God, then it is fitting for God to assume an alien nature.[9] A further question concerns possible contradictions with the standard model of incarnation that follow from the assumption of an alien nature, like the view stated by the Council of Chalcedon.[10] Of modern authors, Brian Hebblethwaite has offered an argument against multiple incarnations that I take to be the best argument available. According to Hebblethwaite, multiple incarnations would lead to incoherence: "One individual subject cannot, without contradiction, be thought capable of becoming a series of individuals, or, a fortiori, a coexistent community of persons."[11] In other words, a divine person cannot become multiple individuals. I offer a summarized argument in the following.

According to the classical doctrine of incarnation, the assumed human nature means a nature consisting of "a rational soul and body." This human nature is then joined together with the divine nature, which is "consubstantial with the Father." Together these natures form one person. Hebblethwaite's concerns seem to be that something goes wrong if we say that there are two or more assumed natures (that is, human nature plus one or more extraterrestrial natures). The exact point is illustrated with the help of eschatological vision: once in heaven, Christ rules at the right hand of the Father, having assumed two natures, but which one of the assumed natures is present in this person?

Tim Pawl has offered reasons to suggest that the situation would not be as problematic as Hebblethwaite suggests.[12] Hebblethwaite thinks that multiple incarnations would lead to a state where there is a "community of persons," but in fact this is not entailed by classical Christology. Namely, assumed human

9. For a formal argument, see Collins, "Extraterrestrial Intelligence."
10. Chalcedon states:
> We, then, following the holy Fathers, all with one consent, teach men to confess one and the same Son, our Lord Jesus Christ, the same perfect in Godhead and also perfect in manhood; truly God and truly man, of a reasonable [rational] soul and body; consubstantial [coessential] with the Father according to the Godhead, and consubstantial with us according to the Manhood; in all things like unto us, without sin; begotten before all ages of the Father according to the Godhead, and in these latter days, for us and for our salvation, born of the Virgin Mary, the Mother of God, according to the Manhood; one and the same Christ, Son, Lord, Only-begotten, to be acknowledged in two natures, *inconfusedly, unchangeably, indivisibly, inseparably*; the distinction of natures being by no means taken away by the union, but rather the property of each nature being preserved, and concurring in one Person and one Subsistence, not parted or divided into two persons, but one and the same Son, and only begotten, God the Word, the Lord Jesus Christ, as the prophets from the beginning [have declared] concerning him, and the Lord Jesus Christ himself has taught us, and the Creed of the holy Fathers has handed down to us. (Quoted in Schaff, *Creeds of Christendom*, 2:62–63)
11. Hebblethwaite, "Impossibility of Multiple Incarnations," 333.
12. Pawl, "Brian Hebblethwaite's Arguments." See also Crisp, *God Incarnate*, 155–75.

nature does not as such constitute a person; Christ did not assume human person but a human nature. Therefore, assuming two natures does not mean that Christ became two persons. Even if Christ assumed a series of individual natures, he would not have become multiple individuals.

Moreover, Hebblethwaite thinks that multiple incarnations would lead to Christ having "a split personality." But given what has been said above, Christ did not assume person even if he did assume a nature, which has a rational soul. Consequently, in the person of Christ there were two rational principles, human and divine. Even though in the classical formulation Christ had two wills, this does not entail any split within his person. Adding one or more wills may sound odd, but if two wills does not constitute a split, then adding another one or more does nothing to change the situation.

Aquinas and Contemporary Accounts of Multiple Incarnations

The debate on multiple incarnations goes back to Thomas Aquinas.[13] In *Summa Theologiae* 3.3, Aquinas offers his sustained argument for the possibility of Christ, or any other person of the Trinity, to assume more than one nature. Regarding the requirement for the nature to be assumed, Aquinas claims that there must be the need for assumption, and the assumed nature must have proper dignity.[14] Human nature possesses the required dignity because it is rational and created to love God. The need for assumption follows from the fall. Therefore, of all natures known to Aquinas, only human nature is assumable. Aquinas did not consider it to be an actual question whether Christ could assume something other than human nature, but his response nonetheless offers a good framework to think about this possibility. If there are other creatures of God with an ability to know and love God, and for

13. Pawl, "Thomistic Multiple Incarnations."
14. *ST* 3.4.1, Resp.:
A thing is said to be assumable as being capable of being assumed by a Divine Person, and this capability cannot be taken with reference to the natural passive power, which does not extend to what transcends the natural order, as the personal union of a creature with God transcends it. Hence it follows that a thing is said to be assumable according to some fitness for such a union. Now this fitness in human nature may be taken from two things, viz. according to its dignity, and according to its need. According to its dignity, because human nature, as being rational and intellectual, was made for attaining to the Word to some extent by its operation, viz. by knowing and loving Him. According to its need—because it stood in need of restoration, having fallen under original sin. Now these two things belong to human nature alone. For in the irrational creature the fitness of dignity is wanting, and in the angelic nature the aforesaid fitness of need is wanting. Hence it follows that only human nature was assumable.

whom the incarnation offers a remedy, then these natures are assumable according to Aquinas's definition.[15]

Regarding the possibility of assuming more than one nature, Aquinas simply affirms God's power to assume anything that in principle is assumable:

> What has power for one thing, and no more, has a power limited to one. Now the power of a Divine Person is infinite, nor can it be limited by any created thing. Hence it may not be said that a Divine Person so assumed one human nature as to be unable to assume another. For it would seem to follow from this that the Personality of the Divine Nature was so comprehended by one human nature as to be unable to assume another to its Personality; and this is impossible, for the Uncreated cannot be comprehended by any creature. Hence it is plain that, whether we consider the Divine Person in regard to His power, which is the principle of the union, or in regard to His personality, which is the term of the union, it has to be said that the Divine Person, over and beyond the human nature which He has assumed, can assume another distinct human nature. (*ST* 3.3.7)

Aquinas compares assuming two natures to how a person owns two garments.[16] As a result, there are not two clothed persons but a person with two sets of clothes. Thereby, the human properties do not limit the divine, but the divine becomes the subject for everything that is assumed. Because God's nature is infinite, no human property can restrict its powers and abilities. However, Aquinas's analogy is somewhat limited; garments and natures are not exactly alike, as human nature seems to have a higher ontological standing than inanimate objects. Closer scrutiny is needed.

If we follow Aquinas in affirming the prima facie possibility of God to assume anything that is worth assuming, we still need to account for how this kind

---

15. Traditional theological anthropology has focused on human life, but we recently have seen new advances in animal theology; the next natural step would be an extension of this to include all possible forms of life. In *Out of the Silent Planet*, Lewis coins the term *hnau* to designate all forms of sentient life, human as well as nonhuman, subsuming them under a common category.

16. *ST* 3.3.7.2:

> For a man who has on two garments is not said to be "two persons clothed," but "one clothed with two garments"; and whoever has two qualities is designated in the singular as "such by reason of the two qualities." Now the assumed nature is, as it were, a garment, although this similitude does not fit at all points, as has been said above [*ST* 3.2.6.1]. And hence, if the Divine Person were to assume two human natures, He would be called, on account of the unity of suppositum, one man having two human natures. Now many men are said to be one people, inasmuch as they have some one thing in common, and not on account of the unity of suppositum. So likewise, if two Divine Persons were to assume one singular human nature, they would be said to be one man, as stated [*ST* 3.2.6, Resp. 1], not from the unity of suppositum, but because they have some one thing in common.

of assumption of multiple natures makes sense. Contemporary philosophical theology has revisited the old debates concerning the person of Christ, deepening our understanding on the matter and also offering new ways of thinking about it.[17] Moreover, several contemporary scholars have argued in favor of multiple incarnations. I offer here the outline of this discussion.[18] Taking up the main versions of contemporary analytical Christology, Robin Collins argues that all except one model are compatible with the idea of multiple incarnations.[19]

According to two-minds theory (mentioned briefly earlier), as a result of assumption Christ now has two centers of consciousness.[20] This is entailed by a central and widely accepted christological maxim: "If anyone has put his trust in Him as a Man without a human mind, he is really bereft of mind, and quite unworthy of salvation. For that which He has not assumed He has not healed; but that which is united to His Godhead is also saved."[21] Thereby, in Christ there are now two minds or centers of consciousness: the eternal, divine mind and the created, human mind. The human mind is limited and does not have access to some of the things that are in reach of the divine mind. This means that Christ could grow in wisdom (Luke 2:52) even though as the eternal Son of God he is all-knowing.

How can we make sense of someone having two minds? The following analogies have been suggested as possible ways of grasping what this could mean, even if it must be borne in mind that they do not constitute an identical situation to incarnation.[22] For example, we can divide our consciousness to perform two tasks at the same time, like speaking to someone while driving a car. In this case, there is only one person or agent who oversees both actions. Another analogy is that of method acting. A talented actor assumes a character of her role and then lets this character guide her actions on the stage. While in character the actor retains her own beliefs, but she is able to enter into the mind of the character she plays. If incarnation is like this, there seems to be no reason why God could not assume more than one nature, as there is no obvious limit to how many roles an actor may assume or how many tasks we can perform simultaneously.

17. On the early twentieth-century debate between E. L. Mascall and E. A. Milne, see Wilkinson, *Science*, 164–66.

18. Pawl, "Brian Hebblethwaite's Arguments"; Collins, "Extraterrestrial Intelligence"; Brazier, "C. S. Lewis"; Fisher and Fergusson, "Karl Rahner."

19. Collins, "Extraterrestrial Intelligence."

20. This view has been defended by, e.g., T. Morris, *Logic of God Incarnate*; and Swinburne, *Christian God*.

21. Gregory of Nazianzus, *Epistle 101*. The quote appears in relation to Apollinarian teachings, according to which Christ did not assume a human rational soul, or mind (*nous*).

22. The general problem with christological and trinitarian analogies is that they typically end up being heretical if taken literally.

The enhypostatic view denies the two-minds view and argues that Christ had only one mind, the human mind, which was deeply interpenetrated by the divine mind. Agency thus belonged solely to Jesus of Nazareth, who through his will brought about actions in accordance with the divine will. The enhypostatic view is supposed to help us solve some christological paradoxes and take seriously certain biblical teachings. Moreover, there is no reason to object to multiple incarnations.[23]

The only contemporary model that does not seem to fit well with multiple incarnations is the kenotic model, according to which God the Son empties himself (Phil. 2:6–8) of his divine properties during incarnation. Kenosis effectively means that God the Son ceases to possess properties like omniscience and infinite power, and as a consequence of this, during his incarnation on Earth in the first century, God the Son had no access to the minds of the other persons in the Trinity and did not share the functions classically attributed to the Logos (Heb. 1:3; Col. 1:17). Therefore, God the Son would be unable to incarnate somewhere else during his incarnation in a particular place (like Earth). Collins argues that if the number of alien races is very high, this model is not very plausible, though not totally impossible.[24]

In sum, nothing in the classical formulations of Christology rules out the possibility of multiple incarnations unless one thinks that the enhypostatic view is the only possible solution to the christological paradoxes. Here I have merely argued that multiple incarnations are possible. I have argued neither that they are actual nor that they should be the way that God must act in the cosmic scenario where multiple other races exist in the cosmos.

No Need for Other Incarnations

Case 2c offers an approach without any need for multiple incarnations, but it raises some problems of its own.

2c. ETs are fallen but included in Christ's redemptive work on Earth.

This view seems to be the one favored by some patristic and medieval thinkers.[25] Christ dies and rises only once here on Earth because it would not be fitting

23. K. Ward, *Religion and Revelation*, 265–73. See also Collins, "Extraterrestrial Intelligence," 219–20. A variation of this view is Karl Rahner's doctrine of incarnation; see Fisher and Fergusson, "Karl Rahner."
24. Collins, "Extraterrestrial Intelligence," 223–24.
25. The biblical basis of this is highlighted in David Bentley Hart's translation of John 3:17: "For God sent the Son into the cosmos not that he might pass judgment on the cosmos,

for Christ to die over and over again.[26] But this seems to lead to problems. First, it seems that humans somehow won in a cosmic lottery. Why did we, not some other race, have the honor of hosting God the Son in our midst? Second, there is a problem concerning epistemic access. Christian theology ordinarily presupposes that the benefit of incarnation needs to be appropriated through conscious faith in order to be effective. Apparently, ETs do not have the same epistemic access to Christ as we do, and this would seem to bar them from the benefits of incarnation.

The first problem does not pose a great challenge. As has been noted previously, God works in mysterious ways. Choosing our planet from millions of planets differs only in degree from electing Israel from among the nations (Gen. 12). In fact, that our planet is nothing special and in the middle of nowhere (from the grand cosmic perspective) fits well with God's revealed character as one who seeks the lost and unworthy.

The second problem is more challenging. How exactly is Christ's work supposed to help ETs?[27] As far I see it, the possible answers boil down to the following options, out of which any one or any combination of 1–4 are prima facie possible.

1. ETs do not need direct epistemic access to Christ.

2. ETs can refer to Christ through a different description.

---

but that the cosmos might be saved through him." Hart, *New Testament*, 174. Hart explains later his choice of words thus:

> For the late antique cultures from which the New Testament came, the "cosmos" was quite literally a magnificent and terribly elaborate *order* of reality that comprehended nature (understood as a rational integrity organized by metaphysical principles), the essential principles of the natural and animal human condition (flesh and soul, for instance, with all their miseries), the spiritual world (including the hierarchies of the "divine," the angelic, and the daemonic), the astral and planetary heavens (understood as a changeless realm at once physical and spiritual), as well as social, political, and religious structures of authority and power (including the governments of human beings, angels, celestial "daemons," gods, terrestrial demons, and whatever other mysterious forces might be hiding behind nature's visible forms). It is a vision of the whole of things that is utterly unlike any with which most of us are today familiar, and that simply does not correspond to any meaning of "world" intuitively obvious to us. (559)

26. For example, William Vorilong (d. 1463) thought that "as to the question whether Christ by dying on this earth could redeem the inhabitants of another world, I answer that he is able to do this even if the worlds were infinite, but it would not be fitting for Him to go unto another world that he must die again." Quoted in Crowe, *Extraterrestrial Life Debate*, 8–9. Origen (*De principiis* 2.3.4–5) also argued that Christ suffers and dies only once.

27. For a good overview of various "astrochristological" positions and an argument for a single incarnation, see Peters, "Astrobiology and Astrochristology." Peters, however, does not explain how exactly Christ's work on Earth is supposed to benefit other races.

3. ETs are offered a way of referring directly to Christ through some special revelation of their own.

4. There is a need to evangelize ETs and to bring the message about Christ to them.

In the first case, there would be no required conscious epistemic stance for ETs to participate in the divine economy. A similar case on Earth might be the fate of higher animals. However, if there are higher races with cognitive skills like ours, it still might be that Christ's incarnation is God's way of dealing with humans only; other races belong to a different kind of divine economy. This may sound odd, but it is not totally unheard of. For example, Christians believe that angels belong to a different economy of salvation. Their fate is decided by a single act of obedience or rebellion, and Christ's sacrifice does not have for them a salvific function (although it may have some other functions).[28]

In the second scenario, it is possible that ETs have their own version of general revelation, which nevertheless guarantees access to Christ's benefits. Maybe they have higher cognitive skills and, consequently, access to a more accurate version of natural theology than humans.[29] When speaking about the divine, they might be referring to the Trinity and Christ but with different terms. For example, I can say "that affluent bachelor," "Bruce Wayne," and "Batman" without being aware that I am referring to a single person.

The third option requires God somehow giving access to Christ's benefits through a special revelation or visitation. There would be no incarnation but merely a messenger who would proclaim the divine revelation to that group of beings. This option would not involve our efforts or rely on our ability to travel to the stars. The fourth option would require us to be cosmic messengers to the other races. This scenario has been depicted in novels like Mary Doria Russell's *The Sparrow* and, to some extent, Lewis's *Perelandra*, where Ransom becomes a kind of Christ figure on Venus.

It is hard to tell which one of these options is the correct one. The cosmic distances are so vast that even if there were other races in the cosmos, we very well might never hear from them, and even if we did hear from them, we would likely never meet or really converse with them. This fact does make the fourth option somewhat unlikely.

28. On classical doctrine of angels, see, e.g., Chemnitz, *Loci Theologici*, 1:172–79; and *ST* 1.50.

29. For example, Anselm of Canterbury argued in the *Monologion* that it was in principle possible to grasp the doctrine of the Trinity without special revelation. M. Brown, "Faith and Reason."

In this chapter, I have laid out all the possibilities that I see as conceivable from the point of view of classical Christology. Because the issue is so speculative, it is hard to evaluate which one of these is the most probable. Each of them has its limits and problems, but in most cases the challenges are not overwhelming. Thus, I think all the options are possible, at least in principle, although some have more plausibility than others. If we ever make contact with an alien race, then and only then will we have access to evidence that narrows down our options.

10

To Boldly Go

Beings in Search of Greater Understanding

In this final chapter, I use C. S. Lewis's theory of the interplay of reason and imagination as an example for how to think constructively about our place in the cosmos. Imagination is for Lewis a medium that reveals to us the structure of the world, although it does not reveal it *simpliciter*. We can also use our imagination to reconstruct things that we know so that we can have new concepts and ideas that we have not yet experienced firsthand. The view of imagination that the mature Lewis embraces takes its cue from multiple sources. As he argues against several false or extreme views, his constructive view closely resembles that of Augustine and Boethius: only God knows things perfectly, while we see things "through a glass, darkly." Nonetheless, the things we perceive are real but imperfect. For Lewis, imagination is not about truth, and therefore an additional source of knowledge—namely, reason—is needed. These mental faculties are tools that require training in order to be used correctly. The refinement of our imagination and reason enables us to adopt a holistic view of reality. Conversely, a corrupted imagination and reason hide reality from us. Together reason and imagination provide us with the greatest epistemic desideratum: understanding. In this way, Lewis offers us a model of the ideal epistemic stance.

Entering a Strange Space

In *Out of the Silent Planet*, when the space traveler Ransom leaves Earth and enters space, his mind captures an image of the universe that he had lost.

> A nightmare, long engendered in the modern mind by the mythology that follows in the wake of science, was falling off him. He had read of "Space": at the back of his thinking for years had lurked the dismal fancy of the black, cold vacuity, the utter deadness, which was supposed to separate the worlds. He had not known how much it affected him till now—now that the very name "Space" seemed a blasphemous libel for this empyrean ocean of radiance in which they swam. He could not call it "dead"; he felt life pouring into him from it every moment. How indeed should it be otherwise, since out of this ocean all the worlds and all their life had come? He had thought it barren: he now saw that it was the womb of worlds, whose blazing and innumerable offspring looked down nightly even upon the earth with so many eyes—and here, with how many more! No: Space was the wrong name. Older thinkers had been wiser when they named it simply the heavens—the heavens which declared the glory . . .[1]

Lewis here uses Ransom's character to illustrate a deep philosophical feature of our understanding: our discursive thinking is constituted by two faculties of mind: reason and imagination. This theme is central in Lewis's writings, and he uses his fiction to give a pictorial form to a theory that is ancient yet still relevant.[2] Lewis draws from very old sources, but he is not alone in doing so. Similar sentiments have been expressed, for example, by Michael Polanyi:

> The book of Genesis and its great pictorial illustrations, like the frescoes of Michelangelo, remain a far more intelligent account of the nature and origin of the universe than the representation of the world as a chance collocation of atoms. . . . The scientific picture denies any meaning to the world, and indeed ignores all our most vital experience of this world. The assumption that the world has some meaning which is linked to our own calling as the only morally responsible beings in the world is an important example of the supernatural aspect of experience which Christian interpretations of the universe explore and develop.[3]

To grasp Lewis's and Polanyi's point, let us take a closer look at how Lewis employs the concepts of reason and imagination. I will first offer a

---

1. Lewis, *Out of the Silent Planet*, 32.
2. Guite, "C. S. Lewis," 425.
3. Polanyi, *Personal Knowledge*, 300.

brief account of reason and imagination as they appear in both his fictional and his philosophical works. Then I will move to examine these themes from the viewpoint of the history of ideas. Lewis's mature vision of imagination is closely related to ancient and medieval philosophers, which he uses to make sense of his own existential condition as a modern person who lives in the world of science but refuses to view the world from the point of view of science alone.

The basic stance of Lewis concerning the world around him is heavily influenced by Platonism.[4] In *The Last Battle*, Professor Digory Kirke exclaims "It's all in Plato!" as he and the children go from Narnia to Aslan's country, where everything is bigger, better, and greater than in the shadowlands they have just left behind. Here Lewis emphasizes one particular ontological feature of his fiction: everything in this world points toward something greater: "The further up and the further in you go, the bigger it gets. The inside is larger than the outside."[5] Also, his philosophical and apologetic works suggest a movement from the world of philosophy and reason to theology and revelation. Here Lewis employs a broadly Thomistic principle: grace does not destroy nature but presupposes it. As he states in "De Futilitate": "You are not moved into a totally new world; you are given more and purer of what you already had in a small quantity and badly mixed with foreign elements."[6] However, there is no necessary or smooth ascension from one world to another. We may be misled by both false images and false judgments of reason. In these shadowlands, science, philosophy, and theology suffer from a lack of direct sunlight. And if the sun may momentarily be gazed upon, it can never be fully grasped.

Corruption of Reason and Imagination

In *Surprised by Joy*, Lewis offers an account of his intellectual and spiritual life with the help of the concepts of intellect and imagination. He characterizes his pre-conversion mindset thus: "Such, then, was the state of my imaginative life; over against it stood the life of my intellect. The two hemispheres of my

4. Good overviews of Platonic themes in Lewis are Fisher, "C. S. Lewis"; and Carnell, *Bright Shadow of Reality*, 67–72.

5. Lewis, *Last Battle*, 160–73. A relatively similar Platonist vision, although even more exuberant, is depicted in the ecstatic ending scene in Lewis, *Perelandra*, 260–82. Thus, both his early and late literary fiction utilize a similar cosmological ontology.

6. Lewis, "De Futilitate," 270. Here Lewis also expresses his hesitation regarding whether the solution to the problems of human knowledge is simply "more reason," because the things of the world are often too complicated as such to be known in the first place.

mind were in the sharpest contrast. On the one side a many-islanded sea of poetry and myth; on the other a glib and shallow 'rationalism.' Nearly all that I loved I believed to be imaginary; nearly all that I believed to be real I thought grim and meaningless."[7] Lewis explains that his problem was an inability to reconcile these two sides of himself with each other, which eventually led to a point where he could enjoy neither the fruits of imagination nor deliverances of reason. Later, his conversion to theism helped him to reconcile these two things.[8]

What would be the actual consequences of not being able to form a union between these? There are several examples in Lewis's works of how both reasoning and imagining can go terribly wrong. Lewis's antagonism to scientism is visible already in his early Ransom Trilogy. Especially Weston, the main evil character in *Out of the Silent Planet*, is depicted as an epitome of modern and abusive scientistic rationalism. Weston is then contrasted with the Martian *soreni*, an alien species that has also mastered advanced technological and philosophical skills, but without the distortions from which Weston suffers.[9]

Another case of reason's corruption occurs when Ransom tastes a delicious fruit in Perelandra (i.e., Venus), and his reason tells him to have another bite. Lewis writes, "Yet something seemed opposed to this 'reason.' It is difficult to suppose that this opposition came from desire, for what desire would turn from so much deliciousness? But for whatever cause, it appeared to him better not to taste again." Here it is not reason but Ransom's renewed vision that sets things straight (it is reason that *tempts* Ransom). He imagines things differently so that he understands (though not consciously) that there are greater things to be desired.[10]

Especially in Weston's character we see an increasing corruption as the story unfolds in three novels. He is first depicted in *Out of the Silent Planet* as seeking only a spread of the human race throughout the stars, while in *Perelandra* his vision of reality is completely taken over by evil; first only the judgments of his intellect are corrupted, while later his complete vision also comes under the spell of the "Bent Eldil" and he leaves his humanity behind, becoming "the Un-man."[11] In *Perelandra*, Weston the Un-man attempts to poison the imagination of the Green Lady by telling stories that are half-truths

7. Lewis, *Surprised by Joy*, 170.
8. For more detail, see Guite, "C. S. Lewis."
9. Lewis, *Out of the Silent Planet*, chaps. 15–16.
10. Lewis, *Perelandra*, 46.
11. On Weston's twisted imagination, see the long dialogues in *Perelandra*, chaps. 13 and 7. It is notable that in chap. 7 Weston describes the world in broadly Blakean terms (God and devil, good and bad, truth and untruth are just different sides of the same coin). Wesley Kort (*C. S. Lewis*, 115) offers a helpful distinction between destructive and creative imagination: "In the first the individual reduces the world to his or her own desires, making it a projection not only of

in order to pervert her conception of her own status. Lewis depicts the effects of Un-man's speech as follows: "It became harder to recall her mind to the *data*—a command from Maleldil, a complete uncertainty about the results of breaking it. . . . The turgid swell of indistinctly splendid images which the Un-man aroused, and the transcendent importance of the central image, carried all this away. She was still in her innocence. No evil intention had been formed in her mind. But if her will was uncorrupted, half her imagination was already filled with bright, poisonous shapes."[12]

A similar process of the corruption of the imagination takes place in *The Lion, the Witch and the Wardrobe* as the White Queen corrupts the mind of Edmund by telling lies about his brothers and sisters.[13] The role of feelings and images is underlined in *The Screwtape Letters* when Screwtape advises Wormwood to use feelings instead of an "intellectual attack" to lure the newly converted man from his faith, since these images (of war) can persuade him to believe that this is the way "the world is *really* like."[14] In *The Magician's Nephew*, the erudite Uncle Andrew cannot understand the language of animals because of his moral corruption, and he seeks to use the magical features of Narnia only for profit and personal gain. In sum, several evil characters are portrayed as seekers of various actual but limited goods who have sealed themselves off from the greater reality.[15] In contrast, Professor Digory Kirke, for example, appears as a positive Socratic teacher of true wisdom,[16] and through his experiences Ransom bit by bit grows to embrace a greater vision.

If we were to locate this very brief overview of Lewis's literary characters in the world of historical theology, where should we look? We know that Lewis was very familiar with Augustine's *Confessions*, as he quotes the Latin original in his writings several times.[17] An important passage in Augustine illustrates well the principles we see in Lewis's characters:

For just as in violent acts, if the emotion of the soul from whence the violent impulse springs is depraved and asserts itself insolently and mutinously—and just as in the acts of passion, if the affection of the soul which gives rise to

---

self but also only of some part of the actual or potential self. In the second a person is placed in a larger or more complex world that calls him or her to be not less than but more than before."

12. Lewis, *Perelandra*, 165. Earlier (p. 154) Lewis writes on the effect of the Un-man's stories on the Green Lady's mind: "What emerged from the stories was rather an image than an idea." Later, in chap. 11, Ransom is also haunted by *images* of doubt.

13. See also M. Ward, *Planet Narnia*, 170.

14. Lewis, *Screwtape Letters*, 153.

15. For a short overview of characters suffering from various forms of intellectual corruption, see Kort, *C. S. Lewis*, 42–43.

16. Lewis, *Lion, the Witch and the Wardrobe*, 46–48.

17. E.g., Lewis, "Christianity and Culture," 74; Lewis, *Surprised by Joy*, 230.

carnal desires is unrestrained—so also, in the same way, errors and false opinions contaminate life if the rational soul itself is depraved. Thus it was then with me, for I was ignorant that my soul had to be enlightened by another light, if it was to be partaker of the truth, since it is not itself the essence of truth.[18]

Here Augustine uses a triadic notion to define the ways in which sin can corrupt our life. Depending on which part of the soul it touches, it can corrupt our actions, desires, and rational judgments. Most notably, Augustine states that not one of the three compartments of our soul is in itself the source of truth. The three compartments are vital to us, even to the extent that without them we would not be fully human; yet they are not sources of truth as such, without divine illumination. For both Augustine and Lewis, what causes our desiring and reasoning to go wrong is inordinate love. Thus, our desires also influence our reasoning. In order to acquire knowledge, we need to learn to love.

Reason and Imagination in Unison

In "Language of Religion," Lewis argues for a view according to which religious language is typically used not in a scientific sense but in an "ordinary" or a "poetic" one. He gives us three sentences that are different responses to the same reality:

(ordinary language)   "It was very cold."
(scientific language) "There was 13 degrees of frost."
(poetry)   "Ah, bitter chill it was!"

Scientific language is very precise, but it does not convey the experience or feeling of a thing, just as looking at the thermometer tells how cold it *is* but does not reveal how cold it *feels*. Because religion involves the whole of the human person, it is only natural that religious language addresses us also in poetic form and with the help of images.[19] But what are these images?

In his essay "Bluspels and Flalansferes," Lewis offers a substantive account of the relation of reason and imagination:

But it must not be supposed that I am in any sense putting forward the imagination as the organ of truth. We are not talking of truth, but of meaning: meaning

18. *Confessions* 4.15.25 (trans. A. C. Outler, 68–69). For a similar account, see also Boethius, *Consolation of Philosophy*, 5.1.

19. Lewis, "Language of Religion," 255–66.

which is the antecedent condition both of truth and falsehood, whose antithesis is not error but nonsense. I am a rationalist. For me, reason is the natural organ of truth; but imagination is the organ of meaning. Imagination, producing new metaphors or revivifying old, is not the cause of truth, but its condition. It is, I confess, undeniable that such a view indirectly implies a kind of truth or rightness in the imagination itself. I said at the outset that the truth we won by metaphor could not be greater than the truth of metaphor itself; and we have seen since that all our truth, or all but a few fragments, is won by metaphor.[20]

This is a very rich passage that requires some patience to unpack. First, it is good to note that Lewis argues that imagination always comes *before* reason because meaning is the necessary condition for speaking about the truth.[21] In his mature discussion of imagination, Lewis seems to employ a broadly medieval view of the faculties of mind. In the medieval model, it belongs to imagination to form the relation to the world through "phantasms" (mental images) before reason starts judging and assessing what has been encountered.[22]

In medieval philosophy, this was the primary function of imagination: it provided direct access to reality. However, already in the writings of Augustine (who was the first to translate the Greek word *phantasma* as Latin *imaginatio*) imagination is understood as a faculty that can construct new knowledge.[23] In *Epistle* 7.3.6, he tells how as a little boy he had never seen the ocean but could form an idea of the ocean by looking at the water in his cup (something similar takes place in *The Voyage of the Dawn Treader* when the painting of the sea and the ship comes alive and absorbs the children).

20. Lewis, "Bluspels and Flalansferes," 265.
21. For Lewis's account of medieval philosophy of mind, see Lewis, *Discarded Image*, 152–97.
22. To put it briefly, imagination has been understood in two different but interrelated senses: imagination can refer to (1) knowledge acquisition in general or (2) construction of new knowledge based on something that has been previously known. Lewis employs both of these. See, e.g., Schakel, "'Feeding the Imagination,'" 3. In the first case, imagination is the first thing that happens in the act of knowing. Aristotle states in *On the Soul* 3.7, "The soul understands nothing without a phantasm." This phantasm is the thing we perceive when we know something. In this first use, imagination simply means the process by which our mind represents the world. If I know that this thing in my hand is a pen, I know this only because I have an experience of a particular sensible image. See Spruit, *Classical Roots*, 37–38, 45–46. Aristotle's influence is apparent when, for example, Aquinas argues that we cannot think *at all* if the phantasm is not in our sensible part of the soul. This is generally known as *conversio ad phantasmata*. *ST* 1.84.7: "It is impossible for our intellect to understand anything actually, except by turning to the phantasms." In medieval Latin, "convert" means, among other things, the adaption of new form. Thus, in the moment of knowledge, we are joined with the thing we know. This joining means that our minds are formed according to the image we perceive. In a very specified sense, we become the things we see. See, e.g., *ST* 1.78; *De veritate* 10.6.7.
23. For a discussion on imagination in the history of Western philosophy, see Palmén, *Richard of St. Victor's Theory of Imagination*.

The reproductive function of imagination is introduced in *De musica* (6.32), where Augustine writes how our mind can create new objects by adding and reducing the properties we have previously sensed. In this way, we can create things that have no counterpart in concrete reality: we can imagine possibilities.[24]

In *Surprised by Joy*, Lewis tells about his friendship with Owen Barfield, whom he regarded as his anti-self, "who had read all the right books but has got the wrong thing out of every one."[25] Lewis coined the term "Great War" to describe his peculiar relationship with Barfield, with whom he vehemently disagreed about the meaning of imagination. Barfield insisted that imagination is a source of truth whereas Lewis came to deny this. Even if for Lewis phantasms reflect the "shape of the reality,"[26] they do not represent reality pure and simple. He describes his mature, post-conversion view thus: "I think all things, in their way, reflect heavenly truth, the imagination not least. 'Reflect' is the important word. This lower life of the imagination is not a beginning of, nor a step toward, the higher life of the spirit, merely an image."[27]

In his mature conception of imagination, Lewis is trying to avoid three very different views that in diverse ways prevent the correct use of reason and imagination. The first is Barfield's idealism, which does not draw a distinction between true and false images. In the idealistic view, everything that we perceive is true since the distinction between the reality and the unreality of the object has been removed. In this way, Barfield could claim that imagination as such is a source of truth. While flirting with absolute idealism for a while, Lewis eventually came to see it as an untenable view: "For take away the object, and what, after all, would be left?—a whirl of images, a fluttering sensation in the diaphragm, a momentary abstraction."[28]

Second, Lewis does not think that we perceive reality simply as it is, called "naive realism." He adopts a sort of Kantian view (to use contemporary terms), which denies that we have direct access to reality.[29] However, images

24. Palmén, *Richard of St. Victor's Theory of Imagination*, 30–31.
25. Lewis, *Surprised by Joy*, 199.
26. Lewis, *Surprised by Joy*, 167.
27. Lewis, *Surprised by Joy*, 167. Lewis adds here an important footnote: "I.e., not necessarily and by its own nature. God can cause it to be such a beginning." In Scholastic theology and philosophy, it was also typical to give warnings for taking imagination too seriously. See, e.g., Ockham's warnings in *Quodlibeta* 3, 20, 3.
28. Lewis, *Surprised by Joy*, 168.
29. On the possibly Kantian influences in Lewis, see *Discarded Image*, 218: "Part of what we now know is that we cannot, in the old sense, 'know what the world universe is like' and that no model we can build will be, in that old sense, 'like' it." However, Lewis's point here seems

can function as partial pointers toward something more real.[30] When Ransom meets the shape-shifting angels Mars and Venus on Perelandra, after they have chosen a form that Ransom is able to perceive, he asks whether they see each other as they are. The answer given by Mars is that "only Maleldil sees any creatures as it really is." Then Ransom inquires whether he is "only perceiving an appearance." The answer of Mars is that, in fact, "you have never seen more than an appearance of anything—not of Arbol, nor of a stone, nor of your own body."[31] Also in *Till We Have Faces*, it is hinted that our images of the divine are slowly developing toward a greater likeness of reality.[32]

It is possible that Lewis was influenced by Boethius (and not by Kant, as Barfield suggested) when presenting this mediated form of knowledge. After all, he did say that *The Consolation of Philosophy* was one of the works that influenced him most.[33] In the fifth chapter, Boethius presents a quick sketch of his philosophy of mind. According to Boethius, only God has perfect knowledge of both particular and universal things. Human knowledge instead proceeds as follows: sense perception (*sensus*) is processed by imagination (*imaginatio*), which is then handed over to reason (*ratio*) for rational evaluation. Ideally, the end of this process is called "understanding" (*intelligentia*), which is perfectly instantiated only by God but in some rare cases by humans as well.[34] In other words, human knowledge is always only partial, and true wisdom is attainable only for those who strive for it. The mediating function of reason and imagination that Lewis adopts to counter Barfield's idealism can be seen not as a resorting to Kantianism but as a view held by one of his most treasured medieval authors. This Boethian account enlightened Lewis's words in "Bluspels," where he claims that "reason is the natural organ of truth; but imagination is the organ of meaning." Also, the understanding that Boethius talks about could easily be seen as an ideal stance toward the

---

to be that the "old sense" primarily refers to nineteenth-century Enlightenment and positivists' views. Also, Barfield argued that Lewis was a Kantian. See Morris and Welding, "Coleridge." Already Plato (*Sophist* 264a) and Aristotle (*On the Soul* 428a20–25), while discussing the role of phantasms in human knowing, argued that phantasms are in a way similar to opinions, as they can be true or false. See Palmén, *Richard of St. Victor's Theory of Imagination*, 20–23.

30. Lewis, *Surprised by Joy*, 197–98.

31. Lewis, *Perelandra*, 255. In *A Grief Observed*, Lewis refers to images by acknowledging that we need them, but also it is God's intention to break our images of the divine. God is "the great iconoclast." See, e.g., Lewis, *A Grief Observed*, 51–53.

32. See especially Lewis, *Till We Have Faces*, chap. 2, sec. 4.

33. For Lewis's brief outline of Boethius, see Lewis, *Discarded Image*, 75–90; Armstrong, "Boethius."

34. Boethius, *Consolation of Philosophy*, 5.4–5. See also Palmén, *Richard of St. Victor's Theory of Imagination*, 35.

universe, which is perhaps most lucidly defined by Lewis in his account of
"enjoyment" and "contemplation."[35]

The third false view that Lewis seeks to avoid is extreme scientism (a view
that denies the role of imagination altogether). The scientistic attitude reduces
our means of thinking about the meaning of things. This is illustrated well by
the above quotation of Ransom's experience of space. His previous scientism
gave him only a very limited perspective of the meaning of the cosmos, which
was not different from the accounts of several twentieth-century scientists and
philosophers whom I quoted at the beginning of chapter 6.

So how can we benefit from Lewis's account of reason and imagination?
I note here four principles that arise from Lewis's writings. First, our proper
stance toward the world is one of both curiosity and epistemic humility. There
are always more things to know, and the things we think we know may be false
after all. We have an epistemic duty to increase our knowledge of the world,
which goes hand in hand with the duty to avoid making claims of knowledge
when we are not entitled to do so.

Second, it is not possible to approach the world from the viewpoint of mere
reason.[36] We always perceive the world through our imaginative faculty, and
reason starts to function only after that. Therefore, the world as we perceive it
is always already an interpretation. This does not mean naive relativism or absolute perspectivism. We can have factual knowledge, but often our knowledge
is only a part of a greater whole and open to improvement and corrections.

Third, reason and imagination are not faculties that are in conflict; instead,
they have different purposes and both are needed. Imagination opens us to
the world of possibilities. With the help of mere reason, we could not think
of other possibilities, some of which may eventually be true. Yet many of
these possibilities turn out to be false. It is the task of reason to analyze the
gifts of imagination.

Fourth, the unison of reason and imagination enables the sense of awe and
wonder that speaks not only to our minds but also to our hearts. However, there
are different kinds of awe. A commandant of a concentration camp may feel
awe when he looks at his little kingdom, where everything runs smoothly or
orderly, and where everything exists to serve his will. A scientist may feel awe

35. Lewis, *Surprised by Joy*, 217–19. Lewis quite early on adopted Samuel Alexander's
distinction between contemplation and enjoyment, and rejected the notion that imagination,
pure and simple, could tell us whether what we experience is true, or that imagination could
by itself reveal to us spiritual truths. The Alexandrian stance, instead, enables us to see reality
in its fullness. See also Schakel, "'Feeding the Imagination,'" 10–11.

36. Lewis, *Miracles*, chap. 3, "The Cardinal Difficulty of Naturalism"; Schakel, "'Feeding the
Imagination,'" 19–21. For a discussion, see Reppert, *C. S. Lewis's Dangerous Idea*; Wielenberg,
God and the Reach of Reason, 93–108.

when she looks in the telescope or microscope and understands how complex the world is, and how far she is from grasping it. In the first case, one approaches the cosmos from the viewpoint of power, control, and benefit. In the latter case, one almost becomes insignificant in light of the whole. This experience, however, helps one to adopt more consciously the three earlier points.

In *Perelandra*, the inhabitants are told by Maleldil (God) not to go to the Fixed Land but to stay on the moving islands. After some trials, the Green Lady understands the meaning of this strange commandment: "And why should I desire the Fixed except to make sure—to be able on one day to command where I should be the next and what should happen to me?"[37] The correct epistemic stance, illustrated by Maleldil's command, creates a space where the person is not in control of what may happen to him or her. This is not a prison. Instead, it secures that persons remain persons when they go about trying to understand the nature of the cosmos. They must remain open to whatever may arise.

Conclusion: The Next Steps

How should these principles be used in our thinking about cosmology from a theological perspective? A critic might argue that the genre of Lewis's Ransom Trilogy is not what is nowadays called "hard science fiction"; that is to say, his emphasis is not on scientific theories and technical detail, and Lewis creatively employs aspects of the pre-Copernican view of the cosmos, which he knows to be scientifically false. Thus, the obvious question is whether Lewis's cosmology is too detached from the scientific worldview to be taken seriously.

I argue that the philosophical point that Lewis is trying to make could easily be incorporated into modern cosmology. As has been noted, Lewis resisted the scientistic worldview that was "all fact and no meaning." By setting his stories within a nonscientific worldview, he wished to underline the meaning that was lost as "mere facts" had taken over our imagination. In *The Voyage of the Dawn Treader*, Eustace observes empirically, and reductively, that "a star is a huge ball of flaming gas." But Ramandu, a personified star, answers that "[that] is not what a star is but only what it is made of."[38]

In February 2017, the journal *Nature* published a short science-fiction story to accompany the announcement of the finding of the Trappist-1 system.[39] In the story, experiences of a future member of the human race are used to translate to us the meaning of the discovery. The three exoplanets somewhere out there

37. Lewis, *Perelandra*, 208.
38. Lewis, *Voyage of the Dawn Treader*, 159.
39. Suhner, "Terminator," 512.

are not just spheres of rock, metals, and possibly water. They are something more. We can grasp this intuitively, and good literature can help us think through the questions of meaning, even if it is often hard for us. Nonetheless, reaching toward this understanding is perhaps the most human thing there is.

Religions and philosophies are not simply ignorant of facts (although they sometimes can be), and hard sciences cannot divorce themselves from the world of meaning, as the example of Trappist-1 shows. A popular description of the advance of science is that as new facts have been found, this has led to a retreat of old, mythic depictions of the cosmos. Consequently, stars are merely "huge balls of flaming gas." Matthew Arnold's poem "Dover Beach," which is often used to give poetic form to secularization, illustrates this withdrawal thus:

> The Sea of Faith
> Was once, too, at the full, and round earth's shore
> Lay like the folds of a bright girdle furled.
> But now I only hear
> Its melancholy, long, withdrawing roar,
> Retreating, to the breath
> Of the night-wind, down the vast edges drear
> And naked shingles of the world.[40]

It would be foolish, and obviously false, to think that Christian faith has sailed smoothly through history without ever encountering serious objections and challenges. However, it is equally foolish to think that science and new discoveries somehow necessarily, like a tide, force the Sea of Faith to withdraw from these shores.

Lewis thinks, perhaps a bit simplistically, that the advance of science in effect means merely extending the imaginative grasp of reality. For him, the scientists do not in fact find new things (as if people before Newton did not know what things like gravity or weight were). The advance of science gives us new ways of testing the things we already knew, which enables our understanding about these things to grow. Contra Lewis, it seems to me reasonable to think that science *does* find new things, like powers and effects—things like black holes and bosons—that we knew nothing of before. Yet Lewis's slightly exaggerated point underlines his conviction that the relation between facts and meanings is not simple.[41]

---

40. Matthew Arnold, "Dover Beach," accessed June 1, 2017, https://www.poetryfoundation .org/poems-and-poets/poems/detail/43588.

41. This is also argued by Ratzinger, *Jesus of Nazareth*, 193–94:

Modern man is tempted to say: Creation has become intelligible to us through science. . . . Indeed, in the magnificent mathematics of creation . . . , we recognize the language

Table 1. Major Changes in Cosmology

	Geocentrism	Heliocentrism	Galactocentrism	Extraterrestrial Life
Origins	Eudoxus, Aristotle, Ptolemy	Copernicus 1543	Shapley 1917	For now, based on inductive speculation
General acceptance	From fourth century BC	1700–	1930–	1750–
Final confirmation	Disproven	1838 (stellar parallax)	1950 (galactic radio maps)	Not confirmed (possible ways of confirmation: radio signals; signs of life on Mars, Europa, meteorites; etc.)
Opposed by	Atomists	Geocentrists, both scientists and theologians	Some scientists	Set of various scientific, philosophical, and theological arguments
Relevance for theology	Easily accommodated with commonsense phenomenology of many biblical accounts of, e.g., sun "rising"	Reinterpretation of some geocentric passages	None	Human significance, christological considerations

The convictions of Christians have typically to do with the meanings of things that are, as such, relatively simple to perceive even if their meaning can be contested. The early Christian cosmology consisted of very few, but important, claims: God is one and different from creation, the created matter is good, and everything has a purpose. Now, we may consider what facts might disprove these claims.

If we look at the changes in our worldview, we can spot three major cosmological changes that lie behind us, as well as one that might be ahead of us.[42]

---

of God. But unfortunately not the whole language. The functional truth about man has been discovered. But the truth about man himself—who he is, where he comes from, what he should do, what is right, what is wrong—this unfortunately cannot be read in the same way. Hand in hand with growing knowledge of functional truth there seems to be an increasing blindness toward "truth" itself—toward the question of our real identity and purpose. What is truth? Pilate was not alone in dismissing this question as unanswerable and irrelevant for his purposes. Today too, in political argument and in discussion of the foundations of law, it is generally experienced as disturbing. Yet if man lives without truth, life passes him by; ultimately he surrenders the field to whoever is the stronger.

42. I have slightly modified here the table from Dick, "Cosmotheology," 196.

All of these changes concern some facts about the cosmos. So far, only the Copernican turn has caused major theological debate, but as we saw in chapter 3, this was both very badly handled and a complex issue that involved additional factors that were neither theological nor scientific in the first place. The actual theological challenge that resulted from the Copernican turn seemed to concern the interpretation of some passages, like Joshua 10:12–13, which were used as proof texts for the geocentric view. The galactocentric turn did not have any mentionable effect on theological deliberation per se, although it might have boosted the discussion about human worth and significance to some extent.

What about the changes that might be ahead of us? Steven J. Dick argues emphatically that "any theology that ignores the facts of cosmic evolution as understood over the last century does so at the peril of being divorced from reality."[43] I agree. Dick laments the lack of reflection on cosmological issues by theologians and offers five points that he thinks are vital for any "cosmo-theology" that takes seriously the new cosmology. Each claim is followed by a suggestion for what this should mean for Christian theology.

1. Humans are not spatially central to the universe. Therefore, doctrines like incarnation smack of anthropocentricism.
2. Humans are not special or unique as biological organisms. Therefore, we should not think that we are objects of special attention of any divine being.
3. Humans are quite likely at the bottom of the great chain of being. This makes the idea of any universal deity obsolete.
4. Cosmotheology needs to be open to radically new conceptions of God. Dick suggests that pantheism would fit more easily with the new cosmology.
5. Cosmotheology needs to have a moral dimension that extends reverence to all species in the universe. This would also enable us to see humanity as one despite our differences.

From what has been said in the previous chapters, it is quite clear that Dick's points 1, 2, 3, and 5 have already been accommodated within orthodox Christian theology a long time ago, without the problems and challenges that Dick lists here. Also, his suggestions in 1, 2, and 3 are non sequiturs, as has already been demonstrated. Point 4 is more interesting. It seems that this

---

43. Dick, "Cosmotheology," 206.

conclusion follows from the ananthropocentric drift of the other claims; that is to say, our current understanding of the cosmos makes any anthropomorphic conception of deity untenable. These points, however, are not related directly to empirical science, as they are philosophical. Moreover, the challenge of 4 seems to rely on the viability of claims 1, 2, 3, and 5. If they are unwarranted, as I think they are, the credibility of 4 is decreased.

The movement from anthropocentrism toward a cosmology where we are not alone mostly concerns our cosmic significance and uniqueness. In chapter 6, we saw both how the discussion about these topics has often been unclear and how Christian theology, in the end, has been able to incorporate these changes quite easily into its narrative. The facts that Christian theologians take to be the grounding of their cosmology are so basic that it is very hard to challenge them, or they are by their nature philosophical, not empirical, which makes it possible for these views to be coupled together with several different cosmologies.[44]

A list of central Christian convictions that have something to do with cosmology includes, for example, those in table 2.

Table 2. List of Christian Cosmological Convictions

Humans	Cosmos	God
Imago Dei	Ordered	One
Purpose	Good	Distinct from creation
Objective moral duties	Metaethical realism	Personal and good
Immortal	Finite	Infinite

We may consider what cosmological finding would challenge some of these views. I underscore that Christians should expect that some of their views will be challenged. In the light of history, some of their views have changed. Therefore, it is to be expected that further challenges and revisions will also happen in the future. But we must not overestimate this. The beliefs that have changed in the past have typically been auxiliary, not core beliefs. By auxiliary beliefs, I mean beliefs that resonate with central Christian convictions, without being themselves the most central convictions. Core beliefs, like the

44. A cross-cultural empirical study found that anthropocentrism correlates more than religiosity with unsettling attitudes toward the existence of other civilizations. See Vakoch and Lee, "Reactions." A high level of religiosity, however, correlates more with the belief that the other cultures are likely not benevolent. The study does not distinguish or explain reasons for this. Interestingly, some Christian theologians have argued that only theists are able to reasonably sustain the belief that other cultures are our "brothers." See Jaki, *Cosmos and Creator*, 124.

convictions listed above, are very resistant to change but not totally isolated, while auxiliary beliefs are more easily challenged and changed.[45]

In the beginning of the book, I listed a set of material and formal criteria for Christian identity.

Formal

1. Understanding of history
2. Coherence of knowledge
3. Intellectual virtue

Material

1. Canonical witness
2. Tradition
3. Ecumenical consensus

The formal criteria concern the epistemic desiderata that should govern dogmatic deliberation. These criteria are not especially Christian, and similar values should be acceptable to anyone, regardless of one's own background beliefs. The material criteria arise from a specific Christian context. If the thinking of a community is supposed to involve genuinely the thinking of *this* given community, it needs to follow the basic convictions of that community.[46]

Robert W. Jenson makes a helpful distinction between doctrine and dogma. Dogma is a creedal statement defined once and for all by ecumenical councils, and it is thus unchangeable. However, there are very few dogmas, while there are many doctrines. These are explications of dogma in a given historical situation; in principle, they are open to change. According to Jenson, this effectively means asking whether saying F instead of G means that we are proclaiming the genuine gospel. The questions typically concern the interpretation of canonical witness: what it is that our tradition teaches. As we have seen, in history it has often been the case that some contingent interpretation of tradition has taken over the witness, so that the church has lost the distinction between auxiliary and core beliefs. The Copernican controversy is a case in point.

The church thinks through different challenges with the help of tradition and an ecumenical point of view. The questions that need to be asked here

45. I ask my reader to note that I am now speaking of Christian cosmology, not about the totality of Christian beliefs. There is a method of public verification and falsification of Christian beliefs, but that is not the topic of this book.
46. For an extended argument for this view, see Marshall, *Trinity and Truth*.

include the following. How have we solved these issues in the past, and on what grounds? Is there something that is obviously wrong about these past decisions, and if so, what and why? How have other churches acted, and what kinds of arguments have they offered?

Theologizing requires balancing between both the apostolic witness handed to the church and intellectual virtues like honesty, truthfulness, steadfastness, and wisdom, which are part of the Christian tradition (Phil. 4:8; 2 Pet. 1:5–8; Prov. 1). Jenson describes the function of theology as follows: "Theology is actual as a continuing consultation. Theology is not the adding of proposition to proposition in the steady construction of a planned structure of knowledge. It is a discussion and debate that as it continues regularly confronts new questions, and from which participants drop out and into which new participants enter." In fact, it is not only natural but imperative that "it is the fate of every theological system to be dismembered and have its fragments bandied about in an ongoing debate."[47]

The perspective, in addition to the aforementioned epistemic stance, Lewis brings to our cosmological and theological inquiry is a vision of a place from which the inquiry can start. For him, humans are standing at the steps of a magnificent cathedral, which welcomes them inside. It most definitely is not a vision of a lonely castaway sailing on a raft on a never-ending sea. The cosmos portrays order and beauty. It gives itself to us to be studied, understood, and enjoyed. Nonetheless, the cosmos can be a perplexing and even dangerous place, but perhaps this is required for it to be a place of endless adventure, where explorers steer their ships toward distant islands and planets, where scientists look deeper and deeper into the fundamental elements of life, and where the great variety of human experience is understood continually better.[48] This is how Lewis contrasts two possible attitudes toward the universe: "Popularized science, the conventions or 'unconventions' of his immediate circle, party programmes, etc., enclose him [an uneducated man] in a tiny windowless universe which he mistakes for the only possible universe. There are no distant horizons, no mysteries. He thinks everything has been settled. A cultured person, on the other hand, is almost compelled to be aware that reality is very odd and that the ultimate truth, whatever it may be, must have the characteristics of strangeness— must be something that would seem remote and fantastic to the uncultured."[49]

Christians believe that their faith has cosmic relevance and every single being has cosmic worth. "Look at the birds of the air; they do not sow or

47. Jenson, *Systematic Theology*, 1:18.
48. For two slightly different meditations along these lines, see Gingerich, "Do the Heavens Declare"; Garcia-Rivera, *Garden of God*.
49. Lewis, "Christianity and Culture," 81.

reap or store away in barns, and yet your heavenly Father feeds them. Are you not much more valuable than they?" (Matt. 6:26). This is not a scientific statement but a philosophical and religious one. It is reached not by experiments but by illumination. Often these are not in tension, but sometimes our experiences raise questions that demand answers. It belongs to theology, as a form critical inquiry that seeks to explain what the church in fact believes, to continuously enlighten the borderline between empirical truths and truths of reason. There is no single general method or solution that shows where the border lies and what belongs to each side. These are defined case by case, as I have tried to do in this book with a few particular questions.

A proper Christian attitude toward the cosmos is one of awe and wonder—and the desire to understand it ever more deeply. Alas, as humans we often fail to live up to the high ideals handed to us by our tradition. The process of understanding requires the unity of intellectual virtues, which are endemic to any good scientific practice. Perhaps the most important of these is the recognition of how little we know.

Bibliography

Adams, Robert Merrihew. *Finite and Infinite Goods*. Oxford: Oxford University Press, 2002.

Alexander, Denis. *Creation or Evolution: Do We Have to Choose?* Oxford: Lion, 2009.

———. *The Language of Genetics*. West Conshohocken, PA: Templeton Press, 2011.

———. "Order and Emergence in Biological Evolution." In *The Future of Creation Order*. Vol. 1, *Philosophy, Sciences, and Theology*, edited by Gerrit Glas and Jeroen de Ridder. Dordrecht: Springer, 2018.

Alfsvåg, Knut. "The Centrality of Christology on the Relation between Nicholas Cusanus and Martin Luther." *Studia Theologica* 70, no. 1 (2016): 22–38.

———. "*Explicatio* and *Complicatio*: On the Understanding of the Relationship between God and the World in the Work of Nicholas Cusanus." *International Journal of Systematic Theology* 14, no. 3 (2012): 295–309.

Ambrose. *Hexameron, Paradise, and Cain and Abel*. Translated by John J. Savage. Fathers of the Church 42. New York: Catholic University of America Press, 1961.

Anderson, Bernhard W. *Creation in the Old Testament*. Issues in Religion and Theology 6. Philadelphia: Fortress, 1984.

Aquinas, Thomas. "Exposition of Aristotle's Treatise *On the Heavens*." On Past Masters website, 1993. http://pm.nlx.com/xtf/view?docId=aquinas/aquinas.25 .xml (subscription required).

———. *Sancti Thomae Aquinatis Doctoris Angelici Ordinis Praedicatorum Summa Theologiae*. Matriti: Biblioteca de Autores Cristianos, 1955.

———. *The Summa Theologiae of St. Thomas Aquinas*. 2nd and rev. ed., 1920. Translated literally by Fathers of the English Dominican Province. http://www .newadvent.org/summa/.

Aristotle. *On the Heavens*. Translated by J. L. Stocks. The Internet Classics Archive, 2009. http://classics.mit.edu/Aristotle/heavens.html.

Armstrong, Chris. "Boethius, *The Consolation of Philosophy*." In *C. S. Lewis's List: The Ten Books That Influenced Him Most*, edited by David Werther and Susan Werther, 135–56. London: Bloomsbury, 2015.

Arnould, Jacques. "Does Extraterrestrial Intelligent Life Threaten Religion and Philosophy?" *Theology and Science* 6, no. 4 (2008): 439–50.

Atkins, Peter. "Atheism and Science." In *Oxford Handbook of Science and Religion*, edited by Philip Clayton and Zachary Simpson, 124–36. Oxford: Oxford University Press, 2006.

Augustine. *City of God*. In *Nicene and Post-Nicene Fathers*, series 1, vol. 2, edited by Philip Schaff. Grand Rapids: Eerdmans, 1983.

———. *City of God*. Translated by R. W. Dyson. Cambridge: Cambridge University Press, 1998.

———. *Confessions*. Translated by A. C. Outler. New York: Barnes & Noble Classics, 2007.

———. "The Literal Meaning of Genesis." Translated by Edmund Hill, OP. In *The Works of St. Augustine: On Genesis*, 155–507. New York: New City Press, 2002.

———. *On Christian Doctrine*. Translated by J. F. Shaw. In *Nicene and Post-Nicene Fathers*, series 1, vol. 2, edited by Philip Schaff. Grand Rapids: Eerdmans, 1983.

Backhaus, Knut. "'Before Abraham Was, I Am': The Book of Genesis and the Genesis of Christology." In *Genesis and Christian Theology*, edited by Nathan MacDonald, Mark W. Elliott, and Grant Macaskill, 74–84. Grand Rapids: Eerdmans, 2012.

Baehr, Jason S. *Intellectual Virtues and Education: Essays in Applied Virtue Epistemology*. New York: Routledge, 2016.

Baggett, David, and Jerry L. Walls. *God and Cosmos: Moral Truth and Human Meaning*. Oxford: Oxford University Press, 2016.

———. *Good God: The Theistic Foundations of Morality*. New York: Oxford University Press, 2012.

Baltes, Matthias. *Die Weltentstehung des Platonischen Timaios nach den antiken Interpreten*. Leiden: Brill, 1976.

Barbour, Ian G. *Religion and Science: Historical and Contemporary Issues*. San Francisco: HarperCollins, 1990.

Barnes, Robin B. *Astrology and Reformation*. Oxford: Oxford University Press, 2016.

Barrow, John D., and Frank J. Tipler. *The Anthropic Cosmological Principle*. Oxford: Clarendon, 1986.

Basil. *Hexaemeron*. Translated by Blomfield Jackson. In *Nicene and Post-Nicene Fathers*, series 2, vol. 8, edited by Philip Schaff and Henry Wace. Grand Rapids: Eerdmans, 1980.

Bellah, Robert N. *Religion in Human Evolution: From the Paleolithic to the Axial Age*. Cambridge, MA: Belknap Press of Harvard University Press, 2011.

Benton, Michael. *When Life Nearly Died: The Greatest Mass Extinction of All Time*. London: Thames & Hudson, 2005.

Betz, John. "After Barth: A New Introduction to Erich Przywara's *Analogia Entis*." In *The Analogy of Being: Invention of the Antichrist or Wisdom of God?*, edited by Thomas Joseph White, 35–87. Grand Rapids: Eerdmans, 2011.

———. "Translator's Introduction." In *Analogia Entis*, by Erich Przywara, 1–116. Translated by John Betz and David Bentley Hart. Grand Rapids: Eerdmans, 2014.

Black, Jeremy. *The Literature of Ancient Sumer*. Oxford: Oxford University Press, 2004.

Blackburn, Simon. "An Unbeautiful Mind." *New Republic* 5, no. 12 (2002): 29.

Blair, Ann. "Tycho Brahe's Critique of Copernicus and the Copernican System." *Journal of the History of Ideas* 51, no. 3 (2010): 355–77.

Bockmuehl, Marcus. "Locating Paradise." In *Paradise in Antiquity*, edited by Marcus Bockmuehl and Guy Stroumsa, 192–208. Cambridge: Cambridge University Press, 2010.

Boethius. *The Consolation of Philosophy*. Translated by W. V. Cooper. New York: Cosimo, 2007.

Bostrom, Nick. *Superintelligence: Paths, Dangers, Strategies*. Oxford: Oxford University Press, 2014.

———. "Where Are They? Why I Hope the Search for Extraterrestrial Life Finds Nothing." *MIT Technology Review* (2008): 72–77.

Bouteneff, Peter C. *Beginnings: Ancient Christian Readings of the Biblical Creation Narratives*. Grand Rapids: Baker Academic, 2009.

Brazier, Paul. "C. S. Lewis: The Question of Multiple Incarnations." *Heythrop Journal* 55 (2014): 391–408.

Brient, Elizabeth. "Transitions to a Modern Cosmology: Meister Eckhart and Nicholas of Cusa on the Intensive Infinite." *Journal of History of Philosophy* 37, no. 4 (1999): 575–600.

Brooke, John Hedley. *Science and Religion: Some Historical Perspectives*. Cambridge: Cambridge University Press, 1991.

Brown, Montague. "Faith and Reason in Anselm: Two Models." *Saint Anselm Journal* 2, no. 1 (2004): 1–12.

Brown, William P. *The Ethos of Cosmos: The Genesis of Moral Imagination in the Bible*. Grand Rapids: Eerdmans, 1999.

Burrell, David, ed. *Creation and the God of Abraham*. Cambridge: Cambridge University Press, 2010.

Calcidius. *On Plato's Timaeus*. Translated by John Magee. Cambridge, MA: Harvard University Press, 2016.

Calvin, John. *Commentary on Genesis*. Grand Rapids: General Books, 2011.

Carnell, Corbin Scott. *Bright Shadow of Reality: Spiritual Longing in C. S. Lewis*. Grand Rapids: Eerdmans, 1999.

Carr, Bernard. "Cosmology and Religion." In *The Oxford Handbook of Religion and Science*, edited by Philip Clayton and Zachary Simpson, 139–55. Oxford: Oxford University Press, 2006.

Catling, David C. *Astrobiology: A Very Short Introduction*. Oxford: Oxford University Press, 2013.

Chan, Man Ho. "Would God Create Our Universe through Multiverse?" *Theology and Science* 13, no. 4 (2016): 395–408.

Chemnitz, Martin. *Loci Theologici*. Translated by J. A. O. Preus. 2 vols. St. Louis: Concordia, 1989.

———. *The Two Natures in Christ*. Translated by J. A. O. Preus. St. Louis: Concordia, 1971.

Chesterton, G. K. *Orthodoxy*. Peabody, MA: Hendrickson, 2006.

Cleland, Carol E. "Life without Definitions." *Synthese* 185, no. 1 (2012): 125–44. https://doi.org/10.1007/s11229-011-9879-7.

Clement of Alexandria. *The Stromata, or Miscellanies*. In *The Ante-Nicene Fathers*, vol. 2, edited by Alexander Roberts and James Donaldson. Grand Rapids: Eerdmans, 1983.

Clifford, Richard J. *Creation Accounts in the Ancient Near East and in the Bible*. Washington, DC: The Catholic Biblical Quarterly, 1994.

Collins, Robin. "Extraterrestrial Intelligence and the Incarnation." In *God and the Multiverse*, edited by Klaas J. Kraay, 211–26. London: Routledge, 2015.

———. "The Fine-Tuning Evidence Is Convincing." In *Debating Christian Theism*, edited by James Porter Moreland, 35–46. Oxford: Oxford University Press, 2013.

———. "The Fine-Tuning for Discoverability." Draft paper, 2014. http://home.messiah .edu/~rcollins/Fine-tuning/Greer-Heard%20Forum%20paper%20draft%20for %20posting.pdf.

———. "The Multiverse Hypothesis: A Theistic Perspective." In *Universe or Multiverse?*, edited by Bernard Carr, 459–80. Cambridge: Cambridge University Press, 2007.

———. "The Teleological Argument: An Exploration of the Fine-Tuning of the Universe." In *Blackwell Companion to Natural Theology*, edited by William Lane Craig and James Porter Moreland, 202–81. Oxford: Blackwell, 2012.

Coloe, Mary L. *Creation Is Groaning*. Collegeville, MN: Liturgical Press, 2013.

Consolmagno, Guy. "Would You Baptize an Extraterrestrial?" In *The Impact of Discovering Life beyond Earth*, edited by Steven J. Dick, 233–44. Cambridge: Cambridge University Press, 2015.

Conway Morris, Simon. "Does Biology Have an Eschatology, and If So Does It Have Cosmological Implications?" In *The Far-Future Universe: Eschatology from a Cosmic Perspective*, edited by George F. R. Ellis, 158–74. Philadelphia: Templeton Foundation Press, 2002.

————. *Life's Solution: Inevitable Humans in a Lonely Universe*. Cambridge: Cambridge University Press, 2003.

Copan, Paul, and William Lane Craig. *Creation out of Nothing: A Biblical, Philosophical, and Scientific Exploration*. Grand Rapids: Baker Academic, 2004.

Copernicus, Nicolaus. *On the Revolutions of the Heavenly Spheres*. Translated by Charles Glenn Wallis. Chicago: William Benton, 1952.

Corcoran, Kevin. "Constitution, Resurrection and Relationality." In *Personal Identity and Resurrection: How Do We Survive Our Death?*, edited by Georg Gasser, 191–206. Farnham, UK: Ashgate, 2011.

Cornford, Francis MacDonald. *Plato's Cosmology*. New York: Liberal Arts Press, 1957.

Cortez, Marc. *Theological Anthropology: A Guide for the Perplexed*. London: T&T Clark, 2010.

Cox, Ronald. *By the Same Word: Creation and Salvation in Hellenistic Judaism and Early Christianity*. Berlin: Walter de Gruyter, 2007.

Coyne, George V. "The Church's Most Recent Attempt to Dispel the Galileo Myth." In *The Church and Galileo*, edited by Ernan McMullin, 340–60. Notre Dame, IN: Notre Dame University Press, 2005.

————. "Extraterrestrial Life and Our Worldview." In *Many Worlds: The New Universe, Extraterrestrial Life, and the Theological Implications*, edited by Steven J. Dick, 177–90. Philadelphia: Templeton Foundation Press, 2000.

Crawford, Jackson, ed. *The Poetic Edda*. Indianapolis: Hackett, 2015.

Crisp, Oliver. *God Incarnate*. London: Continuum, 2009.

Crowe, Michael J. *The Extraterrestrial Life Debate, 1750–1900*. London: Dover, 2011.

Cusanus, Nicholas. *Of Learned Ignorance*. Translated by Germain Heron. London: Routledge, 1954.

Danielson, Dennis R. *The Book of Cosmos: Imagining the Universe from Heraclitus to Hawking*. Cambridge: Perseus, 2000.

————. "The Great Copernican Cliché." *American Journal of Physics* 69 (2001): 1029–35.

Dante. *Inferno*. Translated by Henry Longfellow. New York: Modern Classics Library, 2003.

Davies, Paul. *Are We Alone? Philosophical Implications of the Discovery of Extraterrestrial Life*. New York: Basic Books, 1996.

————. *The Goldilocks Enigma: Why Is the Universe Just Right for Life?* London: Penguin, 2006.

Dawkins, Richard. *River Out of Eden: A Darwinian View of Life*. New York: Basic Books, 1995.

Deane-Drummond, Celia. "God's Image and Likeness in Humans and Other Animals: Performative Soul-Making and Graced Nature." *Zygon* 47, no. 2 (December 2012): 934–48.

———. *The Wisdom of the Liminal: Evolution and Other Animals in Human Becoming*. Grand Rapids: Eerdmans, 2014.

Deane-Drummond, Celia, Rebecca Artinian-Kaiser, and David L. Clough. *Animals as Religious Subjects: Transdisciplinary Perspectives*. New York: Bloomsbury, 2013.

Delio, Ilia. "Christ and Extraterrestrial Life." *Theology and Science* 5, no. 3 (2008): 249–65.

Denzinger, Heinrich. *Compendium of Creeds, Definitions, and Declarations on Matters of Faith and Morals*. 43rd ed. San Francisco: Ignatius, 2012.

Derham, William. *Astrotheology; or, A Demonstration of the Being and Attributes of God from a Survey of the Heavens*. London: Willian Innys, 1715.

de Schrijver, Georges. *Imagining the Creator God from Antiquity to Astrophysics*. Quezon City, Philippines: Ateneo de Manila University Press, 2015.

Dessain, C. S., and T. Gornall, eds. *The Letters and Diaries of John Henry Newman*. Vol. 24. Oxford: Clarendon, 1973.

Dick, Steven J. *The Biological Universe: The Twentieth-Century Extraterrestrial Life Debate and the Limits of Science*. Cambridge: Cambridge University Press, 1996.

———. "Cosmotheology: Theological Implications of the New Universe." In *Many Worlds: The New Universe, Extraterrestrial Life, and the Theological Implications*, edited by Stephen J. Dick, 191–210. West Conshohocken, PA: Templeton Foundation Press, 2000.

———, ed. *The Impact of Discovering Life beyond Earth*. Cambridge: Cambridge University Press, 2015.

———. *Life on Other Worlds: The 20th-Century Extraterrestrial Life Debate*. Cambridge: Cambridge University Press, 1998.

———. *Plurality of Worlds: The Origins of the Extraterrestrial Life Debate from Democritus to Kant*. Cambridge: Cambridge University Press, 1982.

Dick, Steven J., and James E. Strick. *The Living Universe: NASA and the Development of Astrobiology*. New Brunswick, NJ: Rutgers University Press, 2004.

Dixon, Scott C. "Popular Astrology and Lutheran Propaganda in Reformation Germany." *History* 84, no. 275 (1999): 403–18.

Domagal-Goldman, Shawn D., and Katherine E. Wright. "The Astrobiology Primer 2.0." *Astrobiology* 16, no. 8 (2016): 561–653.

Dougherty, Trent. *The Problem of Animal Pain*. London: Palgrave Macmillan, 2014.

Drees, Willem B. *Beyond the Big Bang: Quantum Cosmologies and God*. La Salle, IL: Open Court, 1990.

Dronke, Peter. *The Spell of Calcidius: Platonic Concepts and Images in the Medieval West*. Florence: Sismel, 2008.

Duhem, Pierre. *Medieval Cosmology: Theories of Infinity, Place, Time, Void, and the Plurality of Worlds*. Edited and translated by Roger Ariew. Chicago: University of Chicago Press, 1986.

Dupré, Louis. "The Question of Pantheism from Eckhart to Cusanus." In *Cusanus: The Legacy of Learned Ignorance*, edited by Peter Casarella, 74–88. Washington, DC: Catholic University of America Press, 2006.

el-Aswad, el-Sayed. "Archaic Egyptian Cosmology." *Anthropos* 92 (1997): 69–81.

Enns, Peter. *The Evolution of Adam: What the Bible Does and Doesn't Say about Human Origins*. Grand Rapids: Brazos, 2012.

Epicurus. *Letter to Herodotus*. Translated by C. Bailey. In *The Stoic and Epicurean Philosophers*, edited by Whitney Oates, 3–15. New York: Modern Library, 1957.

Evans, C. Stephen. *God and Moral Obligation*. Oxford: Oxford University Press, 2013.

———. *Natural Signs and Knowledge of God: A New Look at Theistic Arguments*. Oxford: Oxford University Press, 2010.

Everitt, Nicholas. *The Non-Existence of God*. London: Routledge, 2004.

Fantoli, Annibale. *The Case of Galileo: A Closed Question?* Notre Dame, IN: Notre Dame University Press, 2010.

Feldhay, Rivka. *Galileo and the Church: Political Inquisition or Critical Dialogue?* Cambridge: Cambridge University Press, 1995.

Fergusson, David A. S. *The Cosmos and the Creator*. London: SPCK, 1998.

Ferrari, Leo C. "Cosmography." In *Augustine through the Ages*, edited by Allan D. Fitzgerald, 246. Grand Rapids: Eerdmans, 2009.

Finlay, Stephen. "Four Faces of Moral Realism." *Philosophy Compass* 2, no. 6 (2007): 820–29.

Finocchiaro, Maurice A. *Defending Copernicus and Galileo: Critical Reasoning in the Two Affairs*. Dordrecht: Springer, 2010.

Fiorenza, Francis Schüssler, and John P. Gavin, eds. *Systematic Theology: Roman Catholic Perspectives*. Vol. 1. Minneapolis: Fortress, 1991.

Fisher, Christopher L., and David Fergusson. "Karl Rahner and the Intelligence Question." *Heythrop Journal* 47 (2006): 275–90.

Fisher, H. Dennis. "C. S. Lewis, Platonism and Aslan's Country." *Inklings Forever* 7 (2010): 1–16.

Frankena, William K. *Ethics*. Englewood Cliffs, NJ: Prentice-Hall, 1973.

Fretheim, Terence E. *God and World in the Old Testament: A Relational Theology of Creation*. Nashville: Abingdon, 2005.

Frye, Roland Mushat. *Is God a Creationist? The Religious Case against Creation-Science*. New York: Charles Scribner's Sons, 1983.

Galilei, Galileo. "Dialogue Concerning the Two Chief World Systems." Translated by Stillman Drake. Annotated and condensed by S. E. Sciortino. Accessed January 1, 2017. http://www.famous-trials.com/galileotrial/1010-dialogue.

———. "Letter to Madame Christina of Lorraine, Grand Duchess of Tuscany." In *Discoveries and Opinions of Galileo*, edited by Stillman Drake, 173–216. New York:

Anchor-Doubleday, 1957. Available at http://inters.org/galilei-madame-christina
-Lorraine.

Garcia-Rivera, Alejandro. *The Garden of God: A Theological Cosmology.* Minneapolis: Fortress, 2009.

Gerhard, John. *Loci Theologici (1610).* Reprint, Berlin: Schlawitz, 1863.

Gilson, Étienne. *God and Philosophy.* New Haven: Yale University Press, 1959.

Gingerich, Owen. "Do the Heavens Declare the Glory of God?" *Perspectives on Science and Christian Faith* 66, no. 2 (2014): 113–17.

Gioia, Luigi. *The Theological Epistemology of Augustine's "De Trinitate."* Oxford:
Oxford University Press, 2008.

Graf, Fritz. "The Bridge and the Ladder: Narrow Passages in Late Antique Visions."
In *Heavenly Realms and Earthly Realities in Late Antique Religions,* edited by
Ra'anan S. Boustan and Annette Yoshiko Reed, 1–18. Cambridge: Cambridge
University Press, 2004.

Graney, Christopher M. *Setting Aside All Authority: Giovanni Battista Riccioli and
the Science against Copernicus in the Age of Galileo.* Notre Dame, IN: Notre
Dame University Press, 2015.

Grant, Edward. *A History of Natural Philosophy: From the Ancient World to the
Nineteenth Century.* New York: Cambridge University Press, 2007.

———. *Planets, Stars and Orbs: The Medieval Cosmos, 1200–1687.* Cambridge:
Cambridge University Press, 1994.

———. *Science and Religion, 400 B.C. to A.D. 1550: From Aristotle to Copernicus.*
Westport, CN: Greenwood Press, 2004.

Greenwood, Kyle. *Scripture and Cosmology: Reading the Bible between the Ancient
World and Modern Science.* Downers Grove, IL: IVP Academic, 2015.

Gregory, Brad S. *The Unintended Reformation: How a Religious Revolution Secular-
ized Society.* Cambridge, MA: Belknap Press of Harvard University Press, 2012.

Guarino, Thomas G. *Vincent of Lérins and the Development of Christian Doctrine.*
Grand Rapids: Baker Academic, 2013.

Guite, Malcolm. "C. S. Lewis: Apologetics and Poetic Imagination." *Theology* 116
(2013): 418–26.

Gunton, Colin. *The Triune Creator: A Historical and Systematic Study.* Edinburgh:
Edinburgh University Press, 1998.

Halvorson, Hans, and Helge Kragh. "Cosmology and Theology." In *Stanford Encyclopedia of Philosophy* (Summer 2017 edition), edited by Edward N. Zalta. https://
plato.stanford.edu/archives/sum2017/entries/cosmology-theology.

Hanson, Robin. "The Great Filter—Are We Almost Past It?" Unpublished paper,
September 15, 1998. http://hanson.gmu.edu/greatfilter.html.

Harrison, Peter. *The Territories of Science and Religion.* Chicago: University of Chicago Press, 2015.

Hart, David Bentley. *The Hidden and the Manifest*. Grand Rapids: Eerdmans, 2017.

———. *The New Testament: A Translation*. New Haven: Yale University Press, 2017.

Hebblethwaite, Brian. "The Impossibility of Multiple Incarnations." *Theology* 104 (2001): 323–34.

———. *In Defence of Christianity*. Oxford: Oxford University Press, 2005.

Herzfeld, Noreen L. *In Our Image: Artificial Intelligence and the Human Spirit*. Minneapolis: Fortress, 2002.

Hildebrand, Stephen. *Basil of Cesarea*. Grand Rapids: Baker Academic, 2014.

Hintikka, Jaakko. "Gaps in the Great Chain of Being: An Exercise in the Methodology of Ideas." In *Reforging the Great Chain of Being*, edited by Simo Knuuttila, 1–18. Dordrecht: Reidel, 1981.

Hoggard Creegan, Nicola. *Animal Suffering and the Problem of Evil*. Oxford: Oxford University Press, 2013.

Holder, Rodney D. *God, the Multiverse, and Everything: Modern Cosmology and the Argument from Design*. Aldershot, UK: Ashgate, 2004.

Holmes, Michael, ed. and trans. *Apostolic Fathers*. 3rd ed. After an earlier work of J. B. Lightfoot and J. R. Harmer. Grand Rapids: Baker Academic, 2007.

Horowitz, Wayne. *Mesopotamian Cosmic Geography*. Winona Lake, IN: Eisenbrauns, 2011.

Hudson, Hud. *The Metaphysics of Hyperspace*. Oxford: Oxford University Press, 2005.

Hudson, Nancy J. *Becoming God: The Doctrine of Theosis in Nicholas of Cusa*. Washington, DC: Catholic University of America Press, 2007.

Hurlbutt, Robert H., III. *Hume, Newton, and the Design Argument*. Lincoln: University of Nebraska Press, 1985.

Ijjas, Anna, Johannes Grössl, and Ludwig Jaskolla. "Theistic Multiverse and Slippery Slopes: A Response to Klaas Kraay." *Theology and Science* 11, no. 1 (2013): 62–76.

Jaki, Stanley J. *Cosmos and Creator*. Edinburgh: Scottish Academic Press, 1980.

———. *Genesis 1 through the Ages*. London: Thomas More Press, 1992.

Jenson, Robert W. *America's Theologian: A Recommendation of Jonathan Edwards*. New York: Oxford University Press, 1988.

———. *Systematic Theology*. Vol. 1, *The Triune God*. New York: Oxford University Press, 1997.

———. *Systematic Theology*. Vol. 2, *The Works of God*. New York: Oxford University Press, 1999.

John Paul II. *Fides et Ratio* [On the relationship between faith and reason]. September 14, 1998. http://w2.vatican.va/content/john-paul-ii/en/encyclicals/documents/hf_jp-ii_enc_14091998_fides-et-ratio.html.

Johnson, Keith. *Karl Barth and Analogia Entis*. London: T&T Clark, 2010.

Johnson-Laird, Philip. *How We Reason*. Oxford: Oxford University Press, 2006.

Justin Martyr. *Second Apology.* In *The Ante-Nicene Fathers,* vol. 1, edited by Alexander Roberts and James Donaldson. Grand Rapids: Eerdmans, 1981.

Kahane, Guy. "Our Cosmic Insignificance." *Nous* 48, no. 4 (2014): 745–72.

———. "Should We Want God to Exist?" *Philosophy and Phenomenological Research* 82, no. 3 (2011): 674–96.

Kaiser, Christopher B. *Creational Theology and the History of Physical Science: The Creationist Tradition from Basil to Bohr.* Leiden: Brill, 1997.

Kärkkäinen, Veli-Matti. *Creation and Humanity.* Vol. 3 of *Constructive Christian Theology for the Church in the Pluralistic World.* Grand Rapids: Eerdmans, 2015.

Kather, Regine. "'The Earth Is a Noble Star': The Arguments for the Relativity of Motion in the Cosmology of Nicolaus Cusanus and Their Transformation in Einstein's Theory of Relativity." In *Cusanus: The Legacy of Learned Ignorance,* edited by Peter Casarella, 226–50. Washington, DC: Catholic University of America Press, 2006.

Kenny, Anthony. *A New History of Western Philosophy: In Four Parts.* Oxford: Clarendon, 2010.

Kierkegaard, Søren. *Philosophical Fragments, or a Fragment of Philosophy/Johannes Climacus, or De Omnibus Dubitandum Est.* Vol. 7 of *Kierkegaard's Writings.* Edited by Edna H. Hong and Howard V. Hong. Princeton: Princeton University Press, 1985.

Klima, Gyula, Fritz Allhoff, and Anand Vaidya, eds. "Selections from the Condemnations of 1277." In *Medieval Philosophy: Essential Readings with Commentary,* 181–89. Oxford: Blackwell, 2007.

Knepper, Timothy D. *Negating Negation: Against the Apophatic Abandonment of the Dionysian Corpus.* Eugene, OR: Cascade, 2014.

Knuuttila, Simo. *Modalities in Medieval Philosophy.* London: Routledge, 1993.

Kojonen, Erkki Vesa Rope. "The God of the Gaps, Natural Theology, and Intelligent Design." *Journal of Analytic Theology* 4 (2016): 291–316.

———. *The Intelligent Design Debate and the Temptation of Scientism.* London: Routledge, 2016.

Kopperi, Kari. "Theology of the Cross." In *Engaging Luther,* edited by Olli-Pekka Vainio, 155–72. Eugene, OR: Cascade, 2011.

Kort, Wesley A. *C. S. Lewis: Then and Now.* New York: Oxford University Press, 2001.

Koyré, Alexandre. *From the Closed World to the Infinite Universe.* New York: Harper, 1958.

Kraay, Klaas J. "Theism, Possible Worlds, and the Multiverse." *Philosophical Studies* 147, no. 3 (2010): 355–68.

Kraay, Klaas J., and Chris Dragos. "On Preferring God's Non-Existence." *Canadian Journal of Philosophy* 43, no. 2 (2013): 157–78.

Kragh, Helge S. *Conceptions of Cosmos: From Myths to the Accelerating Universe; A History of Cosmology.* Oxford: Oxford University Press, 2007.

Krauss, Lawrence M. *A Universe from Nothing.* London: Simon & Schuster, 2012.

Laato, Antti, and Johannes C. de Moor, eds. *Theodicy in the World of the Bible*. Leiden: Brill, 2003.

Lambert, W. G. "Mesopotamian Creation Stories." In *Imagining Creation*, edited by Markham J. Geller and Mineke Schipper, 15–60. Leiden: Brill, 2008.

Laplace, Pierre-Simon. *A Philosophical Essay on Probabilities*. Translated by F. W. Truscott and F. L. Emory. New York: Dover, 1951.

Laughlin, R. B., and David Pines. "The Theory of Everything." *Proceedings of the National Academy of Sciences of the United States* 97, no. 1 (2000): 28–31.

Leinsle, Ulrich G. *Introduction to Scholastic Theology*. Washington, DC: Catholic University of America Press, 2010.

Lerner, Michel-Pierre. "Aux Origines de La Polémique Anticopernicienne (II): Martin Luther, Andreas Osiander et Philipp Melanchthon." *Revue des Sciences Philosophiques et Théologiques* 90, no. 3 (2006): 409–52.

Leslie, John. *Universes*. London: Routledge, 1997.

Lewis, C. S. "Bluspels and Flalansferes." In *Selected Literary Essays*, edited by Walter Hooper. Cambridge: Cambridge University Press, 1969.

———. "Christianity and Culture." In *C. S. Lewis Essay Collection: Faith, Christianity and the Church*, edited by Lesley Walmsley, 71–92. London: HarperCollins, 2002.

———. *Collected Letters*. Vol. 3. San Francisco: HarperCollins, 2007.

———. "De Futilitate." In *C. S. Lewis Essay Collection: Faith, Christianity and the Church*, edited by Lesley Walmsley, 261–74. London: HarperCollins, 2002.

———. *The Discarded Image: An Introduction to Medieval and Renaissance Literature*. Cambridge: Cambridge University Press, 1964.

———. "Dogma and the Universe." In *C. S. Lewis Essay Collection: Faith, Christianity and the Church*, edited by Lesley Walmsley, 118–26. London: HarperCollins, 2000.

———. *English Literature in the Sixteenth Century, Excluding Drama*. Oxford: Clarendon, 1954.

———. *A Grief Observed*. London: Faber & Faber, 1961.

———. "Language of Religion." In *C. S. Lewis Essay Collection: Faith, Christianity and the Church*, edited by Lesley Walmsley, 255–66. London: HarperCollins, 2002.

———. *The Last Battle*. London: Fontana, 1956.

———. *The Lion, the Witch and the Wardrobe*. London: Fontana, 1950.

———. *Out of the Silent Planet*. New York: Harper, 2005.

———. *Perelandra*. London: HarperCollins, 2005.

———. "Religion and Rocketry." In *C. S. Lewis Essay Collection: Faith, Christianity and the Church*, edited by Lesley Walmsley, 231–36. London: HarperCollins, 2002.

———. *Screwtape Letters*. London: Fontana, 1942.

———. *Studies in Words*. Cambridge: Cambridge University Press, 2002.

———. *Surprised by Joy: The Shape of My Early Life*. London: Fontana, 1955.

———. *Till We Have Faces*. In *Selected Books*. London: HarperCollins, 2002.

———. "Transposition." In *The Weight of Glory, and Other Addresses*, 114–15. New York: Harper, 2001.

———. *The Voyage of the Dawn Treader*. London: Fontana, 1959.

Lewis, Geraint F., and Luke Barnes. *A Fortunate Universe: Life in a Finely Tuned Cosmos*. Cambridge: Cambridge University Press, 2016.

Lewis-Williams, David, and David Pearce. *Inside the Neolithic Mind: Consciousness, Cosmos and the Realm of the Gods*. London: Thames & Hudson, 2005.

Linville, Mark. "Moral Argument." In *The Blackwell Companion to Natural Theology*, edited by William Lane Craig and James Porter Moreland, 391–448. Oxford: Blackwell, 2012.

Losch, Andreas, and Andreas Krebs. "Implications for the Discovery of Extraterrestrial Life: A Theological Approach." *Theology and Science* 13, no. 2 (2016): 230–44.

Lougheed, Kirk. "Divine Creation, Modal Collapse, and the Theistic Multiverse." *Sophia* 53, no. 4 (2014): 435–46.

Louth, Andrew. *The Origins of the Christian Mystical Tradition from Plato to Denys*. Oxford: Clarendon, 1981.

Lovejoy, Arthur O. *The Great Chain of Being: A Study of the History of an Idea*. New York: Harper & Row, 1960.

Lovin, Robin. "Astrobiology and Theology." In *The Impact of Discovering Life beyond Earth*, edited by Stephen J. Dick, 222–32. Cambridge: Cambridge University Press, 2015.

Lucretius. *Of the Nature of Things*. Translated by W. E. Leonard, 2013. http://www.gutenberg.org/files/785/785-h/785-h.htm#link2H_4_0012.

Luther, Martin. The Heidelberg Disputation. In *Triglot Concordia: The Symbolical Books of the Evangelical Lutheran Church: German-Latin-English*. St. Louis: Concordia, 1921. Available at http://bookofconcord.org/heidelberg.php.

———. *Luther's Works*. American edition. St. Louis: Concordia; Philadelphia: Fortress, 1955–1986.

Lutheran World Federation and the Catholic Church. *Joint Declaration on the Doctrine of Justification*. Grand Rapids: Eerdmans, 2000.

Mackie, John Leslie. *Ethics: Inventing Right and Wrong*. Harmondsworth: Penguin, 1977.

Maimonides, Moses. *Guide for the Perplexed*. Translated by M. Friedländer. New York: Dover, 1956.

Mann, Robert P. "Puzzled by Particularity." In *God and the Multiverse*, edited by Klaas J. Kraay, 25–44. London: Routledge, 2015.

Marshall, Bruce. *Trinity and Truth*. Cambridge: Cambridge University Press, 2002.

Martinez, Alberto A. *Pythagoras, Bruno, Galileo: The Pagan Heresies of the Copernicans*. Cambridge: Saltshadow Castle, 2014.

Mawson, Tim. "The Rational Inescapability of Value Objectivism." *Think* 6, no. 17–18 (Spring 2008): 15–21.

May, Gerhard. *Creatio Ex Nihilo: The Doctrine of "Creation out of Nothing" in Early Christian Thought*. Edinburgh: T&T Clark, 1994.

McGrath, Alister E. "Darwinism." In *Oxford Handbook of Science and Religion*, edited by Philip Clayton and Zachary Simpson, 681–96. Oxford: Oxford University Press, 2006.

———. *A Fine-Tuned Universe: The Quest for God in Science and Theology*. Louisville: Westminster John Knox, 2009.

———. *The Science of God: An Introduction to Scientific Theology*. London: T&T Clark, 2004.

McMullin, Ernan. *The Church and Galileo*. Notre Dame, IN: Notre Dame University Press, 2005.

———. "The Church's Ban on Copernicanism, 1616." In *The Church and Galileo*, edited by Ernan McMullin, 150–90. Notre Dame, IN: Notre Dame University Press, 2005.

———. Introduction to *Evolution and Creation*, edited by Ernan McMullin, 1–58. Notre Dame, IN: University of Notre Dame Press, 1985.

———. "Life and Intelligence Far from Earth: Formulating Theological Issues." In *Many Worlds: The New Universe, Extraterrestrial Life, and the Theological Implications*, edited by Steven J. Dick, 151–75. Philadelphia: Templeton Foundation Press, 2000.

Michel, Paul-Henri. *The Cosmology of Giordano Bruno*. Ithaca, NY: Cornell University Press, 1973.

Miller, Fred D. "Aristotle against the Atomists." In *Infinity and Continuity in Ancient and Medieval Thought*, edited by Norman Kretzman, 87–111. Ithaca, NY: Cornell University Press, 1982.

Miller, Patrick D. *The Religion of Ancient Israel*. Louisville: Westminster John Knox, 2000.

Monton, Bradley. "Against Multiverse Theodicies." *Philo* 13, no. 2 (2010): 113–35.

Morris, Francis J., and Ronald C. Welding. "Coleridge and 'the Great Divide' between C. S. Lewis and Owen Barfield." *Studies in the Literary Imagination* 22, no. 2 (1989): 149–59.

Morris, Thomas V. *The Logic of God Incarnate*. Ithaca, NY: Cornell University Press, 1986.

Mulgan, Tim. *Purpose in the Universe: The Moral and Metaphysical Case for Ananthropocentric Purposivism*. Oxford: Oxford University Press, 2015.

Murphy, Mark. "Theism, Atheism, and the Explanation of Moral Value." In *Is Goodness without God Good Enough? A Debate on Faith, Secularism, and Ethics*, edited by Robert K. Garcia and Nathan L. King, 117–32. Lanham, MD: Rowman & Littlefield, 2009.

Murray, Michael. *Nature Red in Tooth and Claw*. Oxford: Oxford University Press, 2008.

Nagasawa, Yujin. *The Existence of God*. London: Routledge, 2011.

Nagel, Thomas. *Secular Philosophy and the Religious Temperament*. Oxford: Oxford University Press, 2010.

Newman, John Henry. *An Essay on the Development of Christian Doctrine*. Westminster, MD: Christian Classics, 1968.

Newton, Isaac. *Opticks; or, A Treatise of the Reflections, Refractions, Inflections and Colours of Light*. London: Willian Innys, 1730.

Nongbri, Brent. *Before Religion: A History of a Modern Concept*. New Haven: Yale University Press, 2013.

Numbers, Ronald L. *The Creationists*. New York: A. A. Knopf, 1992.

———, ed. *Galileo Goes to Jail, and Other Myths about Science and Religion*. Cambridge, MA: Harvard University Press, 2009.

Oakes, Kenneth. "The Cross and the *Analogia Entis* in Erich Przywara." In *The Analogy of Being: Invention of the Antichrist or Wisdom of God?*, edited by Thomas Joseph White. Grand Rapids: Eerdmans, 2011.

O'Meara, Thomas F. "Christian Theology and Extraterrestrial Intelligent Life." *Theological Studies* 60, no. 1 (1999): 3–30.

———. *Vast Universe: Extraterrestrials and Christian Revelation*. Collegeville, MN: Michael Glazier, 2012.

Oord, Thomas Jay, ed. *Theologies of Creation: Creatio Ex Nihilo and Its New Rivals*. London: Routledge, 2015.

Origen. *De principiis*. Translated by Frederick Crombie. In *The Ante-Nicene Fathers*, vol. 4, edited by Alexander Roberts and James Donaldson. Grand Rapids: Eerdmans, 1982.

Osborn, Ronald E. *Death before the Fall: Biblical Literalism and the Problem of Animal Suffering*. Downers Grove, IL: IVP Academic, 2014.

Paine, Thomas. "Age of Reason." In *Thomas Paine: Collected Writings*, edited by E. Foner. New York: Library of America, 1995.

Paley, William. *Natural Theology; or, Evidences of the Existence and Attributes of the Deity: Collected from the Appearances of Nature*. Boston: Gould & Lincoln, 1852.

Palmén, Ritva. "The Experience of Beauty: Hugh and Richard of St. Victor on Natural Theology." *Journal of Analytic Theology* 4 (2016): 234–53.

———. *Richard of St. Victor's Theory of Imagination*. Leiden: Brill, 2014.

Pascal, Blaise. *Pensées*. Indianapolis: Hackett, 2005.

Pasnau, Robert. *Metaphysical Themes, 1274–1671*. Oxford: Oxford University Press, 2013.

———. *Thomas Aquinas on Human Nature*. Cambridge: Cambridge University Press, 2002.

Pawl, Timothy. "Brian Hebblethwaite's Arguments against Multiple Incarnations." *Religious Studies* 52, no. 1 (2016): 117–30.

———. "Thomistic Multiple Incarnations." *Heythrop Journal* 6 (2014): 359–70.

Penrose, Roger. *The Emperor's New Mind: Concerning Computers, Minds, and the Laws of the Universe*. New York: Oxford University Press, 1989.

Peters, Ted. "Astrobiology and Astrochristology." *Zygon* 51, no. 2 (2016): 480–96.

Peters, Ted, and Nathan Hallanger, eds. *God's Action in Nature's World*. Aldershot, UK: Ashgate, 2006.

Philipse, Herman. *God in the Age of Science: A Critique of Religious Reason*. Oxford: Oxford University Press, 2012.

Philo of Alexandria. *On the Creation of the Cosmos according to Moses*. Edited by David T. Runia. Leiden: Brill, 2001.

Plato. *Gorgias*. Translated by W. R. M. Lamb. Cambridge, MA: Loeb, 1925.

———. *Timaeus*. Translated by R. G. Bury. Cambridge, MA: Loeb, 1929.

Polanyi, Michael. *Personal Knowledge: Towards a Post-Critical Philosophy*. London: Routledge, 1973.

Polkinghorne, John. *The Trinity and an Entangled World: Relationality in Physical Science and Theology*. Grand Rapids: Eerdmans, 2010.

Pongratz-Leisten, Beate, et al. "Creation and Cosmogony." In *Encyclopedia of the Bible and Its Reception*. Berlin: Walter de Gruyter, 2016.

Porter, Jean. *Nature as Reason*. Grand Rapids: Eerdmans, 2005.

Pruss, Alexander R. "The Leibnizian Cosmological Argument." In *The Blackwell Companion to Natural Theology*, edited by William Lane Craig and James Porter Moreland, 24–100. Oxford: Wiley-Blackwell, 2012.

Przywara, Erich. *Analogia Entis: Metaphysics; Original Structure and Universal Rhythm*. Grand Rapids: Eerdmans, 2014.

———. "Gott in uns oder Gott über uns? (Immanenz und Transzendenz in heutigen Geistesleben)." *Stimmen der Zeit* 105 (1923): 343–62.

Quirke, Stephen. "Creation Stories in Ancient Egypt." In *Imaging Creation*, edited by Markham J. Geller and Mineke Schipper, 61–86. Leiden: Brill, 2008.

Ratzinger, Joseph [Pope Benedict XVI]. *Jesus of Nazareth, Part Two, Holy Week: From the Entrance into Jerusalem to the Resurrection*. San Francisco: Ignatius, 2011.

Rea, Michael C. "Gender as a Divine Attribute." *Religious Studies* 52, no. 1 (2013): 1–17.

Redford, Donald B., ed. *The Ancient Gods Speak: A Guide to Egyptian Religion*. Oxford: Oxford University Press, 2002.

Reno, R. R. *Genesis*. Brazos Theological Commentary on the Bible. Grand Rapids: Brazos, 2010.

Reppert, Victor. *C. S. Lewis's Dangerous Idea: In Defense of the Argument from Reason*. Downers Grove, IL: InterVarsity, 2003.

Rice, Hugh. *God and Goodness*. Oxford: Oxford University Press, 2000.

Ritchie, Angus. *From Morality to Metaphysics: The Theistic Implications of Our Ethical Commitments*. Oxford: Oxford University Press, 2012.

Roark, Rhys W. "Nicholas Cusanus, Linear Perspective and the Finite Cosmos." *Viator* 41, no. 1 (2010): 315–66.

Roberts, Robert C., and W. Jay Wood. *Intellectual Virtues: An Essay in Regulative Epistemology*. Oxford: Clarendon, 2007.

Robinson, Dominick. *Understanding the "Imago Dei": The Thought of Barth, von Balthasar and Moltmann*. London: Routledge, 2011.

Robinson, Marilynne. *Absence of Mind*. New Haven: Yale University Press, 2010.

Ross, Hugh. *Improbable Planet: How Earth Became Humanity's Home*. Grand Rapids: Baker Books, 2016.

Rubenstein, Mary-Jane. *Worlds without End: The Many Lives of the Multiverse*. New York: Columbia University Press, 2014.

Russell, Bertrand. "A Free Man's Worship." In *The Meaning of Life*, edited by E. D. Klemke and Steven Cahn, 55–57. Oxford: Oxford University Press, 2008.

Russell, Jeffrey Burton. *Inventing the Flat Earth: Columbus and Modern Historians*. Westport, CT: Praeger, 1997.

Sagan, Carl. *Cosmos*. London: Abacus, 1995.

Saler, Robert Cady. *Theologia Crucis: A Companion to the Theology of the Cross*. Eugene, OR: Cascade, 2016.

Schaff, Philip. *Creeds of Christendom, with a History and Critical Notes*. Vol. 1, *The History of Creeds*, 1877. http://www.ccel.org/ccel/schaff/creeds1.

———. *Creeds of Christendom, with a History and Critical Notes*. Vol. 2, *The Greek and Latin Creeds, with Translations*, 1877. http://www.ccel.org/ccel/schaff/creeds2.

Schakel, Peter J. "'Feeding the Imagination': Lewis's Imaginative Theory and Practice." In *Imagination and the Arts in C. S. Lewis: Journeying to Narnia and Other Worlds*. Columbia: University of Missouri Press, 2011.

Scharf, Caleb. *The Copernicus Complex: The Quest for Our Cosmic (In)Significance*. London: Allen Lane, 2014.

Schneider, Susan. "Alien Minds." In *The Impact of Discovering Life beyond Earth*, edited by Steven J. Dick, 189–206. Cambridge: Cambridge University Press, 2016.

Schupbach, Jonah N. "Paley's Inductive Inference to Design: A Response to Graham Oppy." *Philosophia Christi* 7, no. 2 (2005): 491–502.

Schwartz, Sanford. *C. S. Lewis on the Final Frontier*. Oxford: Oxford University Press, 2009.

Sedley, David. *Creationism and Its Critics in Antiquity*. Berkeley: University of California Press, 2007.

Shafer-Landau, Russ. *Moral Realism: A Defense*. Oxford: Oxford University Press, 2003.

Sheridan, Mark. *Language for God in Patristic Tradition*. Downers Grove, IL: IVP Academic, 2015.

Shklovskii, I. S., and Carl Sagan. *Intelligent Life in the Universe*. San Francisco: Holden-Day, 1966.

Shults, F. LeRon. *Reforming Theological Anthropology: After the Philosophical Turn to Relationality*. Grand Rapids: Eerdmans, 2003.

Smith, Mark. *The Priestly Vision of Genesis 1*. Minneapolis: Fortress, 2010.

Sorabji, Richard. *Matter, Space, and Motion: Theories in Antiquity and Their Sequel*. London: Duckworth, 1988.

Soskice, Janet Martin. *The Kindness of God: Metaphor, Gender, and Religious Language*. Oxford: Oxford University Press, 2008.

Southgate, Christopher. *The Groaning of Creation: God, Evolution and the Problem of Evil*. Louisville: Westminster John Knox, 2008.

Sparks, Kenton L. "Enūma Elish and Priestly Mimesis: Elite Emulation in Nascent Judaism." *Journal of Biblical Literature* 126, no. 4 (2007): 625–48.

Spruit, Leen. *Classical Roots and Medieval Discussions*. Vol. 1 of *Species Intelligibilis: From Perception to Knowledge*. Leiden: Brill, 1994.

Stannard, Russel. *Science and Wonders: Conversations about Science and Belief*. London: Faber & Faber, 1998.

Stanovich, Keith. *Rationality and Reflective Mind*. Oxford: Oxford University Press, 2011.

Steenberg, M. C. *Irenaeus on Creation: Cosmic Christ and the Saga of Redemption*. Leiden: Brill, 2008.

Stein, Edith. *Finite and Eternal Being*. Translated by Kurt F. Reinhardt. Washington, DC: ICS Publications, 2002.

———. "Ways to Know God." In *Edith Stein, Knowledge and Faith*. Translated by Walter Redmond, 83–145. Washington, DC: ICS Publications, 2000.

Stenger, Victor J. "Fine-Tuning and the Multiverse." *Skeptic* 19, no. 3 (2014): 35–42.

Stenmark, Mikael. *How to Relate Science and Religion: A Multidimensional Model*. Grand Rapids: Eerdmans, 2004.

———. *Scientism: Science, Ethics and Religion*. Aldershot, UK: Ashgate, 2001.

Stock, Gregory. *Redesigning Humans: Choosing Our Genes, Changing Our Future*. New York: Mariner, 2003.

Stump, Eleanor. *Aquinas*. London: Routledge, 2003.

———. *Wandering in Darkness: Narrative and the Problem of Suffering*. New York: Oxford University Press, 2010.

Suhner, Laurence. "The Terminator: Dreams of Another World." *Nature* 542 (2017): 512.

Swinburne, Richard. "Bayes, God, and the Multiverse." In *Probability in the Philosophy of Religion*, edited by Jake Chandler and Victoria Harrison, 103–23. Oxford: Oxford University Press, 2012.

———. *The Christian God*. Oxford: Clarendon, 1994.

Taliaferro, Charles. "The Project of Natural Theology." In *The Blackwell Companion to Natural Theology*, edited by William Lane Craig and James Porter Moreland, 1–23. Oxford: Wiley-Blackwell, 2012.

Tarter, Jill Cornell. "SETI and the Religions of the Universe." In *Many Worlds: The New Universe, Extraterrestrial Life, and the Theological Implications*, edited by Steven J. Dick, 143–50. Philadelphia: Templeton Foundation Press, 2000.

Tattersall, Ian. "Origin of the Human Sense of Self." In *In Search of Self: Interdisciplinary Perspectives on Personhood*, edited by J. Wentzel van Huyssteen and Erik P. Wiebe, 33–49. Grand Rapids: Eerdmans, 2011.

Taylor, Charles. *A Secular Age*. Cambridge, MA: Belknap Press of Harvard University Press, 2007.

———. *Sources of the Self*. Cambridge, MA: Harvard University Press, 1992.

Tegmark, Max. "Parallel Universes." *Scientific American* 883 (2003): 40–51.

Tertullian. *The Apology*. Translated by S. Thelwall. In *The Ante-Nicene Fathers*, vol. 3, edited by Alexander Roberts and James Donaldson. Grand Rapids: Eerdmans, 1980.

———. *The Prescription against Heretics*. Translated by Peter Holmes. In *The Ante-Nicene Fathers*, vol. 3, edited by Alexander Roberts and James Donaldson. Grand Rapids: Eerdmans, 1980.

Theophilus. *To Autolycus*. In *The Ante-Nicene Fathers*, vol. 2, edited by Alexander Roberts and James Donaldson. Grand Rapids: Eerdmans, 1983.

Toomer, G. J., ed. *Ptolemy's Almagest*. Princeton: Princeton University Press, 1998.

Vainio, Olli-Pekka. *Beyond Fideism: Negotiable Religious Identities*. Farnham, UK: Ashgate, 2010.

———. "Salvation and Religious Diversity: Christian Perspectives." *Religion Compass* 10, no. 2 (2016): 27–34.

Vainio, Olli-Pekka, and Aku Visala. "Varieties of Unbelief: A Taxonomy of Atheistic Positions." *Neue Zeitschrift für Systematische Theologie und Religionsphilosophie* 57, no. 4 (2015): 483–500.

Vakoch, Douglas A., and Matthew F. Dowd, eds. *The Drake Equation: Estimating the Prevalence of Extraterrestrial Life through the Ages*. Cambridge: Cambridge University Press, 2015.

Vakoch, Douglas A., and Y. S. Lee. "Reactions to Receipt of a Message from Extraterrestrial Intelligence: A Cross-Cultural Empirical Study." *Acta Astronautica* 46, no. 10 (2000): 737–44.

van Huyssteen, J. Wentzel. *Alone in the World? Human Uniqueness in Science and Theology*. Grand Rapids: Eerdmans, 2006.

Veldhuis, Henri. "Ordained and Absolute Power in Scotus' 'Ordinatio' I 44." *Vivarium* 38, no. 2 (2000): 222–30.

Vidal, Clement. "Multidimensional Impact Model for the Discovery of Extraterrestrial Life." In *The Impact of Discovering Life beyond Earth*, edited by Steven J. Dick, 55–75. Cambridge: Cambridge University Press, 2015.

Vilenkin, Alex. *Many Worlds in One: The Search for Other Universes*. New York: Hill and Wang, 2006.

Vincie, Catherine. *Worship and the New Cosmology: Liturgical and Theological Challenges*. Collegeville, MN: Liturgical Press, 2014.

Wainwright, William J. "In Defense of Non-Natural Theistic Realism: A Response to Wielenberg." *Faith and Philosophy* 27 (2010): 457–64.

———. *Religion and Morality*. Aldershot, UK: Ashgate, 2005.

Walsh, Denis. "Teleology." In *Oxford Handbook of Biology*, edited by Michael Ruse, 113–34. Oxford: Oxford University Press, 2008.

Walton, John H. "Genesis." In *Zondervan Illustrated Bible Backgrounds Commentary*, edited by John Walton, 1:10–42. Grand Rapids: Zondervan, 2009.

———. *Genesis 1 as Ancient Cosmology*. Winona Lake, IN: Eisenbrauns, 2011.

———. *The Lost World of Genesis One*. Downers Grove, IL: IVP Academic, 2009.

Ward, Keith. *Religion and Revelation: A Study of Revelation in the World's Religions*. Oxford: Clarendon, 1994.

Ward, Michael. *Planet Narnia: The Seven Heavens in the Imagination of C. S. Lewis*. New York: Oxford University Press, 2008.

Ward, Peter D., and Donald Brownlee. *Rare Earth: Why Complex Life Is Uncommon in the Universe*. New York: Copernicus, 2000.

Webb, Stephen. *If the Universe Is Teeming with Aliens . . . Where Is Everybody? Fifty Solutions to the Fermi Paradox and the Problem of Extraterrestrial Life*. New York: Praxis, 2002.

———. *Measuring the Universe: The Cosmological Distance Ladder*. Dordrecht: Springer, 1999.

Wegter-McNelly, Kirk. *The Entangled God: Divine Relationality and Quantum Physics*. London: Routledge, 2011.

———. "Fundamental Physics and Religion." In *The Oxford Handbook of Science and Religion*, edited by Philip Clayton and Zachary Simpson, 156–71. Oxford: Oxford University Press, 2006.

Weinberg, Stephen. *The First Three Minutes: A Modern View of the Origin of the Universe*. New York: HarperCollins, 1977.

Weinrich, D. M., N. F. Delaney, M. A. Depristo, and D. L. Hartl. "Darwinian Evolution Can Follow Only Very Few Mutational Paths to Fitter Proteins." *Science* 312, no. 5770 (2006): 111–14.

Weintraub, David A. *Religions and Extraterrestrial Life: How Will We Deal with It?* Heidelberg: Springer, 2014.

Wielenberg, Erik J. *God and the Reach of Reason: C. S. Lewis, David Hume, and Bertrand Russell*. Cambridge: Cambridge University Press, 2007.

———. "In Defense of Non-Natural, Non-Theistic Moral Realism." *Faith and Philosophy* 29, no. 1 (2009): 23–41.

———. *Robust Ethics: The Metaphysics and Epistemology of Godless Normative Realism*. Oxford: Oxford University Press, 2014.

Wilkinson, David. *Alone in the Universe? The X-Files, Aliens and God*. Crowborough, UK: Monarch, 1997.

———. *Science, Religion, and the Search for Extraterrestrial Intelligence*. Oxford: Oxford University Press, 2013.

Williams, Rowan. "Creation." In *Augustine through the Ages*, edited by Allan D. Fitzgerald, 251–54. Grand Rapids: Eerdmans, 2009.

Williams, Thomas. "The Doctrine of Univocity Is True and Salutary." *Modern Theology* 21 (2005): 575–85.

Yates, Frances A. *Giordano Bruno and the Hermetic Tradition*. London: Routledge, 1964.

Zuckerman, B., and M. H. Hart, eds. *Extraterrestrials: Where Are They?* Cambridge: Cambridge University Press, 1995.

Name Index

Adams, Robert Merrihew, 126–28
Alexander, Denis, 57n48, 81n53, 95n20, 96
Alexander, Samuel, 178n35
Alfsvåg, Knut, 66n18
Ambrose of Milan, 33n13, 37
Anderson, Bernhard W., 18n12
Anselm of Canterbury, 157
Aquinas, Thomas, 23, 61–62, 66–68, 143, 146–52, 155, 162–64, 175n22
Aristotle, 3n4, 7, 11, 23n42, 24–27, 30–31, 36–38, 43–46, 49, 55, 58, 59–62, 64, 91, 103, 160, 175n22, 177n29, 181
Armstrong, Chris, 177n33
Arnold, Matthew, 180
Arnould, Jacques, 2n3
Atkins, Peter, 108, 199, 120n27
Augustine, 8, 23, 29, 32–35, 37–39, 60–61, 73–74, 91–92, 136, 146n8, 169, 175–76

Backhaus, Knut, 31n6
Baehr, Jason S., 7n15
Baggett, David, 122n31, 123n35, 128n50
Baltes, Matthias, 24n43
Barberini, Maffeo, 47
Barbour, Ian G., 55n40
Barnes, Luke, 73n37
Barnes, Robin B., 46n9
Barrow, John D., 72
Basil the Great, 35–37
Bellah, Robert N., 12n3, 102n39

Bellarmino, Roberto, 47
Bentley, Richard, 69
Benton, Michael, 97n27
Betz, John, 137–38
Black, Jeremy, 14n4
Blackburn, Simon, 108
Blair, Ann, 48n16
Bockmuehl, Marcus, 66n16
Boethius, 41–42, 169, 174n18, 177
Bostrom, Nick., 89n6, 154n29
Bouteneff, Peter C., 17n12, 31n6, 32n9, 40n33
Brazier, Paul, 159n5, 164n18
Brient, Elizabeth, 63n11
Brooke, John Hedley, 48n17, 53, 57n48
Brown, Montague, 167n29
Brown, William P., 19n18, 19n23
Brownlee, Donald, 74n40
Burrell, David, 19n18

Calcidius, 40–41
Calvin, John, 45n8, 46n8, 146n6, 146n8
Carnell, Corbin Scott, 171n4
Carr, Bernard, 12n2, 41n36
Catling, David C., 88n4
Chan, Man Ho, 82–83
Chemnitz, Martin, 145
Chesterton, G. K., 6, 110n12
Clarke, Arthur C., 88
Cleland, Carol E., 87n3
Clement of Alexandria, 33–34
Clifford, Richard J., 16n10
Collins, Robin, 73n37, 79, 161n9, 164–65

Coloe, Mary L., 19n23
Consolmagno, Guy, 103n42
Conway Morris, Simon, 75n40, 81n53, 103n42
Copan, Paul, 19n18, 19n21
Copernicus, Nicolaus, 25, 43–49, 52, 67–68, 93, 181
Corcoran, Kevin, 152n23
Cornford, Francis MacDonald, 21n28
Cortez, Marc, 144n1
Cox, Ronald, 30n4
Coyne, George V., 50n24, 88n4
Craig, William Lane, 19n18, 19n21, 100–101, 126
Crawford, Jackson, 16n8
Crisp, Oliver, 161n12
Crowe, Michael J., 2n3, 50n25, 90n9, 93n13, 93n14, 166n26
Cusanus, Nicholas, 48, 63–68, 92–93, 110n12

Danielson, Dennis R., 51n28, 52n31, 93n15
Dante Alighieri, 64–65
Davies, Paul, 1n1, 75–77, 87n2, 101–2, 105
Dawkins, Richard, 108–9
Deane-Drummond, Celia, 147n11, 152n24, 153n26
Delio, Ilia, 158n2
de Moor, Johannes C., 14n5
Denzinger, Heinrich, 19n19
Derham, William, 69–70
Descartes, René, 53
de Schrijver, Georges, 53n35

Subject Index